The Allotment Chronicles

The Allotment Chronicles

A social history of allotment gardening

Written and illustrated by
Steve Poole

Foreword by Terry Walton
'Adopted allotmenteer'
of Radio 2's Jeremy Vine Show

• A SILVER LINK BOOK •
from
The NOSTALGIA Collection

First published in 2006

British Library Cataloguing in Publication Data

A catalogue record for this book is available from the British Library.

ISBN 1 85794 268 X
ISBN 978 1 85794 268 2

Silver Link Publishing Ltd
The Trundle
Ringstead Road
Great Addington
Kettering
Northants NN14 4BW

Tel/Fax: 01536 330588
email: sales@nostalgiacollection.com
Website: www.nostalgiacollection.com

Printed and bound in Great Britain

Front cover The inset postcard photograph of plot 114 at Shakespeare Street Allotment Gardens, Stoke, Coventry, originally belonged to Mr Fred Whitmore, who had been gardening on this site for more than 50 years. The little girl in the picture is Olive Bullock, the dog is Rogie, and the man with the fork is the girl's uncle, Mr Bill Unsworth. The man on the left is also a member of the Unsworth family, but the man in the centre with the spade is unknown. Some time in 1916 the photograph was made into a postcard, which Olive sent to her uncle serving in the trenches. Fortunately, both the uncle and the photograph returned safely after the war.

Frontispiece *A productive post-war allotment garden in the early 1950s.*

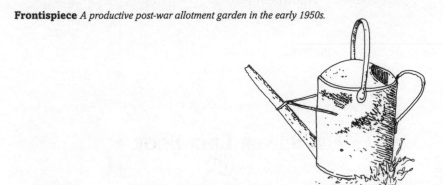

Contents

Feeding the family: a plot-holder brings his produce home, circa 1905.

Foreword

by Terry Walton
'Adopted allotmenteer'
of Radio 2's Jeremy Vine Show

I t is astounding to think that allotments have been in existence for more than 300 years – yes three centuries of tilling, sowing, growing and harvesting.

What also is remarkable is that if one of those allotmenteers of the early 18th century was to walk in through the gates of a 21st-century allotment, the person they would meet would almost certainly be of the same nature as themselves. They would be friendly, talkative and would pass on tips and information in a non-protective way. Their passion for growing their own vegetables, herbs or even flowers would in no way be diminished by the passing of those 300 years.

The other commonality, which still exists and has bridged the centuries, was born of the 18th and 19th centuries, and is the feudal system of bartering that exists in the allotment community. This system is going strong today and no allotmenteers worth their salt will ever go short of some fresh produce to go home with. The average 10-perch plot that most allotment keepers rent always provides more than you or your family can consume, hence the need to swap your excess produce for some you do not have available at that time. A handful of runner beans will purchase a large cabbage or lettuce, a few beetroot an early bunch of carrots, a few pounds of freshly dug potatoes a large marrow. The extent of the exchange system is limitless, thus providing your own kitchen with a variety of allotment produce, though not always grown by your own fair hand. The range of barter also goes beyond the allotment gates, and people with other interests within the community will readily supply bread, wine, eggs, fish and even, on one occasion, a brace of partridge for a supply of freshly picked produce.

In allotment life, like the laws of physics, many of the well-proven methods of cultivation remain the same as they have always been. Rotation of crops is essential to avoid pests and diseases, where to manure and where not to is essential in the growing of root crops, and where to lime soil and the areas where lime is to be avoided at all costs. These practices have been used through the centuries and still apply today has much as the did three centuries ago.

The practices of growing also change and are influenced by what is available at any period of time. Many of the allotment keepers of the 18th and 19th centuries would have grown completely organic, using manure and home-made composting. The use of green manures and leaving ground fallow for periods would have been widely used.

However, during the mid-20th century many man-made fertilisers became cheaply and widely available. This meant that the substances that crops need to grow quickly, such as nitrogen and potash, could be added to the soil in large doses very quickly, which also meant that crops grew large and speedily, and were harvested looking very good. However, beware – looking good and tasting good are two different things. They may lack the flavour and nutrition of crops grown more slowly in rich fertile soil, taking in the natural goodness of the soil and sun.

Also during the mid-20th century came the advent of insecticides. These 'nuked' every insect that moved, friend or foe. DDT and Lindane were seen as the saviours of allotment gardeners, giving us perfect clean crops. But what were they doing? The residues were building up in the ground and acting as a time-bomb, poisoning us and our offspring.

Come the 1980s and the reversion to organic growing was again becoming the norm, and this revolution is gaining momentum every year with allotment growers wanting flavour and insecticide-free crops. Long live the revolution.

When I began my allotment career in the 1950s the allotment was the domain of older, retired men in flat caps who gardened to supplement the food on the kitchen table. Allotments at this time were in great demand with a long waiting list. The 'Swinging Sixties' and the lazy 1970s reversed this trend, and many allotment sites became derelict. There was a big demand for more homes as the population grew, and unused sites became concrete and tarmac jungles. The once fertile soil would never again see a little green shoot push up through its surface. Allotment acreage dropped dramatically as the growth of supermarkets provided cheap pre-packaged food to the masses. Why grow your own when clean products in plastic bags are readily available?

The early 1990s did, however, see a reverse of this trend. The allotment sites were in big demand from younger, professional people who saw them as a place to relax after the pressures of modern-day life. They became places where the whole family could come along, enjoy themselves and grow natural food under their own control. They were no longer the traditional allotment, but were becoming an extension to the leisure garden.

This has meant a large uptake of allotments, and waiting lists are now becoming the order of the day. Long may it continue!

Don't forget that it is everyone's right to have a piece of their own land to grow their own produce. Go out and pressure your local authority to provide more allotment sites and let's revert to the heady days when this hobby was the right of the masses and readily available to all.

Introduction

Before 1900 the term 'allotment' was defined as a parcel or plot of land allocated to an individual on the division of an estate in lands, and it gained special significance during the main period of the enclosure of the common fields between 1760 and 1845. In the enclosure awards it was constantly used to describe the parcels of land granted to individuals from the common estate of the common fields and pastures. During the later part of this period the word was best described as 'an allotment for the labouring poor'. From around 1820 onward the term gained an economic meaning, as the small plot or parcel of land was occupied by a working man and constituted a supplementary source of income, in addition to his regular, though often insufficient, wages.

In the early part of the 19th century the Allotment Movement was largely a rural issue, implemented for three main reasons. First, allotments were envisaged as a way to reduce parochial poor rates in agricultural districts. Second, benevolent landlords were anxious to alleviate the chronic poverty and state of distress that prevailed among the peasant classes, especially after 1830. Third, when labourers were given plots to rent, they were tempted to stay on the land rather than migrate to the expanding towns in search of better-paid work. Landlords and farmers feared a severe labour crisis when greater numbers of workers quit their rural origins. Thus was born the Allotment Movement.

Until the wave of unrest among rural workers in the autumn of 1830, the provision of land was a very haphazard and localised affair that was usually to the advantage of the landlord concerned. After the 'Swing Riots' the Movement gained in momentum. However, the Poor Law Commissioners noted in their 1834 report that labourers were mistrustful of allotments provided under parochial control, fearing that tenancy would lead to a debasement in their wages. Allotment land provided by regional landlords was generally warmly accepted by the labourers, who were eager to procure a rood of land and willing to pay exorbitant rents and comply with the range of finical restrictions that applied to the terms of tenancy.

'It is admitted on all hands that the poor man who has an allotment ungrudgingly bestows labour upon it before and after his regular hours of work, and that the result of this additional labour, both for his own and his family's part, is shown by a material improvement in his social as well as

9

financial position. The farmers do not complain that labour bestowed on small allotments is to the detriment of that for which they receive wages.'
(Lord Onslow, *Landlords and Allotments*, 1886)

Allotments in the Victorian era were of four main types. Plots provided by landlords usually took the form of a garden ranging from 10 to 40 rods, for the cultivation of vegetables. Field allotments awarded under the Enclosure Acts often resembled the surrounding farmland, and were usually of 1-4 acres apiece. On field allotments, tenants raised crops of wheat, barley, millet, potatoes and beans. There were also potato patches, which were often let by farmers at a rack rent. Cow runs were also regarded as an extension to allotments, and generally operated as a communal scheme.

It was not until the 1880s that the Allotment Movement received wider recognition, following further unrest among labourers, who only wanted higher wages, better living conditions and a plot of ground. A successive range of Allotment Acts, together with much speculation, turned the Movement into a political one. The Allotment Act of 1887 conferred special powers on regional Sanitary Authorities to provide allotments. However, this Act proved to be ineffectual as there were no regulators to enforce the Sanitary Authorities to comply. In the following year even the newly established County Councils could do little to influence the decision of the Sanitary Authorities. Then in 1894 the Local Government Act (also known as the Parish Council Bill), which established Parish and Urban District Councils, unlocked the gate to the provision of land by public authorities.

During the 1880s great argument commenced regarding the provision of allotments through compulsory as against voluntary means. Numerous landlords (including Lord Onslow) were horrified by this prospect, fearing that the Movement would degenerate into support for indolent and unwelcome settlers, at the expense of the 'public purse'. Such fears were groundless, for the terms of tenancy on compulsory allotments were equally as stringent as those on voluntary ones. Other spokespersons within the Movement insisted that too little was done to enable labouring folk to secure land. Mr Impey, Hon Secretary for the Allotments & Smallholders Association, received voluminous quantities of correspondence from agitated labourers complaining of the lack of provision and access to land that they so desperately wanted. Since the 1860s there had been an ever-increasing outcry for larger tracts of land in addition to allotments, and they were loosely referred to as smallholdings. Much debate ensued as to whether labouring folk were capable of traversing the immense gulf between hiring a rood (a quarter of an acre) of allotment garden and managing a smallholding. At the time labourers felt that possession of an allotment was the first rung up the social ladder towards gaining a smallholding and thus independence. Throughout the late 19th century the distinction between allotments, smallholdings and small-scale farming was a very ill-defined one.

By the early 20th century the Allotment Movement was very much an urban matter, enhanced by the necessity of producing foodstuff in wartime.

In 1916 the Board of Agriculture asked the Inspectors of their Horticultural Branch to conduct surveys regarding allotment cultivation across the country. All the reports confirmed that the standard of cultivation on rural allotments was much lower than those in urban regions. The Board realised that, for the agricultural worker, the cultivation of an allotment was merely a continuation of the day's work; he had little spare time and the activity did not appeal as a recreation.

On the other hand, for the industrial worker in the towns allotment gardening served as a healthy pastime that was made more attractive because it was remunerative. Town workers earned better wages and had money to spend on the essential items for the allotment, such as seeds, fertilisers and tools. Rural allotments were usually between ¼ acre and 1 acre in extent, and were let at £1 10s to £2 10s an acre. Urban allotments were generally smaller, between one-tenth and one-eighth of an acre, the average rent being 1s a rod (£8 per acre). While rural workers adopted a rough and ready approach to their plots, town workers managed their allotments with greater forethought, resulting in a wider variety of crops and a more continuous supply. The inspectors found that 80% to 90% of urban allotments were skilfully cultivated, while in rural areas only 20% to 30% of plots were worked well. Frederick Ernest Green commented upon the changing tenancy of allotments:

'The ordinary urban allotment holder has invariably been the man of the artisan type: the railway worker, the mill hand, the carpenter and the bricklayer. It is doubtful whether these men with their ten or twenty rods have ever thought much about their allotments as supplementary to wages. The love of gardening and the desire to be in the open air, besides the ambition to grow vegetables for their own table, have been the incentive rather than cash returns. Probably overtime at their own particular trade would have been financially more remunerative.' (F. E. Green, *The Allotment Movement – Contemporary Review*, 1918, Vol 114, p92)

A series of Allotment Acts passed between 1907 and 1931 improved the conditions of tenancy for plot-holders and promoted the Movement further. Both the Government and the Ministry of Agriculture realised the social and economic benefit that allotments provided for town workers, and were quick to approve of schemes to supply tools, seeds and fertilisers at reduced rates. Although there was no fixed maximum rent for plots, under the various Acts local authorities were required to charge a 'full fair rent'. Even so, rents varied considerably in different locations, though 1s a rod (£8 per acre) remained an average rate within towns and cities until the end of the 1960s. Throughout the first half of the 20th century the number of allotments in the British Isles remained consistently high, apart from a temporary dip during the late 1930s when figures dropped to 815,000.

Throughout the second half of the 20th century allotment cultivation tapered away dramatically, though figures evened out slightly during the

1970s. Until the mid-1970s the produce raised on an allotment still made a considerable saving toward the household budget. During the post-war years greater social freedom and affluence within society eradicated the need or desire to grow food on allotments. Public opinion had also changed toward allotments, which had become connected with wartime, shortages, poverty and exertion. Only a core of dedicated enthusiasts continued to embark on allotment gardening, though they often faced an uphill battle to continue. What had once been envisaged as a means to counteract the worst social evils prevalent in society, came to be regarded as a social evil by people with little or no love of gardening. At the end of the 1990s there were fewer allotments across the UK than the figure given for the 1890s.

The story of the Allotment Movement is a long and complex one that was often shaped by political events, and encapsulates the social history of the common people, with their daily struggle against poverty, hardship, injustice and even hostility from enemy nations. Unravelling the facts and delving into historical records has been just as intriguing. Research has included hours spent foraging the pages of dusty volumes or scanning endless reels of microfilm in the quest to uncover the 'Allotment Story'. In order to avoid cumbersome footnotes, sources are incorporated within the text or, as in the case of citations, at the end of the relevant paragraph. Acknowledgements and gratitude for permission to source material and for contributions received are expressed at the end of the Bibliography. However, very special thanks must go to *Horticulture Week*, the HMSO, *The Times* newspaper, the RHS, and the countless allotment tenants who have their own ideas about gardening on their little patches of no-man's-land.

1
The pioneers

A llotments and their provision arose indirectly from the social upheaval caused through the enclosure of the English countryside between 1750 and 1850. Aristocrats, land-owners and the larger tenant farmers viewed the enclosures as the ultimate achievement. Without the agrarian change that resulted in greater productivity, the extensive industrialisation that took place during the 19th century would never have been possible. However, for the small peasant farmers and common land squatters, the impact was devastating. Bereft of the right to pasture a cow or keep pigs and geese on the commons and cut gorse or wood, the peasants were left with nothing other than to sell their labour and that of their families. Although rural poverty had always existed, it had, until enclosure, been lessened by the right to 'common'.

Gorse was a free source of kindling for the commoners before the Enclosure Acts.

Between 1770 and 1845 approximately 10 million acres of land were enclosed, comprising roughly a third of all the agricultural land in the country. At the time the enclosures were justified on the ground that it was for the good of the country. However, since the Acts were always passed privately though Parliament, it was quite impossible for any but the very wealthy to oppose them. As late as 1845 Lord Lincoln stated before the Enclosure Committee that the rights of the poor folk had been systematically swept aside. Henry Fawcett noted that of 320,000 acres enclosed, only 2,119 were set aside for the benefit of the needy. Lawyers, naturally, placed their services with the wealthy and the powerful (landlords and prosperous farmers). In order to justify the obvious robbery of the peasants, they implied that the commons were but 'wastes of the manor'.

Professor Pollock, in his work *The Land Laws*, insisted that the rights of the peasant villager to utilise the common land was far more ancient than the rights of the Lord of the Manor, while Frederic Impey abhorred the injustices connected with the enclosing of the commons and wrote in 1887:

'Nothing shows more clearly the folly and wickedness of depriving the poor of the benefit of the commons than the fact that after settling the rates of wages at quarter sessions, as was the law to our own time [1887], it was necessary to supplement the amount by recourse to the parish funds, so that in 1835, when the new Poor Law was passed, the greater part of the rural population were in the degraded position, little above slavery, of being kept by the funds raised out of the land of which our ancestors had been robbed, whilst by the Law of Settlement it was almost impossible for a poor man to seek a fresh home.' (Frederic Impey, *Allotments and Smallholdings*, 1887)

Almost 60 years beforehand, William Cobbett, the radical journalist and political agitator, acidly commented on the provision of the earliest allotments:

'It is a very curious thing that the enclosing of the commons, that the shutting out of the labourers from all share in the land has produced effects so injurious and so dangerous that the grinders have, by their own accord, and for their own safety, begun to take steps towards this ancient system. This is, I verily believe, the worst used labouring people upon the face of the earth.' (William Cobbett, *Rural Rides*, 1830)

The economic and political importance of allotments far exceeded the benefit to the individual concerned. Allotments came to be regarded as the answer to the chronic state of distress that prevailed in agricultural districts, especially between 1815 and 1830. The allocation of land may have eased the misery and destitution endured by the pauperised proletariat, but the idea was not a new one.

As far back as 1770 the Lord of the Manor at Tewksbury noted that people with a plot of land affixed to their cottage were far superior in neatness and decency toward others than workers that lived in dwellings without any land. As an experiment, he set out 25 acres of land for the use of the poor. The outcome was remarkably successful and even the most idle of labourers took an industrious turn. The parish poor rates dropped to 4d in the pound as against 2s 6d to 5s 0d in adjoining parishes.

When the wool-carding industry at Tetbury died out in 1795, hundreds of women and children were left without employment. The local landlord, Mr Sotheron Estcourt, noted the extent of distress among the peasants and, having decided to clear some land of gorse, he divided the work up among the labourers. After each had finished his allotted task, the labourer was given the opportunity to rent a patch of the cleared ground as an allotment for cultivation in the odd hours of leisure time. Consequently, the regions of Tewksbury and Tetbury became the 'cradle' of the Allotment Movement. As time went on, the 'Poor Plots', as they came to be known, spread to every village in the region and all were kept in a high state of cultivation until the middle of the following century.

Toward the end of the 18th century, questions were being asked about the state of the landless labouring poor. Although there was much in the way of conciliatory noises, there was very little action. In 1775 Nathanial Kent advocated that, with each enclosure award, every labourer should have 3½ acres of land affixed to his cottage. No records exist to prove that such measures were ever implemented. In 1782 an Act was passed that enabled the Guardians of the Poor to enclose up to 10 acres of waste ground near the poor house for cultivation by the paupers, but no mention was made that any land should be allocated to any particular individuals. In many cases the apportioning of land to the poor folk was not greeted with any degree of enthusiasm.

In 1786 Joseph Townsend made a scornful attack on parochial charity in his report 'A Dissertation on the Poor Laws', and asked:

'What cause have the poor to fear, when they are assured, that by their indolence...., by their drunkenness and vices, they should be reduced to want, they shall be abundantly supplied, at the expense of others? In general, it is only hunger which can goad and spur them on to labour: yet our laws have said that they shall never hunger.' (Joseph Townsend, 'A Dissertation on the Poor Laws', 1786, pp9-10)

This outlook persisted throughout the late 18th and early 19th centuries and invariably led to the social unrest and rioting in 1830 and 1831. In 1790 a Private Member's Bill proposed to supply small plots of land to the poor. The General Enclosure Bill of 1796 would have compelled future Acts to set aside land for the benefit of the destitute. Both acts were renounced outright.

While the idea of providing allotments for the labourer was very much at the embryonic stage, another kind of detached garden started to develop in Midlands towns such as Birmingham, Coventry, Warwick and Nottingham. Such plots became known as the Guinea Gardens, due to the initial ground rent of one pound and one shilling per annum. These detached gardens were not mere allotments for the labourers, but were pleasure grounds for craftsmen, artisans, traders, businessmen and shopkeepers and their families.

During the 1700s, when rural folk decided to settle in these towns, enterprising landlords hit upon a new way to acquire an economic ground rent by providing sites for detached gardens. The settlers, used to a rustic way of life and obviously missing their cottage gardens or smallholdings, were only too willing to procure a piece of land to cultivate a garden. As the gardens advanced they took up increasingly large tracts of land, and for the next hundred years or so towns like Birmingham were magically transformed into a leafy green oasis. With the gardens, life became much more bearable for the settlers and very profitable for the town's landlords. By the end of the 18th century a succession of gardens surrounded the centre of the town, and travellers entering Birmingham would have to pass by one or more clusters of them.

By 1731 there was a considerable acreage of detached gardens in

Birmingham, on the site where St Bartholomew's Church now stands. In almost every direction other garden schemes could be seen. In fact, there was no other town in the country to rival the extent of the gardens in Birmingham, and they were to become increasingly important for the citizens, for this was the age when townsfolk worked within walking distance of their place of employment. The provision of a garden served in much the same way as a country retreat, but within a few minutes' walk of the town centre. During this era means of travel were very limited, the majority of roads were in a dreadful state, and the railway system was yet to be invented. A vacation away from home was an unknown indulgence among the working classes. The majority of Birmingham's townsfolk had never been to London or looked upon the mountains or the sea. Faraway places and things like ships were only known from pictures or from descriptions in books, and they were regarded with a sense of wonder.

The gardens were owned in much the same way as a leasehold house. It often took families many years of frugal scrimping in order to save before they managed to purchase a garden, and when they achieved their goal they regarded their plot as a treasured possession. Such gardens often remained in the same family for decades, passed down from one generation to the next, and were only sold off when the need was extremely pressing. Invariably there were times when the occupants were forced to sell up and, because demand for the gardens was very high, sales were usually conducted by auction after notification in the local press.

An advertisement for the sale of a garden in 1805 reads as follows:

'GARDEN – To be sold by Auction, by W. Goode on Wednesday next, April 24th 1805, precisely at three o'clock in the afternoon, an excellent garden, well fenced and planted with fruit trees and vegetables, in a high state of cultivation, with brick summerhouse and other conveniences, pleasantly situated, being No 145 in the Cottage Field, the central walk leading from the Cottage of Content to the Sand Pits.' (*Aris's Gazette*, 1805)

Another local press advertisement for the sale of a garden in 1816 clearly depicts the amount of attention and detail applied to the creation of the gardens:

'To be sold by auction – a remarkable choice garden, at present in the occupation of Mr J. Mason. This delightful garden is situated in The Avenue, leading from the Deritend Brewery to Vaughton's Hole, is well stocked with fruit trees selected with the greatest care and judgement, having produced the finest fruit within several miles of the place, and for a number of years gained first prize at the Annual Show of Fruit, abounding in choice flowers and shrubs and abundance of vegetables, a capital brick summerhouse and a well always supplied with water. The whole enclosed in a remarkably strong double fence, the soil is in high condition, and in no probability of ever being disturbed for building.' (*Aris's Gazette*, 1816)

Many of the Guinea Garden occupants were highly skilled craftsmen and they applied their expertise to construct attractive summerhouses, pavilions, glasshouses and rustic arbours. Most of the tenants quickly realised that their garden was as an investment and were unstinting with their devotion and attention to details. The market value of these gardens rose in accordance with the state of cultivation. The provision of a well-constructed summerhouse or pavilion together with a shed and access to a reliable water supply also enhanced the property value of the garden. Tenants that lacked the necessary skill to build their own summerhouse would pay to have a building of their choice constructed on their site. Since the tenants owned their little gardens, security of tenure was assured and as a result the care and attention was often lavish. Occupants with rural knowledge and skills took full advantage of the opportunity to exploit their talents, and planted hedges, shrubs and fruit trees on their plots. Fruit trees in particular were regarded as an added bonus; fresh fruit was something of a premium among townsfolk. Many of the gardens resembled a miniature orchard and were far superior to the common labourer's allotment.

Although the gardens were highly decorative, they were also functional. Quite apart from cultivating fruit trees and ornamental shrubs, most gardens had up to a third of the land devoted to raising vegetables, including crops of asparagus. Since the tenants treasured their gardens, they chose to plant

Many of the Guinea Gardens had a brick summerhouse or pavilion where families would spend their leisure time.

thick hedges around their plots, which were kept well trimmed and tidy. The borders between each garden were very distinctive, though the gardens interlocked together to provide a pleasing aspect. There were lawns, and pathways of York stone that often incorporated blue brick pavers by the thousand. Miles of blue scalloped edging tiles surrounded the flowerbeds and herbaceous borders. Over the years a vast array of individual features were installed by different tenants, which included seats, bird-baths, sundials, weather vanes, statues and pump troughs. Although the Guinea Gardens provided the opportunity for townsfolk to cultivate fruit, flowers and vegetables, together with the chance to keep pigs, chickens and occasionally pigeons, this was not the primary reason for cultivating the garden.

Ownership of a garden had an incredible influence on the character and social position of the artisan tenants. Workers and businessmen alike found their involvement with the garden to be a wholesome form of relaxation and a way to indulge in social intercourse. The gardens were so arranged that at one time or another tenants would frequently be seen at work on their land, most often during summer evenings when the daylight lasted longer. Very often a neighbourly camaraderie developed between different tenants. Some families spent their few precious days of holiday entirely within the confines of their garden, treating the summerhouse rather like a chalet. A large number of the summerhouses and pavilions were fitted with cast-iron

Some of the Guinea Gardens were very flowery.

'tortoise' stoves, and the gardens generally had a well with a hand pump. So the tiny gardens served as a country retreat, although they were only a mile or less from the town centre.

A map of Birmingham, drafted by J. Pigott Smith in 1824, depicts the town surrounded by gardens, which resembled an enormous patchwork quilt. Throughout the late 18th century and the early part of the 19th, Birmingham remained a town full of gardens that were created, not through any vast municipal expenditure, but by the unstinting efforts of hundreds of ordinary working families, who gained much health and happiness while doing so. By the early 1800s the development of the gardens was regarded as a considerable achievement, and visitors from other regions often admired the state of the grounds.

In 1831 the landscape gardener and writer J. C. Loudon made an excursion into Birmingham and noted the scale and scope of the gardens:

'The detached town gardens are situated in the suburbs of towns, generally collected together, and separated by hedges. There are upwards of two thousand of such gardens in the neighbourhood of Birmingham ... in one of these gardens, occupied by Mr Clarke, chemist and druggist, we found a selection of hardy shrubs and plants which quite astonished us.' (J.C. Loudon, 1831)

The Select Committee on public walks also commented very favourably on the gardens, and in 1833 noted that it was a regular custom for families to spend their evenings and Sundays in their little gardens.

In 1849 Robert Rawlinson made a report on the town and stated that there were at least 250 separate gardens around Edgbaston and noted great swathes of gardens along the Rea Valley and in the direction of Handsworth and Moseley. He noticed that the majority of plots were let to workmen and tradesmen, who took great pride and joy in their plots and carefully fenced them in. He added that a majority of gardeners cultivated vegetables, fruit and flowers. Apart from working on their garden in all spare hours, they also made them the scene of family festivals.

By the middle of the 19th century the glory of the gardens had passed its peak and a considerable number had vanished from the landscape due to the expansion of industry and housing. A small site along Westbourne Road, known as Malthouse Meadows, remained unchanged throughout the period of industrial expansion, and some gardens still existed as late as 1889. This was largely due to the site remaining in private ownership. The third Lord Calthorpe, an MP well known for his altruistic ideals and radical notions, originally laid out the gardens in the 1840s, and they were the last site to be developed. They remained in the Calthorpe family and were later amalgamated into the Calthorpe Estates Trust. Although the family moved away from Birmingham, they remained held in high esteem by the tenants of the gardens until the time of granting of a short lease to Birmingham City Council, the Lord Mayor and the Citizens of Birmingham. Although built later, they followed the same format as the earlier gardens and were generally purchased as a leased property. A varied assortment of summerhouses and pavilions were constructed, which added to the richness of the site. Each of the gardens was enclosed by a hedge of hawthorn, privet or holly, and a range of native fruit trees was also planted. Some of the gardens even resembled miniature orchards with up to 20 or so apple and pear trees.

By the 1860s and 1870s the gardens nearest Westbourne Road had completely disappeared, replaced by a series of large Victorian villas set in formal grounds. In turn the villas were demolished to make way for Lucas Industries. Further encroachment occurred in 1871 when the Birmingham & West Suburban branch of the Midland Railway was formed and a track was established along the Worcester Canal, which led to the destruction of 11 gardens. By 1878 additional losses were incurred along Summer Lane, Holloway Head and Digbeth. Bunce noted that, apart from the gardens at Edgbaston, town expansion had swept most of them away.

In September 1886 the Local Committee of the British Association published a handbook of Birmingham, the precursor to many town guides, and Samuel Timmins wrote:

'Near the Botanical Gardens a group of small gardens may be seen, which are the only "survivals" of the acres of Guinea Gardens, which surrounded Birmingham within a mile from the centre as late as 1830-1840. Birmingham was in fact a town of gardens fifty years ago, not merely as to the gardens attached to the houses, but of the groups of gardens rented by workmen and their families, who could reach their gardens easily from their homes by a short walk and devote their leisure time to them. The site of the Kent Street Baths, those opposite St. Thomas Church, at Ladywood, Spring Hill, Hockley, Handsworth, Digbeth and Aston Road, all within the parish boundary, formed a continuous belt of gardens where the workmen and their families often spent the summer evenings and enjoyed the (then) country air. All is now changed, and the land too valuable to let out in readily accessible gardens for the workers of the town.' (Samuel Timmins, Local Committee of the British Association, 1886)

The height of the Guinea Gardens' popularity was around the end of the 18th and early 19th centuries, when they were almost unique. Industrial development took its toll and by the early 19th century emphasis on letting land lay with development and industrial expansion. The demise of the large pleasure gardens coincided with the rise of the ordinary allotment, which was aimed at relieving poverty among the labouring classes.

In 1795 the newly formed Board of Agriculture asked numerous landowners to proclaim the effects of an allotment system on the cottager, the parish and the public. Lord Brownlow replied:

'To the cottager it affords the comforts of life, to the parish it lowers the poor's rates: the man who keeps a cow has seldom been known to be troublesome to the parish; and to the public it gives an increase in hands (by parents teaching children) from infancy to work to their advantage.' ('Queries Concerning Cottagers, with Answers', Board of Agriculture, Vol 1, 1796, pp87-8)

In 1796 William Wilberforce formed the 'Society for Bettering the Condition and Increasing the Comforts of the Poor'. In a paper to the Society, the Earl of Winchester stated:

'From what I have seen of them, I am more and more confirmed in the opinion I have long held, that nothing is so beneficial to them and the landless owners (labourers) as their having land to be occupied either for the keeping of cows or as gardens, according to the circumstances.' (Lord Fortesque on Poormen's Gardens)

Lord Winchelsea was particularly influential in providing land for the labouring poor, and many landlords followed his example. In the 'Annals of Agriculture' for 1796 (later re-printed in *The Labourer's Friend* magazine of 1835) he noted the different state of affairs and the subsequent advantages to the labouring classes.

1. Those with enough enclosed grassland to enable them [the labourers] to keep one or more cows winter and summer, and a garden near the house. This was much the best situation, for, except for haymaking, the rest of the labour could be done by the wife, thus the man's wage-labour was not interrupted. However, this is only feasible in counties with abundant grassland.
2. Those with summer pasture for a cow, and arable land on which its winter provision could be grown. This was not so advantageous as (1) since some time would be taken up by the arable land.
3. Those with the right to common for the summer keep of a cow, and meadow or arable ground or a meadow in common for winter provision. This would be as good as (2) were it not for the fact that nine out of ten commons are so overstocked that the summer keep is very bad.
4. Those with the right to common, and a garden. This was beneficial; geese and pigs might be kept on the common and the pigs fed with the produce of a garden and a small quantity of purchased food.
5. Those with the right of common, but no garden. Unless fuel was obtained, it was of little value.
6. Those with several acres of land but no summer pasture for a cow. This was of no great value since the continual labour that would be required to stall-feed a cow through the year would so fully occupy the labourer's time that on balance he might lose.
7. Those with a garden near the house: 'The best thing that could be done for labourers in arable counties; and when there are other reasons which prevent them from keeping cows.'

8. Those with no land whatsoever: 'A very bad situation for the labourer to be placed in,' which ought to be rectified by providing gardens. (J. Thirsk & G. E. Mingey, *The Agrarian History of England & Wales 1750-1850*, 1989, p726)

Throughout the 1790s an increasing number of landlords decided that enough had been taken from the peasant classes, and they set aside plots of land on their estates where labouring folk could grow food to supplement their meagre incomes. The movement was not widespread or evenly distributed and varied considerably in different parts of the country.

In some regions following enclosure, plots were set aside for peasants to gather dead wood and cut gorse or bracken for tinder. These early allotments were let in lieu of fuel rights and, in the recital made by the Commissioners, there was often a clause such as:

'A claim of right to cut gorse on waste ground having been delivered on behalf of the poor ... the Commissioners allot to such as do not occupy any part of the land to be enclosed:...'

This was followed by the description of the parcel of land to be let. Such awards were made to the Lord of the Manor or Churchwardens in trust for the poor of the parish. In regions where fuel rights did not exist, riots frequently broke out around the village following enclosure, especially in the winter months.

During the1790s garden allotments were under the jurisdiction of private landlords. William Danby was one of the first mine-owners to enclose plots

Cutting firewood from a fuel allotment.

*Rural poverty has always existed, but it was softened by the peasants'
right to ancient common land to gather tinder and graze their livestock.*

of unproductive moorland around his colliery at Swinton so that miners
could cultivate vegetables to feed their families. James Croft, one of the
miners, was so enthusiastic about his allotment that he worked the night shift
down the pit in order to cultivate his allotment during the day, leaving just
four hours for sleep in every 24. His supreme effort paid off and he
eventually became a prosperous tenant farmer.

The Earl of Egremont was even more generous and provided each of his
estate workers with an allotment of 3 acres. In 1797 his steward noted that
with resources such as a warm cottage and a plot of land to grow vegetables,
the labourers were the most contented of workers. In the majority of cases
allotments were located on unproductive land of little benefit to the landlord.
One villager in Tysoe, Warwickshire, complained bitterly that his allotment
was on a slope so steep that it was almost impossible to stand, let alone dig.
The size of allotments varied tremendously: many were so small or on
ground that was so impoverished that cultivation was not worth the effort. In
Norfolk one Enclosure Commissioner noted that few plots were larger than
an acre, which proved to be insufficient for a labourer to keep a cow. At St
Neots in Huntingdonshire, several labourers were known to have sold off
their plots to farmers for £5 since the cost of fencing them in would have
exceeded this sum.

Arthur Young was only too well aware of how the enclosures had severed the labourers from the land. When the General Bill for enclosures was due for consideration in 1801 he stated that a labourer with several children should be allocated up to 4½ acres for potatoes and perhaps the keep of a cow. Shortly afterwards he put his plan to utilise the common wastes for potato ground into solid form in the 'Annals of Agriculture'. He advised his readers:

'Go to an alehouse kitchen of an old-enclosed country, and there you will see the origin of poverty and the poor-rates. For whom are they to be sober? If I am diligent, shall I have leave to build a cottage? If I am sober, shall I have land for a cow? If I am frugal, shall I have half an acre of potatoes? You offer no motives! You have nothing to offer but a parish officer and a workhouse! Bring me another pot.' (A. Young, 'Annals of Agriculture', Vol XXXVI, 1800, p508)

In locations where there was no waste ground left and benevolent land-owners lacking, Young suggested that the Parish purchase some land from the finances gained from the rates, fence it in, stock it and let it to the poor. Young's plan may have prevented anguish and debasement among the workers, but it could not cope with the escalating numbers. Young noticed that when settled on holdings and allotments, the workers tended to multiply in large numbers, 'so that pigs and children fill every quarter'. Though Young was particularly enthusiastic about implementing allotment schemes, his exhortations with regard to the utilisation of parochial land largely fell on deaf ears. As a result, the provision of allotment land largely depended on the compassionate disposition of regional landlords.

In 1800 Mr Thomas Estcourt established around a hundred allotments in the parish of Long Newnton in Wiltshire. Cottagers and labourers eagerly applied, even though the rent for a small plot (size unspecified) amounted to £1 14s an acre, which was let on a 14-year lease. However, the holders had to refrain from accepting poor relief and had to agree to plant more than a quarter of their plot with potatoes. So effective was this early allotment system that the entire parish was lifted from a state of chronic debt and poverty, and by 1805 the parish poor rate had dropped from £212 16s to £12 6s. It was even claimed that the farmers of the parish said that they never had their work better done, that servants were more able, willing and sober, and that their property was never so free from depression as at present.

In 1805 Mr Estcourt wrote of the allotment system to the Board of Agriculture, stating:

'Some persons have conceived that inconveniences would arise out of this from circumstances of their being in a better situation in life than formerly, that it would put them above the necessity of labour, and would render them idle, insolent and immoral; to which it may be answered that, having given up all claim to parochial relief, they feel themselves obliged to look forward and to provide against occasional distress, which stimulates them to increased industry and economy: besides which, if, with a numerous family, by the occupation of 1½ acres of land only, they could obtain more than a bare sustenance it must be by a very superior exertion and frugality: it is not unlikely that what is so obtained will be spent by the same person in vice and extravagance, in fact three years' experience proved the contrary.' (Mr Estcourt's communication to the Board of Agriculture, 1805)

The Rev Stephen Demainbury, rector of Broad Somerford in Wiltshire, was a another pioneer in the establishment of allotments, and was instrumental in having half-acre gardens attached to cottages in his parish, following enclosure in 1806. The clergy were a leading authority in the argument for (and against) allotment schemes. Clergymen often provided advice on the rents that should be charged and the terms on how the ground should be let.

During the early 1800s the development of the Allotment Movement coincided with the acceptance of the potato as food, due to the high price of flour. The early allotments were largely implemented as one of general economic policy rather than as a benefit for the labourers. At the time it was a widely held belief that labouring folk should be encouraged to cultivate potatoes for their own consumption and reduce their intake of the more expensive wheaten bread. This idea was extremely popular among the gentry in regions where arable farming predominated.

Many labourers became extremely skilled at raising potato crops, and neighbouring workers often exchanged small tubers for use as seed. In some regions the desire to cultivate potatoes reached pandemic proportions. In 1818 labourers in Bedfordshire were so desperate to cultivate the tubers that they dug up wayside verges to plant potatoes. During the early 19th century the term 'allotment' often meant little more than a potato patch.

Although potatoes were widely accepted among the labouring classes, William Cobbett, the radical journalist, would not share enthusiasm for their cultivation, preferring instead to extol the merits of corn (maize). In his book *Cobbett's Corn*, he suspected motives of economic coercion in regions where labourers had made the potato their staple diet. He thought the general adoption of the potato would lead the agricultural labourers to the edge of a chasm. In some places it had become the custom to allocate labourers with a potato patch as part payment of wages. During successive years, when the plight of the labourers worsened, Cobbett never failed to indicate (repeatedly) where the pitfall lay. Cobbett realised that the greatest majority of labourers would not lightly relinquish bread, cheese and meat in place of a monotonous diet based on potatoes. Cobbett was not entirely against their cultivation, and in his book *Rural Rides* he noted that potatoes were widely cultivated in cottage gardens around Hexham. When grown as garden herbage, he thought their cultivation was good. What Cobbett feared most was that the potato should become a total substitute for both bread and meat.

Many of the agriculturists and garden writers of the day regarded the potato as a valuable food crop and, next to wheat, of great importance, both as a source of nutrition and of finance to those that grew them. Such views were not held by J. C. Loudon, who, like Cobbett, doubted the merits of potato cultivation, at least on an agricultural scale. In his *Encyclopaedia of Agriculture*, Loudon pointed out that although potatoes yielded more foodstuff per acre than wheat or barley, they required vast amounts of manure. Since the bulky tubers were difficult to transport, they could only be freely sold when cultivated near the larger towns. Loudon stated that due to such difficulties they were an unprofitable crop. Farmers were not overly enthusiastic about cultivating potatoes as a main crop, which came to be reflected in the rapid expansion of the Allotment Movement. During this early period almost half the land designated for allotments was used for the cultivation of potatoes.

The Select Vestry Act of 1819 was the first to bestow power on public authorities (Parochial Overseers) to purchase or hire up to 20 acres of land and let it to labourers. The Act also gave permission for the Overseers or Churchwardens to enclose and improve waste ground, with consent from the Lord of the Manor, and let it for the benefit of the paupers. Very little use was made of this Act since there were few overseers willing to put its provisions into operation.

Some years later, Assistant Commissioner Captain Chapman deduced that allotments under parochial control were far less beneficial to the labourers since the land was taken with suspicion and distrust. For the most part, the labourers feared that the taking of an allotment from parochial authorities would lead to a reduction in their wages. Consequently, the land was rarely attended to by either the parish or the tenant. Other Commissioners noted that the overseers of parochial allotment land were often eager to escape, with as little effort as possible, from the thankless office that had been enforced upon them. Therefore they were less inclined to bestow attention to the needs of the tenants in framing of the rules or observing that they were adhered to.

Although labourers were more receptive to the provision of plots under private management, every scheme did not ensure success, as Captain Chapman later discovered. In 1820 the Marquis of Bath let 6 acres of quality grassland at Frome, Somerset. The land was divided into small portions (size unspecified) and seed was supplied free to poor folk on condition that they refrained from taking all or part of their parish pay (depending on the individuals' circumstances). Industrious people were selected, and no rent, poor rates or tithes were paid by the tenants. Each plot was let for one year and no manure was required. During the first year, under careful management, the venture went well. However, by the second year complaints were voiced. It was said that the poor folk robbed each other and some started to demand their poor pay as before. Others refused to cultivate the ground, claiming that their minimal leisure hours were consumed by travelling to and from their gardens. Finally the experiment was relinquished as of no advantage to the parish or the paupers.

Where the allotment system worked, benefactors were often quick to highlight their success. In 1822 an article in an East Anglian newspaper drew attention to the difficulties of extending the allotment system, and maintained that the answer lay in the formation of societies:

'Let central and branch organisations be formed immediately in every large town and its surrounding neighbourhood. Such associations regularly organised will collect information, digest plans, and stand ready to embrace every eligible opening for engaging land. Especially when farms become vacant and are about to be re-let it may be hoped that such associations will find little difficulty in inducing the proprietor to set off 10 acres out of 500 for the use of the poor, seeing that the rent is guaranteed by a respectable association, which will kindly come between the landlord and the labouring occupier and collect it by instalments or in small sums and be answerable for deficiencies.

If two respectable individuals would unite with zeal in attempting to establish such central associations, they could not but succeed. Let them look round and invite half-a-dozen persons like-minded and form at once a provisional committee. The way would then gradually open before them, and their exertions would entitle them to be ranked among the best benefactors of their country. Let the motto of a successful doer be adopted "Begin directly and never give it up".' (Anonymous article, 'Ministry of Agriculture Journal', 1933)

Another article, published around 1823, highlighted an allotment experiment at Britlington on the Essex coast:

'At the above mentioned period, the moral and physical circumstances described to have been the most wretched description; their earnings being generally spent at the ale-house, and when the fishing was prosperous they never thought of saving any part of their earnings; in consequence, when the fishery, being their only resource, in any ways failed, their condition was truly pitiable; even a profession of religion was scarcely recognised among them. Their abodes were miserable in the extreme; in fact, they could scarcely be said to enjoy the comforts of civilised society.

After entering upon their little allotments of land, having been instructed on how to manage it to the best advantage, a spirit of emulation sprang up among them. They began to perceive what benefits might be derived from the cultivation of the soil during those hours, which formerly had been spent in dissipation, or wasted in idleness. By these means they not merely saved the money wasted in spirituous liquors, but realised a considerable sum of money by their industry, as well as health from their salutary employment. The Lord's Day is now observed by them; a place of worship has been erected; and those individuals whose feet never before trod the floor of a place of worship, now rejoice at the sound of a church-going bell; a day-school has been established, in which, as well as Sunday-school, their children are trained to industry, virtue, and religion. They are now comparatively neat and clean in their persons, their houses exhibit a greatly improved system of domestic economy, and it is a delightful sense to those that knew them thirteen years ago, to see them on an evening busily occupied on their little plots, and vying with each other who shall produce the best crops of cabbages, potatoes, grain and who shall rear the finest pigs.' (Article, 'Ministry of Agriculture Journal', 1933)

In 1827 Dr Carlyon, a Truro magistrate, wrote in a leaflet of the benefit that local miners gained from their little plots of land:

'Above all, no industrious cottager should be allowed to remain unprovided with such a spot of ground as he is capable of cultivating at leisure hours; and from one-eighth to a quarter of an acre will generally be better than more; for without the aid of a lucky start in mining, or some other piece of good fortune productive of means beyond the proceeds of daily labour, no poor man should attempt to cope with several acres, especially of a coarse description. After years of hard struggling, a severe winter sooner or later will arrive, and find him ill-provided for the maintenance of his little stock, and a petition, such as may be seen in circulation, will soon inform the humane and charitable that the loss of a horse or a cow has brought him to great distress. Besides, when there is too much to be done at home the labourer will seldom be worthy of his hire elsewhere; so that, whatever we have regard to the interests of the labourer himself, or of his employer, or of the parish, with reference to the poor rate, in which he lives, it will equally, I believe, be found that he cannot be placed better for the maintenance of a family than where the produce of a well-cultivated garden goes to help out the earnings of regular daily labour.' (Poor Law Report, 1834)

In spite of the provision of allotments, and schemes to alleviate the poverty, the rural labourers were being policed in an increasingly oppressive manner. In 1770 poaching was punishable with six months imprisonment. By 1803 a poacher resisting arrest was liable to face the death penalty. In order to protect the game, a lethal array of mantraps and spring guns were set up on the once open commons. Consequently, docile game birds strutted in the newly enclosed fields, within sight of half-starved labourers who toiled away for less than half-a-crown a day.

Pheasants and other game strutted about on the once open commons, in sight of half-starved labourers who earned a few shillings a week.

Some land-owners and the majority of farmers expressed grave anxiety on the question of supplying labourers with plots of land. Farmers often said that their labourers with plots became too saucy by far. In reality, the labourers had little reason to be mirthful or impertinent. This was the period when a rift began to develop between the farmer and the labourer. The gulf ever widened, as farmers sought to become more efficient, adopted mechanised farming techniques and attempted to limit the amount labourers could earn. While the farmers endeavoured to become richer, the labourers slid deeper into a chronic state of poverty. Numerous contributory factors aggravated the dire situation still further. The collapse of the French Wars after 1815 led to the demob of thousands of soldiers, which created a serious and permanent glut in the labour market. Consequently, the rate of pay among the workforce declined dramatically. The severity of the game laws and the harsh treatment of labourers by local overseers fuelled the seething discontent among the workers. The implementing of the threshing machine also robbed labourers of their much-needed winter work. Bad harvests and low productivity in 1829 and 1830, together with the labour surplus, led to a general state of distress in agriculture.

The agricultural labourers in particular suffered more than most, working for longer hours on more days than anyone else. Gangs of agricultural labourers were even hired out to the highest bidder, to perform menial tasks such as weeding, picking fruit and field clearance. Not surprisingly, vast numbers turned to the poor relief fund in order to survive. The fund for 1750 stood at £700,000, but by 1800 the figure had swelled to £8 million. As productivity fell, poor relief, which was much hated, was cut as a deterrent. Attempts to reduce it still further only aggravated the anguish and destitution among the labourers. For years the labourers had been victimised and bullied into submission, largely through the Speenhamland System, which discouraged labourers from being industrious in order to implement a system of low pay. Originally introduced in 1795, the Speenhamland System only gave the scantiest of relief and a guarantee of a minimum wage (usually about 6 shillings a week). This strategy was exploited by the farmers, who were anxious to keep the labourers dependent on their paltry wages. Then in the autumn of 1830 the smouldering discontent among the rural workers exploded.

The Agricultural Revolt of 1830-31, often referred to as the 'Swing Riots', was a terrifying new spectacle. The rioters smashed agricultural machines, set hayricks alight, threatened the Justices of the Peace and distributed inflammatory handbills and posters. Some of the riot leaders were skilled craftsmen and artisans from townships intent on mischief, and they deliberately incited the labourers to rebel. The greatest majority of the rioters were labourers and, though destitute, were of good character. Labourers that were married had previously (before the uprising) been regarded as stable and even respectable. Acts of arson usually occurred when the guilty party bore hostility toward a localised target, which often followed a dispute. The smashing of threshing machines was a new feature of unrest, and about 100 were wrecked in East Kent alone.

A farmstead at the time of the Swing Riots.

Assistant Poor Law Commissioner Ashurst Majendie noted that the riots in East Sussex were particularly violent. The independently minded labourers were joined by farmers smarting over the war duty on hops and the high tithes. He commented:

> 'Beyond all doubts the practice of smuggling has been a main cause of the riots and fires in Sussex and East Kent: labourers have acquired the habit of acting in large gangs by night, and of systematic resistance to authority. High living is become essential to them, and they cannot reconcile themselves to the moderate pay of lawful industry.' (Ashurst Majendie, Poor Law Report, 1833, p26)

The uprising was not a universally co-ordinated campaign: action was swift, erratic and occurred in the counties where wages were lowest. The riots commenced in Kent and continued in that county extensively. It was not long though before rioting spread to other counties, notably Sussex, Wiltshire, Hampshire, Berkshire, Buckinghamshire and Dorset. Hobsbawm and Rudé noted that out of 1,475 incidents in 36 counties, 21% entailed arson, 29% machine breaking, 16% robbery and burglary, 7% riot and assault, and 7% involved the dispatch of threatening letters.

The Agricultural Revolt was the first full-scale demonstration by agricultural labourers, who agitated for a pay rise to 13s 6d a week in winter and 15s a week in summer. Their demand was not met. The Government accused radicals of stirring up the trouble and left local authorities to deal with the matter, and they came down hard on the rioters. Overall there were 1,976 trials related to the Swing Riots, of which 252 men were sentenced to death, 19 executed, 505 transported, 644 imprisoned and 233 commuted to life transportation. The Agricultural Revolt died down in 1831, almost as suddenly as it had arisen. The Government, though much relieved, quickly diverted attention to the forthcoming General Election, and the social unrest

*Little was done to provide allotments until workers
set farmers' hayricks alight at the end of 1830.*

prevalent in France. In spite of the uprising the agricultural labourers remained as the lowest-paid, poorest-fed and worst-housed of all the workers. During the first quarter of the 19th century the spread of the Allotment Movement had been rather slow. It took the Agricultural Revolt to trigger the movement into operation, which grew and flourished throughout the remainder of the 19th century ... and beyond.

2
Those redeeming allotments

After the Agricultural Revolt sporadic rioting still persisted in many rural regions. The political situation of the time was precarious and an unsettled state within agriculture existed across much of the country. In the Horsham district of Sussex, Henry Burstow noted that between 1831 and 1834 five young men were hanged for rick-firing offences that had been committed in different parts of the county. Further disturbances occurred between 1834 and 1835 caused by the introduction of a new Poor Law, which proved to be very unpopular with the labouring classes. Magistrates in the Horsham district were unable to contain order through the local constabulary and frequently sent to Brighton for a troop of cavalry to do so. Mr Henry Burstow recollected:

'I can see them now – one captain, one lieutenant, one sergeant, two corporals and usually about 25 troopers marching around the town and often frequenting Broadbridge Common for drill and sword exercise.' (Henry Burstow, *Recollections of Horsham*, 1911)

The soldiers, of course, were untouched by the grinding industrial conditions of the time, though they sympathised with the labourers. But it was the labourers in their poverty that were taxed for the soldiers' upkeep. The grim situation was summed up in a verse that followed Henry Burstow's account:

'In former days the labourers were all called happy men,
As well they might be; labourers could keep a grunter then;
But in these days a grunter is but to a poor man lent –
Hard times – now he must kill and sell his pig to pay the rent.'

The Government, though unaffected by the Agricultural Revolt, realised that measures needed to be taken to counteract further insurrection from the rural workers. In 1831 an Act of Parliament empowered Church Wardens and Poor Law Overseers to supply land for the benefit of the labouring poor, which was not to exceed 20 acres in extent. This was later extended to 50 acres where demand outmatched supply. A further Act was passed in 1832, which made it lawful for the Overseers of Allotments in the Parish Vestry to

32

apportion allotments of land not above an acre but not less than a quarter of an acre to an individual. The land was let on an annual basis from Michaelmas to Michaelmas to industrious cottagers, labourers, and journeymen of good character who were legally settled within the parish.

In 1832 Charles James Bloomfield, then Bishop of London, consented to the enclosure of 20 acres of commonland at Ealing Dean Common for use as allotments. Each of the plots was usually an eighth of an acre, though many ended up being sub-divided owing to various tenants' inability (or disinclination) to keep their plots in good order. The annual rent for a plot of an eighth of an acre amounted to 5 shillings. Considerable allowance was made as some of the tenants were engaged in professional labour for 12 hours a day, and had little time to tend their plots as gardening on the Sabbath was contrary to the conditions of tenure. The official responsible for collecting the rents also acted as an inspector, and reported the condition of each plot to the Management Committee. Demand for allotments at Ealing Dean Common was considerable, even though the Management Committee insisted that all cultivation be with the spade and that space had to be provided for paths, roads and frontages to nearby houses.

By December 1832 the merits of the allotment system were widely noted by the Poor Law Officials. In the Sussex town of Hastings, Mrs Mary Ann Gilbert had introduced 35 allotments of land for the benefit of labourers in 1830. By 1832 the number of plots had been extended to 117. All the tenants paid punctually and many unemployed labourers, convinced of the benefit, offered to give up part of their parish allowance if allotments were let to them. Mrs Gilbert also undertook a daring experiment, on advice from the Archbishop of Dublin. A large portion of shingle on the seashore was covered with clay from the adjacent marsh and good-quality topsoil was spread upon the surface. This land was then hired out to labourers at 3d per rod (40 shillings per acre), which exceeded the rent for the best arable land in the parish. A crop of potatoes was raised in the autumn from land that in the previous spring was unproductive beach.

Mrs Gilbert illustrated that destitution among the workers could be diminished if they were provided with plots of land on which to grow their own food. She later sent some specimens of potatoes cultivated on the beach allotments to Lord Liverpool. By 1835, 213 tenants gardened upon the beach allotments and Mrs Gilbert provided them with advice on using liquid manure, forking the soil and the stall-feeding of cows. Mrs Gilbert also established two agricultural schools to offer the children of allotment-holders the chance to learn the basics of cultivation, together with the three Rs.

In 1830 spade husbandry was introduced to Saffron Walden in Essex. Before that year great distress prevailed in the region and a general meeting among the inhabitants was held to consider the best course of action to alleviate the poverty among the labouring classes. Lord Braybrooke presided over the meeting, which was attended by the Mayor, several members of the Corporation and numerous parishioners. Among the resolutions the following were unanimously accepted:

'That, both to encourage the industrious labourer and to try the experiment of whether or not land can be tilled on the parish account with benefit to the parochial funds, the said committee be authorised to hire a parcel or parcels of land not exceeding in the whole twenty acres [the quantity then limited by Parliament], and to apportion any part there of in small allotments at an equitable rent, to be let to the labouring poor having families or otherwise, as may be deemed advisable, and to appropriate the residue to the purposes of tillage, for the growth of potatoes, pulse &c. on the parish account; and that in order to stimulate the land-owners in the parish to offer ground for this purpose, the proportion to be paid by them to the parochial officers, on account of work actually done, be two-fifths of the outlay per rod.' (Lord Onslow, *Landlords and Allotments*, 1886, pp11-12)

Lord Braybrooke received invaluable assistance from Messrs Gibson & Co, the bankers of the town, who had long advocated the introduction of allotments for the labouring classes in order to enable them to earn an additional income through their own exertions. At the start of 1830 there were 136 men claiming on the parish at a weekly expense of £40. By 1832 only 86 souls were dependent on the parish and the annual rate (overall) was £560. Many factors influenced the rapid reduction, but the most competent judges attributed the improvement to the inception of allotments. When the allotment system was implemented in November 1830, rick-burning and riotous behaviour prevailed in many adjoining parishes, but Saffron Walden escaped. Not only did labourers with allotments refrain from joining the angry mobs, but they went out on orders of the magistrates to assist in putting down the riots.

Sixteen landlords participated in this venture. Fifty-two acres of land were dug by parochial labourers and the rents varied from 2d to 4d per rod, the land-owner being charged for the work at the rate of 16s to 21s 4d per acre. The labourer obtained considerable remuneration for his effort and well beyond that earned from the farmer or upon the road. The experiment of whether land could be cultivated on the parish account never actually took place. There were so many applications for allotments that the Committee was able to acquire the entire tract of land. The co-operation of landlords and members of the Corporation in letting plots enabled the system to be extended without intervention from the parochial authorities. The additional area covered 33 acres, and by 1833 the entire site was divided into 157 plots, which were let to 144 tenants. Shortly afterwards it was estimated that 700 people were interested in and derived benefit from this successful enterprise.

The profit from each allotment, after deducting the rent and charge for seed, was estimated to be £3 per annum. There was a constant creation of capital, which would otherwise have been non-existent. The attachment of the labourers to their little plots (varying from 20 to 40 rods) increased. Many labourers spent their leisure hours there, and sometimes the whole day, and had now something to call their own.

In 1834 the Poor Law Commissioners were asked to comment upon the subject of allotments. In their report, published on 21 February, the Assistant Commissioners declared their findings. Assistant Commissioner Mr Okeden, having surveyed the West Country, found that there was not a labourer in Wiltshire or Dorset that did not have the use of the land. He added:

'The allotment of land to the labourers divided itself into two chief points: first, as to that quantity of land just sufficient for the cultivation of a labourer and his family during their spare hours; and second, as to that larger quantity which requires to be worked by the assistance of others, or by the entire dedication of the labourer's time. The day is not long past since in every industrious cottage family the wheel and the distaff, the shuttle and the knitting needles were in full activity. At present to compete with machinery would be a useless waste of time, money and labour. I cannot suggest any mode of doing so more profitable to the agricultural labourer and his family than the cultivation of exactly that quantity of land which will occupy these hours as well as his own spare time. This quantity of land is calculated to be one sixteenth of an acre, or ten lug or rods, to each individual capable of work.' (Poor Law Report, 1834, pp278-279)

Mr Okeden calculated that the labourer's expenses in maintaining a 10-rod plot, including the rent at £8 per acre (10s for a 10-rod plot), the labour of setting and storing the crop at home at £3, and the cost of five sacks of potatoes valued at 6s 6d per sack, to be £16 5s 0d, together with a further £1 worth of small potatoes for the feed of a pig. From the total value of £17 5s 0d, the deduction of outgoing expenses of £12 12s 6d left a net profit (per acre) of £4 12s 6d.

Commissioner Mr Walcott, in his report on allotments in North Wales stated:

'The quantity of land, which a labourer can beneficially occupy without interfering with his ordinary labour, is admitted, with scarcely an exception, to be about a quarter of an acre, and certainly not more than half an acre. I examined, on this subject, several small farmers, who from working on their own land as labourers were the best judges of the matter, and in giving the testimony of one or two, I may in effect give all. A farmer in the parish of Guildsfield, in Montgomeryshire, stated that a labourer could not do justice to his master and the land if he had more than half an acre, and that he must be a very industrious and good workman, and be assisted by his wife and family, to work upon even that quantity, which he thought was too much. He added that if he wanted a labourer, and two men, equally strong and equally skilful, were to apply, one of whom had a quarter of an acre, and the other of one or two acres of land, he should without hesitation prefer the former. A farmer in Kerry likewise stated that if a labourer had more than a quarter of an acre he is not a valuable servant, since he is apt to curtail the time which belongs to his master in order to attend to his own land; this, he said, he had found to be the case.' (Poor Law Report, 1834, p282)

Mr Walcott found that throughout most of North Wales labourers were allowed, on payment of so much a bushel, either in money or in kind, to plant as many potatoes as they needed on fallow land owned by the farmer, who in most instances supplied the manure and prepared the ground ready for use. However, if the labourer supplied the manure (many kept a pig), he had the use of the land without charge. This plan was regarded as advantageous to both parties since the labourer gained a cheaper crop than if he rented a plot in the usual way and manured the land. The farmer gained a useful source of income, produce and manure, but had his fallow ground cleared in the process.

Potatoes have always been the number one crop on allotments, and their acceptance as food for the workers coincided with the spread of allotments, especially after 1830.

Mr Walcott continues:

'Where a labourer was possessed of a small portion of land, sufficient, and not more than sufficient, to occupy his leisure time and furnish his children with employment, I found a striking improvement in the general condition of the whole family. The children were early and practically taught the benefits of industry, and the man appeared to be more content with his lot, and had less inducement to keep loose company. From what I witnessed, therefore, I cannot too strongly recommend that every facility should be granted to encourage the occupation of land to this extent by the labouring classes. The measure was warmly advocated by all classes, and is universally popular.' (Poor Law Report, 1834, pp282-283)

Mr Power observed in Cambridgeshire that allotments were generally disliked by the farmers, who were jealous of their deductions and objected to the increased independence of the labourers. However, he added that the movement was much to the credit of the land-owners, and that the system was generally adopted across the county. He said that if the allotment system was to be regarded in its proper light, as a cheap charity on the part of the landlords, there should be little reason for its trenching on the large farms. He added that the instant the allotment was viewed as a source of rent, the influence that caused the small farms to be absorbed into the larger ones would check the breaking up of large farms into small ones again. He also added that although the shortage of leisure hours, including the lack of half-day holidays or complete days, must not only deduct from the labour market, it must place the allotment occupier on a better footing with regard to the terms of employment with the farmers. Mr Power concluded by saying that although he found numerous cases where the allotment system was excluded, eventually, following a successful introduction of the system, the prejudices against providing land yielded to humanity and good sense.

Assistant Commissioner Captain Chapman observed the provision of land at Wells, West Looe, St Germans, Warminster, Frome, Westbury, Bradford and other locations in the West Country. He stated:

> 'At Wells, fifty acres are now granted by the Lord Bishop of Bath and Wells to 203 persons, in quantities varying from one-twelfth to half an acre, at a rent of 12s 6d the quarter acre. Of these persons, not above ten are unmarried, and many are widows. The average of each family being taken at five, upwards of a thousand persons are thus benefited.' (Poor Law Report, 1834, p284)

Captain Chapman noted that in general the plots at Wells were less than an acre, the land was let tax and tithe free, and that the holders paid their rent regularly, prior to the crops being harvested, unless the agent permitted half the crops to be removed first for the purpose of paying the rent. The land was to be kept properly manured, and the hedges and fences were to be left undamaged. To encourage prompt payment, the sum of 2s 6d was refunded to the tenants who paid punctually and adhered to the rules, reducing the rent to 10 shillings for a quarter of an acre. Premiums were also given to the tenants that raised the largest quantity of potatoes on their quarter acre plots. Unlike many other allotments, there were no rules regarding the forfeiture of parish pay, though only three souls took relief, two of whom were infirm.

The Wells plots were established in 1826 with three portions covering 30 acres, which were let to 109 families. In 1831 a fourth portion was added, and a fifth in 1832, thus making a total of 50 acres. The land agent estimated that the value of produce, including 20 sacks of potatoes at £4 10s 0d with other vegetables at £1, yielded a total of £5 10 0d. After deducting the cost of labour and other expenses, estimated to be £2 15s 6d, the labourer was left with a clear profit of £2 14s 6d, assuming that he hired and paid for everything. However, if all the work was undertaken by the labourer, the return was estimated to be £4 4s 6d. Captain Chapman added:

> 'The opinion expressed by the agent was that a man who works for a farmer for twelve hours, six to six, with the help of his wife and family, can manage half an acre, supposing it half potatoes, keep a pig, and support his family, and that a mechanic can do more. The continued increase in the demand for allotments is the best proof of the advantage derived from them. There is a general improvement in the character of the occupiers, who are represented as becoming more industrious and diligent, and as never frequenting those pests, the beer-houses. Frequently, they have been known to work by candle-light. Not a single instance has occurred in which any one thus holding land has been taken before a magistrate for any complaint.' (Poor Law Report, 1834, p286)

At West Looe a portion of common waste had been enclosed within the previous five years, which covered some 22 acres. The land was let in 1 acre, half-acre and quarter-acre plots, at a fixed price of 20s to 15s an acre. Originally the plots were only let to the poor folk within the borough. The only conditions that applied to tenancy were that the rent was paid annually to a committee and, if in default, the occupier was to give up the land. Captain Chapman added:

'The effect on the poor rate has been a diminution from 10s in the pound to 3s; but the moral effect upon the poor is beyond calculation, the population being principally seafaring men who, in bad weather, had no occupation, and who idled about, a dead weight upon the poor rate; but who now have occupation, and who are happy, contented and laborious. I went over the land and found it in excellent condition; the men can pick up seaweed and procure lime on easy terms, so that they can do justice to a larger portion of land than under ordinary circumstances.' (Poor Law Report, 1834, p287)

Assistant Commissioner Ashurst Majendie maintained that the system was beneficial:

'There is no class in society whose feelings and opinions are so much known to each other as the labourers; it can be no secret to them that the crops, which may be raised by their exertions on small plots of land, are infinitely greater than those produced by ordinary cultivation. The denial of land to them will constantly produce an increase of ill-feeling on their part. It is to the proprietors that they must look to for this boon; and it seems probable that nothing can more effectually restore their good feeling, which formerly prevailed between the different classes of society, than the allotment system under prudent regulations.' (Ashurst Majendie, Poor Law Report, 1834, p280)

From 1831 onwards the provision of allotments was largely undertaken by landlords and rectors, and this increased after 1832. After that date there were no further moves to implement allotment schemes through public Acts until 1882, except for the General Enclosure Act of 1845.

By 1833 two out of five parishes in Norfolk had allotments, although there had been considerable delays from the outset, caused by much stubbornness on the part of the farmers. They were still smarting from the effects of the Agricultural Revolt and viewed allotment schemes with deep-seated suspicion. The farmer classes were loath to encourage the labourers, whom they often regarded as troublesome, to gain a foothold toward independence. Many farmers automatically did everything in their power to dissuade labourers from taking allotments.

In 1850 a group of farmers at South Lindsey in Suffolk assembled at Toynton St Peter Vestry to order four labouring tenants on the Duke of Ancaster's estate to sell off their cows and cease all grazing activity in the lanes during summertime. The farmers' fears were largely groundless, because the labourers' lacked security of tenure over their allotments.

Between 1830 and 1850 landlords and other observers recognised the vast social difference between wage-earning labourers who cultivated a plot in their spare time and people who relied entirely upon their cottage gardens for a living. Such gardens only provided cottagers with the barest means to remain above the poverty line. The status of the cottager was seriously undermined by the advent of enclosure. In some regions cottagers managed to retain use of common land that was not enclosed. These were the few that could survive, but even they were less well off than the wage-earning labourers. At Skelton in Cumbria cottagers were described as freeholders poorer than labourers, and that was as late as 1885. Some cottagers turned to enterprises such as market gardening, horticulture, orchards and poultry rearing, which enabled them to survive in post-enclosure villages such as Waterbeach in Cambridgeshire and Sandy in Bedfordshire. Holdings of around 8 acres allowed cottagers to earn a living by cultivating onions, potatoes, French beans and carrots.

Landlords and members of the clergy concluded that wage-earning labourers with an allotment or pasture for the keep of a cow were in a far stronger position. However, many labourers still saw their allotments as the first rung up the social ladder of progress toward achieving a smallholding and thus independence.

A benevolent clergyman wrote on the merits of the allotment system in 1832:

'The advantages attending this system [ie. of allotments not exceeding a quarter of an acre], besides the comfort of the poor man, are the diminution of the Poor's Rate and the moral improvement of the labourer. Since this plan has been in operation the Poor Rate has been steadily declining from about £320 to about £180 per annum, with the prospect of still further diminution. When the farmer's work is scarce the poor man finds profitable employment on his plot of ground, which if he had not to occupy him he would be sent to idle upon the roads at the expense of the parish. The system has the further, and very important, effect of improving the character. When the labourer has his little plot of ground, from which he feels he shall not be ejected as long as he conducts himself with propriety, he has an object on which his heart is fixed; he has something at stake in society; he will not hang loose on the community, ready to join those who would disturb it; so much so that in the late riots no man in the parish showed any disposition to join them.' (*Christian Observer*, 1832)

The Agricultural Revolt stimulated noblemen and landlords to hold numerous meetings across the country to discuss ways of improving the social condition of the labourers. In 1834 they formed an association, known as the Labourers' Friend Society, with the aim of acquiring small plots of land at a moderate rent in addition to a fair price for their labour. Mr Benjamin Willis, the founder member, received support from many prominent landlords, which included the Duke of Bedford, the Duke of Shrewsbury and the Bishops of Bath and Gloucester. The Society flourished for many decades and numerous branches were established throughout the country. The West Surrey branch called to attention the advantages of the allotment system, furnished hints, and gave assistance to those who were willing to accept it. Before the West Surrey branch of the Society began its operations in the county there were only 400 allotments in 24 parishes. In the years following the Society's activities, the number of allotments increased dramatically throughout the county. Numerous other landlords were inspired by the call to supply plots of land.

Sir Henry Bunbury managed the Society's West Suffolk branch, and in 1843 he began to assign small plots of land to a few labourers. He found that labourers with allotments became more respectable in conduct as their social standing and economy improved. By 1845 Sir Henry had more than 100 allotments of varying sizes on his Mildenhall estate. He saw little reason to doubt the merits of the system and stipulated that there should not be any tedious or hard and fast rules governing the amount of land allocated or on the methods of working it. For beginners and labourers with little or no money set aside, Sir Henry let a rood (a quarter of an acre). As the labourer improved the value of his plot, he was granted half an acre in place of his original rood. A few exceptionally industrious tenants held plots of up to 2 and even 4 acres. Sir Henry maintained that half an acre was the ideal plot size and that, with assistance from his wife and children, the labourer could keep his plot in good condition without becoming diverted from his daily wage-earning chores.

Sir Henry thought that far too many landlords interfered with the finer points of their allotments. He advocated giving the labourer free rein on his plot, and to dispense advice only when the tenant made mistakes. He estimated that a well-managed plot of half an acre could yield a net profit of between £3 10s and £5 per annum. At first the tenants mainly cultivated potatoes and wheat, but gradually other crops were introduced, especially beans, which consolidated the ground.

In order to highlight the merits of the allotment system, Sir Henry quoted one of his tenants:

> 'I cannot tell you sir, what my land is worth to me in money. It helps in so many ways: a bit here and a bit there. It helps the children: it feeds the pigs and fowls. It is the best thing that was ever done for a poor man.' (Sir Henry Bunbury on the allotment system in J. Thirsk & G. E. Mingey, *The Agrarian History of England & Wales*, 1989, p725)

A very benevolent lady (who at the time wished to remain un-named) also devoted much attention to the letting of allotments to poor folk, who would otherwise become a burden to society. She started with 50 allotments on her estate in 1830, and by 1843 there were 404. The plots ranged in size from 8 rods to 5 acres. Previous good conduct was, unusually, not a prerequisite for gaining an allotment. All that was necessary was to comply with a specific set of rules and belong to one of several parishes in the vicinity. Failure for adhering to the rules resulted in forfeiture of the allotment and (in theory) any crops on the plot.

Tenants were not allowed to sub-let their plot or any part of their plot without consent from the owner. The removal of straw, hay or manure from the premises was forbidden, and tenants were not permitted to cut gorse or tinder on land that was not hired. Cultivating the land with a horse and ploughshare incurred a fine of 2d per rod. Two crops of the same kind were not to ripen their seed without green or root crops intervening. The produce cultivated was only for consumption by the tenant and his family or his livestock and was not to be sold off the premises. The killing of game was expressly forbidden. Any damage resulting from careless negligence, such as an unfastened gate, was to be redressed within seven days or produce equal to the sum of the damage would be seized from the guilty tenant's plot. For scaling a wall or leaving a hole in a hedge a fine of 6d was imposed. Manure or rubbish was not to be left in the road and there was to be no trespassing on adjoining land. All fines were to be split between the neighbouring tenants, and the land-owner was entitled to re-enter without recourse to legal proceedings. In 12 years there were only four defaulters on this allotment site, and even they were entitled to remove their crops first.

In October 1844 Walton Kent, a surgeon at Bury St Edmunds, described in a lengthy letter to the *Bury Post* the merits of the local allotments. He endeavoured to disprove allegations that the allotments at Town Farm near Walsham le Willows had failed, in spite of their being the largest site in the county. Critics of the system had been very anxious to claim that the Town Farm allotments were unsuccessful. Mr Kent, who lived in the village and knew many of the tenants, refused to accept any criticism of this enterprise.

The allotments were established in November 1833 when part of the farm was allocated for use by the poor. So successful was the venture that the following year further land was added. By 1837 the entire farm was converted into allotments for the villagers, and the effect on the local poor rate was a reduction from 12 shillings in the pound to 6 shillings. There was also a vast reduction in local crime. Although the Town Farm allotments were about 2 miles from the village, the plot-holders became very attached to their land and were frequently to be seen carting away manure to the plots. Mr Kent stated that it was 'very gratifying sight to see 50 or 100 men, women and children all busily employed in clearing the land, digging and planting their little patches of wheat.'

Mr Kent collected statements from 56 of the holders, who all agreed that they were satisfied with their land, though some expressed a desire for larger plots. Some of the plot-holders had work, though much of it was seasonal and quite insufficient on which to keep a family.

John Nunn, a tenant with half an acre of ground, said, 'I am quite satisfied with my allotment; wish I had more; got 14½ bushels of wheat and 14 bushels of Windsor beans: I employ a man for three weeks a year.'

Widow Rebecca Callow cultivated half an acre and had five children to look after. Her eldest son usually dug the land, though when he fell ill she employed another casual labourer. During her son's illness Rebecca had very little help from the parish. Richard Lammas cultivated a little over three-quarters of an acre and said, 'I have a very large family and could not pay my way without my land; I should be out of work for two months of the year if it were not for my land.'

Edward Nice also cultivated three-quarters of an acre and stated, 'I should not want to give it up, for if I did I should be starved; I got 4 coombes of white bread off ¼ acre and 4½ coombes of Windsor beans off the same quantity of land. I and my sons work the land and I always have bread in the house.'

Lydia Hunt, a widow, cultivated 1½ acres and had a large family. She worked the land herself, dug it and cut her wheat, and said that if she should lose it she would be unable to pay her rent. Having lost two husbands accounted for her occupying so much land, as they both had allotments. All the tenants expressed similar views, though in a few cases rents were in arrears and some land was left uncultivated.

Mr Kent ended his letter my stating that:

'The evidence being thus clear and satisfactory as to the benefit of the allotments to the labourers, I will next enquire into the effects which they system has produced upon the general interests of the parish; upon the trades, the payment of the rents of cottages; the finances of the parish and of the alleged increase of pauperism.' (*Bury Post*, 1844, courtesy of the Walsham Village History Group)

The pages of the *Maidstone Journal* for 1844 highlighted the benefits of another allotment scheme at Bearsted in Kent. Around 40 tenants gardened upon this site, which was established by Major Wayth in 1834. The plots ranged from 30 rods to half an acre in extent, the rent being 40 shillings per acre. A plentiful supply of manure from the nearby cottages was greatly appreciated by the gardeners, for they realised that without fertiliser their effort would be a waste of time. The use of liquid manure proved to be exceptionally popular on this site and was considered to give the best results. On the evening of rent day (23 October) the tenants were treated to a hot supper, together with plenty of ale at the Royal Oak on Bearsted Green. The supper, provided for by subscriptions from the local landed proprietors, clergy and gentry, quickly became an annual custom. The whole event was good-natured and Mr Streatfield, the Allotment Committee Treasurer, noted that not one farthing was lost through non-payment of the rent.

In November 1844 the Duke of Marlborough set aside some land for allotments on his estate at Waddesdon at Lady Day. Cultivation was to be with the spade. A correspondent for the *Aylesbury News* stated that for years the land had been bad and the tenants had been 'done good'. The lowest rent was 48 shillings an acre, which was regarded as a 'stiff rent for stiff land'. Even though the tenants did not take their plots until after Lady Day, they were expected to pay up at Michaelmas. The correspondent implied that asking for poor folk to pay six months in advance was little short of sharp practice.

The General Enclosure Act of 1845 allowed for the development of a field garden for the benefit of the labouring poor following enclosure of land within a parish. After this Act, enclosures, Poor Laws and allotments were inextricably connected. These allotments were placed under the management of parish officials or clergymen who acted as wardens and let them on yearly tenancies. Rents were free of rates, taxes and tithes. The construction of any type of buildings on field allotments was expressly forbidden.

Allotments awarded under the 1845 Enclosure Act did not solve the problem of rural poverty and the Enclosure Commissioners frequently found that there was not always a strong desire for them. The allotments were often some distance from the village, situated on heavy clay or stony ground, and their use was peppered with finical restrictions. Their rent was often far above that of the surrounding farmland and, unless a tenant could keep a pig for the manure, they were not particularly productive. To many labourers and their families, such allotments were still an asset and the produce raised supplemented their meagre diet, though at a cost of hard labour after long hours spent in professional toil. Demand for allotments was always strongest in districts where wages were particularly low. Where regions remained un-enclosed there were usually no allotments at all, unless a benevolent landlord provided them.

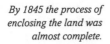

By 1845 the process of enclosing the land was almost complete.

In 1845 Lord Mount Temple introduced a Bill to enable the election of field wardens in parishes that decided to adopt the Act, which gave the wardens the power to hire land and re-let it as allotments, giving a security of rates to the land-owner for his rent. The Government warmly supported the Bill but it failed to pass into law.

The discussion raised many questions in Parliament, and attracted a great deal of attention, which in later years led to the general practise of attaching half an acre or so of land to or near the labourer's dwelling. The aim was to enable the labourer and his family to fill their leisure hours without turning him into a small farmer or leading him to place less dependence on his

Field allotments awarded under the Enclosure Acts were often far from the village. Here tenants raised arable crops.

A rural labourer reaping his meagre harvest from his allotment.

wages. The matter of cultivating a plot while managing to earn a regular income was even raised in the press and periodicals.

'The object of making such allotments is moral rather than economic: the cultivation of a few vegetables and flowers is a pleasing occupation, and has a tendency to keep a man at home from the ale-house. Any extension of the allotment system beyond what a labourer can cultivate easily at his leisure hours ... in the end will be an injury to himself and to others. If he becomes half a labourer and half a cultivator, he runs the risk of failing in both capacities.' (*The Penny Magazine*, 1845)

While the greatest majority of labourers looked upon allotments as a great blessing and were very eager to obtain them, a growing number began to voice their discontent over the high rents charged and of the additional effort required to maintain their plots after a day of work in the fields. In 1850 Oxfordshire farmers were still critical of allotments and insisted that they were 'injurious to the steady industry of the labourer and a heavy tax on themselves'. Labourers were often given the poorest land, which was rented exorbitantly.

In 1846 a 'Dorset Labourer' complained bitterly on the matter of allotment rent, stating that 1 shilling a rod, or £8 an acre, was little more than an imposition. If allotments were thought of as such a great blessing, why were they so over-rented? He argued that if the cottager could afford to pay £8 per acre, then why shouldn't the tenant farmer be asked to pay £4,000 for his 500 acres? Of course, no landlord ever conceived of asking for such a vast sum.

The labourer also questioned whether it was fair that a labourer should have to cultivate an allotment after a lengthy working day. He likened the

*The Dorset Labourer's cottage. He maintained that
a rent of £8 per acre was an imposition.*

situation to a weary traveller who, having walked 30 miles in the course of a day, would think of another 5 miles to go as rather invigorating. He complained that the majority of farmers looked upon their labourers with less concern than a steam engine in full throttle, and that the landlords had painted the Allotment Movement so delightfully that it was little wonder that they regarded themselves as beneficiaries. He stated:

> 'But I speak for experience when I say, if a man works for 10 or 11 hours a day, he is not able, giving himself justice, to work another four or five hours, although for himself. Ever, since I was able, I have been employed in cultivating the ground with the sweat of my brow, and am certain that, if I had the labour to perform night and morning, which I see others perform, I would have been ill-fitted for giving a fair day's work for a fair wage. I know I could not, and know not one in ten who is able to do it.' (*The Agricultural Gazette*, 1846, p363)

He insisted that people who had never had to graft upon the land or put their hands to the plough were not in a position to judge whether labourers could manage further exertion to maintain their plots during their spare hours.

Such was the argument put forth by 'Dorset Labourer' that an 'Industrious Labourer' from Northampton was compelled to reply. He was fearful that such comments would dissuade landlords from letting further land for use as allotments. 'Industrious Labourer' said that allotments let at 1 shilling a rod were rather scarce, and where one was let at that price there were 50 others let at 3d-6d a rod. He also said that allotment cultivation did not necessarily entail a four or five hour stint on the plot every day, and elaborated:

> 'Supposing the allotment consist of 40 rods, the occupier in all probability apportions it off thus, 15 rods for wheat, 20 rods for potatoes and the remaining 5 rods for peas, cabbages and onions. The wheat ground is dug and set by the end of October or November, and the remainder is dug and cropped by the end of March. After that there is very little work to be done by the man, for the weeding can be done by the children; for nothing remunerates a cottager more than picking weeds by hand and burning them; 20 rods of potatoes do not take a long time to earth up, not is it a very fatiguing job; and it is done about the end of May when the evenings are long and the weather is fine.' (*The Agricultural Gazette*, 1846, p587)

'Industrious Labourer' claimed his Dorset counterpart's worries of overwork were largely theoretical. Mowers often worked from three in the morning to nine at night with a two-hour break around midday, and from Monday to Saturday without pausing. A hay-pitcher worked from six in the morning to nine at night, and this was considered (by 'Industrious Labourer') to be light work. He said that most labourers thought little of working for 16 hours a day if it was asked of them during busy times. He also stated that the diligent man who cultivated an allotment well was far more likely to bear the strain of the day's toil, for he was able to afford a larger bit of bacon and bread than the indolent labourer with bread and very little bacon.

Robert Castelles, a Wiltshire landlord, weighed up the points posed by both labourers and was inclined to agree with the Industrious one. Mr Castelles said the real question centred on whether the labouring man received enough payment for his 10 or 12 hours of work in order to support his wife and children. He stated that if it were the case, why was there such a burning desire among labourers to gain an allotment?

Mr Castelles advocated the allotment system, and said that they were of unquestionable benefit to the labouring man. For instance, in a little under two hours an able-bodied worker could plant a rood of potatoes without undue strain. On favourable ground, between 8 and 12 bushels of potatoes could be raised, which were worth 6d a bushel. So even at 1 shilling a rod, the allotment provided better value for effort than labour for the farmer. With regard to overwork, Mr Castelles said it was up to the labourer to decide when to call it a day. Most of his estate workers had allotments, and whether they had been at work on their plots their strength never seemed to alter. He added that if the workers were dispossessed of their plots, they would consider it a bitter blow, but maintained that 60 rods was the maximum size the regular wage earner could manage in his spare time. For the jobbing labourer, he thought as much land as possible should be allocated as would fill up his time when not employed, and that all workers should have the opportunity to rent a piece of land at a reasonable rate. Mr Castelles concluded that cultivation of an allotment reduced crime, encouraged younger generations to become industrious, and lured the worker away from the beer-shop, from poaching and a string of other vices.

By 1846, 5 acres of Birmingham's Botanic Gardens were turned into allotments of 576 square yards (or, as the working class called it, 9 roods). Every 64 square yards was let at 3 shillings per annum, so the rent for each portion totalled 27 shillings. Lord Calthorpe, the land-owner, gained a return of £11 5s per acre every year. Some asked whether this sum amounted to profiteering and thought a reduction should be made possible. Prominent citizens noticed that workers who took allotments improved considerably in their behaviour. The provision of an allotment enabled the workers to breathe fresh air after hours spent in the foul and polluted atmosphere of the factories. The workers also collected all manner of decomposing waste matter from every part of their dwellings and carted it away to their allotments every day. Consequently, the health and the cleanliness of the townsfolk improved considerably. Many hoped that landlords would take such matters into consideration.

Another 'Enterprising Landlord' deduced that provision of an allotment could raise the moral character of the labourer and vastly improve his domestic life, which was often appalling. He noted that the labouring classes rarely appreciated the free gift that extended to money, and all too often the given shilling ended up being squandered in the ale-house. When the labourer earned his shilling it was far more valued and less likely to be frittered away. In support of his theory, 'Enterprising Landlord' conducted an experiment on one of his less discerning labourers. This working man of 45 was prone to be uncivil and indulge in vices of every kind. He was shunned by those around him and considered to be shameless.

One day 'Enterprising Landlord' offered this immodest rogue the chance to cultivate an acre of land. The labourer said he was not sure how to go about it but didn't want to lose anything by it. Generously, but for the sake of the experiment, the landlord agreed to bear any loss incurred and, if there was a dividend from the venture, the labourer could keep it.

Without any kind of gift, not even a shilling, the labourer set about cultivating his acre. He covered his outgoing expenses through a loan from one of his few friends. Costs included £3 for the rent of an acre of land that was free of rates and tithes, 12 shillings for seed oats to plant half an acre, and 13 shillings for the purchase of a pig. Other costs included 17s 3d for potato plants for half an acre and £2 8s 0d for manure to enrich the potato ground. Running costs mounted to 8s 6d for ploughing half an acre of oats and half an acre of potatoes, 18s 6d for cartage, 1 shilling for mowing half an acre of oats, and 3 shillings for threshing half an acre of oats.

The total sum loaned to the labourer amounted to £8 2s. The labourer re-paid his advances in the following manner, with two quarts of oats valued at £2 4s and 105 bushels of potatoes at £5 5s, together with a cash sum of 13 shillings. The total repaid was £8 2s, and all was achieved without so much as a day's work from the labourer, who was engaged in employment elsewhere. A jobbing labourer was hired to sow and gather the oats, while his wife and children undertook the planting and harvesting of the potato crop and looked after the pig. When questioned on the profits, the labourer said:

> 'I have 90 bushels of potatoes on my land and upwards of a quarter, that is 8 bushels, of oats and a stone hog in my sty – a thing I never had in my life before. I have potatoes enough for my family for winter, and for seed next year.' (*The Agricultural Gazette*, 1850, p156)

However, 'Enterprising Landlord' was not done, for he noticed that his new tenant had spent a considerable sum on manure. He suggested that the labourer offer to empty the town cesspit and so gain an abundant supply of manure to enrich the ground. The labourer undertook the chore and his children gathered dung from the roads and lanes.

The following year, instead of having to purchase manure, he sold three loads to nearby residents and neighbours and reduced his overheads from £8 2s to £4 13s, and no longer owed his friend a shilling. The labourer became a reformed character, much to the delight of his employers and family.

By the 1850s the rural population was still diminishing at the rate of 30,000 a year. Since 1840 an escalating demand in the rapidly expanding towns for gardeners, servants, porters, policemen and factory workers offered the labourers the chance to escape the life of grinding poverty. A worker on the railway could earn three times as much as a labourer on the land. In the country towns and larger villages new industries sprang up, such as brick and tile manufacture, stone quarrying, brewing, cement manufacture and corn and seed milling, influenced by urban development. Other labourers enlisted in the Army, while some undertook to migrate when developing lands were opened up overseas.

By the mid-Victorian period wages for agricultural labourers were still less than 12 shillings a week, although north of the coal-line labourers generally received 15 shillings a week together with perks such as potatoes, potato patches and free beer or cider.

Considerable differences existed between allotments under statute of a local landlord and 'potato patches' that were let by farmers within their fields. Allotment-holders enjoyed continuous tenancy, were free to cultivate the crops of their choice, and retained full advantage of their time, effort and manure applied to the land.

For working on a potato patch the ground rent charged by the farmer was often four or five times what the farmer paid to his landlord. Labourers working potato patches were also under obligation to keep the land manured and clean during the growing season. Although many farmers still objected to allotments, they regarded potato patches as an asset. In a small way the labourers gained through this policy. Until the establishment of potato patches, there was considerably less food for the labourers, especially in regions devoted to arable production.

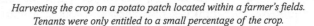

Harvesting the crop on a potato patch located within a farmer's fields.
Tenants were only entitled to a small percentage of the crop.

By the mid-1800s another form of allotment became extremely popular in the West Country, especially in Cornwall and parts of Devon. These grounds bore much resemblance to the Irish conacre. Farmers let out portions of land to labourers and 'potato jobbers'; the farmer ploughed and manured the land and the tenant was responsible for sowing the seed and cultivating the crop, which was usually potatoes. Tenants paid the farmer £5-£7 per acre, though they were only entitled to a small percentage of the harvest. By adopting this method of work, numerous men were able to elevate themselves to become small farmers with several acres of land. Similar developments took place in potato-growing regions of Lincolnshire, and parts of East Anglia.

By the 1840s and '50s the potato had become an essential commodity around the labourer's abode, but dependence on this one crop was to spell disaster.

In 1845 potato blight was found on the Isle of Wight. By 1846 the disease had arrived in mainland Britain and its spread during the warm wet summer was far-reaching and swift. No region escaped the virulent disease. By the end of the growing season Ireland was severely infested with blight, which resulted in widespread famine, death and mass migration to the Americas. At about the same time there was a distinct drop in allotment cultivation in many regions, and some attributed this fact to the arrival of blight. So devastating was the situation in Ireland that little attention was given to the English farmsteads, smallholdings and allotments.

In the 1880s an agricultural correspondent for *The Times* recalled the demise of allotment cultivation at Ebrington in Gloucestershire some 40 years earlier, and conjectured that the possibility of potato disease in the ground may have discouraged labourers from taking plots. After the potato murrain, allotment rental in the region had fallen and by 1847 one in 15 allotments had been given up. Not long afterwards other plots began to fall vacant, and some were taken by a small diary farmer. By Lady Day 1854 the dairy farmer took another 12 unoccupied allotments. During this period a considerable number of allotments stood vacant, thick with weeds and grasses. The allotments, once so eagerly sought after, in many regions remained un-applied for. On one estate, seven batches of allotments were laid to grass, one was turned over to a small farmer, and a further two converted to arable fields. Only three remained in use as allotments, and one was vastly reduced in acreage. The small farmers that applied for the unwanted plots were ready to pay the same rent for them collectively, rather than as separate allotments as previous occupants had done.

Many of the labourers said that it did not pay to take allotments. Consequently, some politicians and landlords inferred that it would be downright rash to provide allotments on a compulsory basis everywhere, at the expense of ratepayers.

Even in the 1860s there was little demand for allotments in the region. Sir Michael Hicks-Beach conducted an experiment to determine how little allotments were sought after. He placed an advertisement in the village shop at Coln St Aldwyns:

'Any householder in Coln St Aldwyns desirous to rent a piece of land of from one to six acres, can learn from Mr G. N. Woolley, Coln Lower Mill, the terms on which it would be let. Early application is necessary.'

Sir Michael displayed the rules of tenancy:

'It will be necessary for tenants to show –

That they are able to command a certain amount of money, say at the rate of £3 per acre.

That their gardens or allotments are well cultivated, and their rents not in arrears.

The land will be let free of tithe, rates and taxes.

Rents to be paid half-yearly; and some simple provisions against exhaustion from over cropping agreed to.

If three acres are taken the rent will be 25s or 20s per acre, according to the situation.

For a piece of land less than three acres a higher rent will be charged; above three acres, rather less; in each case in proportion to the acreage.'

(Lord Onslow, *Landlords and Allotments*, 1886, pp28-29)

Sir Michael also stated that as each of the fields was between 17 and 18 acres, no promise could be made to give it up to that purpose, unless there was a sufficient number of applicants to take it all between them. If only one or two tenants came forward, Sir Michael said that he would accommodate them within existing allotment ground. Not a single application for an allotment was ever made, though the parish consisted of a population of more than 430 of all classes. So the cradle of the Allotment Movement had become the grave. However, elsewhere the story was rather different.

By the middle of the 1860s allotments gained a new level of popularity. This time the earlier resentment and hostility toward the Allotment Movement had largely vanished. Instead it was the general opinion among benevolent landlords and some members of the clergy that possession of an allotment would instil the virtues of thrift and industry among the working classes.

3
Cowgates and gardens

In the 1850s and '60s British farmers prospered, harvests were good and the price for cereals was favourable. During this golden age of farming, questions were being asked about the number of children of minor years being employed in agriculture. In the late 1860s the evils of the gang system were heavily criticised. This led to the passing of the Gangs Act of 1867, which established a licensing system for gang leaders and forbade the employment of children under the age of 8 to work on the land. In 1867 a Royal Commission was appointed to ascertain the extent of women and children working in agriculture. After a short spell this was extended to include men. The Commission also looked closely at the provision of allotments and whether they improved the labourer's welfare. Before the

In the mid-19th century children were employed in agricultural gangs.
An outcry eventually led to the passing of the Gangs Act of 1867.

Commission no one was really sure exactly how many allotments existed across the country. The Commission found that the practise of letting land varied immensely in different parts of the country.

In Kent, allotments were less plentiful as the majority of the cottages had large gardens, some of which were considered to be massive. Lord Harris undertook a survey in the county to determine whether labourers would like a larger garden. Few labourers expressed such a wish, but for those that did provisions were made. Lord Radnor granted a huge quantity of land (size unspecified) at Folkestone to be let as allotments ranging from 10 rods to half an acre, which were situated around the Junction railway station. The plots proved to be very popular and by 1880 there were more than 100 tenants.

In Sussex the Reverend John Goring of Wiston Park allocated considerable tracts of land for labourers, as they were able to stock and farm it. By the middle of the 1800s there were around 30 tenants, who were originally day labourers, and the rents varied from £4 to £60. Lord Gage also took immense interest in the subject and was a warm supporter of the Labourers' Friend Society. The agent to his Firle estate noted that arable allotments were in excess of demand and assumed that pasture allotments, as long as they did not interfere with the labourer's wage-earning chores,

*Many labourers did not require allotments as
they had a large garden affixed to their cottage.*

A farm labourer's wife plants potato seed in their large garden.

would be of great benefit to him. Sussex was one of the few counties to escape the noxious gang system.

The efforts of the Labourers' Friend Society also bore fruit in the neighbouring county of Surrey, and hardly a village was without some form of allotment. On Mr Cubitt's estate, just outside Dorking, a large field was set aside and handed over to a committee consisting of town tradesmen for usage as gardens for the benefit of the poorer inhabitants. Wages in Surrey varied considerably and could be as much as 15 shillings a week within the vicinity of London, while to the west of the county the rate dropped to around 12 shillings.

In Hampshire allotments were generally let at about 32 shillings an acre, and by 1867 the county was well presented with them. On Lord Winchester's extensive estates the Committee of Allotment Holders, which were self-appointed, settled the amount of compensation to be paid by the incoming to the outgoing tenant. His Lordship was of the opinion that, provided the tenants were of good character, the duty of deciding compensation, in case of disturbance, could be entrusted to the Committee. Rent for allotments in the county was considered to be low by comparison with other regions. Mr Chamberlayne of Cranbury devoted extensive tracts of land for allotments on the outskirts of Southampton, not only for poor labourers but also for artisans and craftsmen from the town.

In Wiltshire there was no shortage of allotments or tenants wanting to garden upon them. Wages were as low as 9 to 11 shillings a week, so the opportunity to cultivate a plot of land was warmly received by labourers. Lord Pembroke, who had 900 allotments on his estate, thought that there was still room for the system to be extended. Lord Pembroke was also of the opinion that the matter of providing allotments by landlords and their agents should be set on more of a business footing to generate a profit, rather than just as a benefit to the labourers. On average the annual rent for allotment land in Wiltshire was 5d per rod. On the Marquess of Ailesbury's estates there were in the region of 268 acres and 39 rods devoted to allotments, which were divided into 973 plots varying in size from 20 to 100 rods each. Such provision was not exceptional in the county. The Marquess's agent, Mr Woolcott, stated that allotments were very popular and they appeared to exist on all similar estates.

In 1830 Lord Carnarvon wrote that almost every cottager occupied a sufficient portion of land to cultivate vegetables for his family, as well as to fatten his pig. Lord Nelson further elaborated on the development of allotments and holdings:

'Let me give a short account of how my smallholdings have been formed. In one parish I asked the farmer of a 400-acre farm to give up some 40 acres near the village for allotments: this he did gradually, as he had taken the wheat crop off the land. It is now let to 85 tenants in portions varying from 20 rods to 2 acres apiece, 15 having over an acre, at a rent of £3 per acre. Losing a little over 2 acres in paths and roadways, I get, after paying £24 for rates and taxes, about £2 per acre. The men who have it do not grumble: there are hardly ever any vacant allotments, and though outsiders say the rent should only be £1 instead of £3, I well know if I sold it in 2-acre pieces for building purposes I could easily get £100 an acre for the land.

In another parish, in the middle of the parish being given up, I divided it into cow-land, fencing and building cowsheds, paying rates and taxes, and giving the tenant the permanent grasses to lay down in pasture where not already meadow land. Part of another farm, about 40 acres, falling in, I similarly divided it in agricultural allotments to four tenants, as it was also within easy reach of the village.' (Lord Nelson writing to Lord Onslow)

On Sir George Jenkinson's estate in 1856, around 56 acres were let as allotments of one-third of an acre, and they were all taken immediately. In 1863 a further 11 acres were added. As the local population was somewhat scattered, portions of 11 different fields situated as near to the cottages as possible were chosen. Tenants were charged 3½d per rod and in every case the landlord was responsible for payment of tithes, taxes and other expenses. By the 1880s, when wages rose and the price of corn fell, around 10½ acres of the original 48 were given up, and almost 3 acres lay unoccupied. Another 12 acres were re-let to small tradesmen, who had cultivated allotments before.

The Commissioners discovered that in Berkshire allotment rents were very much higher than the surrounding land, on average 3d to 6d per rod. Lord Wantage had done much to help smallholders across the region, and in 1854 the Wantage Society also provided the poor with allotments. Of the 35 plot-holders, the Society reported that during the first year 18 tenants cultivated their plots well, six more than well, six very well indeed, four in a middling fashion, and only one rather badly.

In Buckinghamshire allotments were very numerous on Lord Carrington's estate, though many said that the rent charged was rather high, which may have led to some disinclination to take them. When a reduction in the rent was made the allotments became more popular than ever. At Steeple Claydon, Sir Harry Verney, Bart, established 7 acres of allotment land on Stifflands Farm. The plots of quarter of an acre were let at 10 shillings to the local cottagers, who had previously undertaken a trek of 2 miles to reach their allotments. The land was let on condition that only vegetables would be cultivated. Near Henley, on the Berkshire border, there was little demand for allotments. Mr Mackenzie of Fawley Court offered some 200 acres of land close to the town for allotments, but there were very few applications. In the more rural districts the system was on the increase. The Duke of Buckingham found plenty of occupiers for the land, which his farm-tenants surrendered for the purpose. In regions where there was difficulty in establishing allotments, farmers often gave potato ground.

The West Country was extremely well provisioned with allotment gardens of one sort or another. In Dorset, Lord Allington hired suitable tracts of land and sub-let it (at a loss to himself) in 144 allotments as well as providing allotments on his own land. Close to Blandford, land was let at £2 an acre. On Lord Rivers's estate allotments had been in existence for many years and he granted tenancy not only to labourers but also to anyone interested in cultivating them. Lord Sherborne took a great deal of interest in the question of supplying allotments and drew up the first written record for the letting of allotment land around 1840. Entry was to be on 15 November, and notice to vacate was to be given on 1 August; the incoming tenant was permitted to plant his winter crops on the plot from the latter date. Each tenant was entitled to keep one pig but not to grow unchanged crops on the same land for two successive years. Under-letting by tenants was expressly forbidden. No work was to be conducted on the allotment during the hours of farm labour without the master's consent. All rents were to be paid within 10 days of 15 November. Any conviction of a crime resulted in forfeiture of the allotment. In Dorset, wages were generally around 8 to 9 shillings a week, and the Commissioners failed to see how the family could earn sufficient to support life without the granting of a potato patch or allotment. The Commissioners noted that the usual rent was around £4 per acre.

Devon was another county where the system of providing allotments reached near perfection, due to the low wage rate. When Canon Girdlestone became Vicar of Halberton, near Tiverton, he found that the labourers were forced to live on 7 to 8 shillings a week, with additional allowances such as cider, and sometimes a cottage. Carters and shepherds, who worked longer hours, usually received a shilling more. For extra work at harvest time, labourers usually received payment in the form of their supper. Additional cash payment was rarely made, except in the case of piecework. Fuel was only given to the labourers when they grubbed up a hedge. In numerous cases, labourers were forbidden by the farmer to keep a pig or poultry for fear that they would steal the food for fattening them.

Sir Thomas Dyke Acland took great interest in the welfare of his tenants, and at Broadclyst had more than 250 allotments in 24 different regions. They varied from 20 to 40 rods in extent. The total rent paid for 55½ acres amounted to £127 8s. The expenses and outgoings amounted to £44, leaving a net rental of £83, or 30 shillings per acre. The allotments were taken by 170 agricultural labourers, 48 mechanics, six tradesmen, ten gardeners, 18 widows and other persons. The rents remained unchanged for half a century, though the time of entry was changed to November in the 1880s. Sir Thomas, who had very liberal views on the land question, also had numerous allotments close to the town of South Molton, which were let to 113 tenants. The rent for the allotments was generally 9d per rod or 7s 6d per annum, but 1s 6d was refunded to the tenant for prompt payment, which reduced the rent to 7¼d per rod or 6 shillings per acre a year. The return per acre amounted to £4 16s gross, but the outgoings, which were paid for by the tenant, amounted to 18 shillings per acre; the net rent was £3 17s 6d per acre. The adjoining agricultural fields were let as accommodation land at rents of 5 shillings per acre, the tenants paying the outgoings. When compared to the fields, the allotments were not thought of as highly rented, but one tenant thought that they should not pay proportionately more than the average rent of the farm, which was about £1 per acre.

Inquiries were also made of other allotments around South Molton and it was discovered that some were let at 1 shilling and others at 9d, and those let by the Town Council were 4d to 4½d per rod. However, the quality of Sir Thomas's plots was very high while those let by the Town Council was generally inferior; the latter were not fully taken up owing to the poor quality of the ground and the exposed nature of the site. A longstanding tenant on Sir Thomas's estate said that the allotment, if managed properly, could yield a fair return, and calculated that the crops following the potato harvest should cover the rent costs and other expenses, leaving the potato crop as pure profit. He estimated his expenses as follows: rent at 6 shillings per annum, manure at 10s 6d and labour at 15 shillings, resulting in a total of £1 11s 6d. This tenant grew a bag of potatoes with a profit of 35 to 40 shillings, and the aftercrop was sufficient to pay the expenses. The tenant, naturally, was quite happy with the rent charged.

In the 1860s the Hon Mark Rolle devoted more than 1,000 acres of his estate to the development of field allotments. Plots ranged from 1 to 12 acres apiece and there were almost 1,000 tenants. The average size of each allotment was an eighth of an acre and the rent of 5 shillings to 6s 8d was paid in advance in January each year. Mark Rolle was firmly convinced, as many landlords were, that a plot of 20 rods was the maximum amount of land for which a working man could find manure and could cultivate during after-work hours. He also noted that the greatest number of his tenants also had gardens attached to their cottages. Mark Rolle had plans to extend the system of allotments on his other estates. On a neighbouring estate, belonging to Lord Clinton, the tenants had allotments of a quarter of an acre each and their social condition was vastly improved as a consequence.

In Cornwall miners on higher wages were less interested in the chance to obtain allotments, though many were enthusiastic about taking up a few acres of grassland.

In 1873 the Parliamentary returns showed that Northampton had a greater number of allotments than any other county. The rent for plots was roughly 3s 6d per rod. Lord Henley noted that there were many complaints that allotments were left in a bad state of cultivation. During his 40 years of involvement with the allotment system, he had rarely encountered cases of badly neglected allotments. Lord Spencer also implemented a scheme to allow labourers to cultivate smallholdings on a farm of 300 acres. The inhabitants made the choice of tenants by ballot. Eventually eight men worked on the farm, together with one manager, who received wages of 14 shillings a week. The tenants were entitled to split the profits between themselves after repaying 4% of the original capital, back to Lord Spencer.

In Worcestershire and Herefordshire the farm labourer received a wage of 10 to 12 shillings a week and in addition got two rows of potatoes in one of the fields, a supply of skimmed milk and the occasional rabbit. Even so, the provision of allotments was not gregarious, partially due to the region being a major fruit-growing area. On Sir H. F. Vernon's estate, allotments were let and trees were even supplied to the tenants. The rental value was the same as that of the surrounding farmland plus outgoing expenses. The tenants had to pay an additional amount when their trees began to bear fruit, which enabled the landlord to recoup his initial expenditure on supplying the trees. When the balance was met there was no further increase in the rent. The land was exceptionally good for the culture of fruit trees and close to a railway station. Gardens close to the town of Wellington were let at £8 an acre, while less than a quarter of a mile away in the same town allotments went begging at 64 shillings an acre with tithes of 16 shillings an acre, which were paid by the landlord.

Oxfordshire was one of the counties least affected by industrial expansion and consequently the labourer's wages remained low, at between 10 and 11 shillings a week, so there was considerable demand for allotments. During the early 1800s parochial authorities in this county appear to have been unreceptive to the provision of allotments. Between 1846 and 1866 some 20 enclosure awards were made in 40 parishes, under the General Enclosure Act of 1845. The highest percentage of allotments was supplied through private agreement by landlords, including the Duke of Marlborough, Vernon J. Watney Esq, Lord Bertie, the Earl of Ducie, and the Earl of Jersey. The Duke of

Marlborough was the largest and most eminent provider of allotment land in the county; in 1867 there were more than 900 plots on his Oxfordshire estate.

By 1886 only one-seventeenth of the labourers in Oxfordshire were given potato patches and no cow pasture was provided. In 1873 there were 9,088 allotments, but by 1889 this figure reached 17,947. Between 1883 and 1889 the majority of allotments were of the small garden type ranging in size from an eighth to a quarter of an acre.

In Bedfordshire it became customary to let allotments at the same value as ordinary agricultural land. On the Duke of Bedford's estate allotments of 20 rods to a quarter of an acre were let to tenants and cultivated in addition to cottage gardens. The Duke, who owned 1,116 cottages, was anxious to provide allotments for the cottagers and extend the existing gardens as the allotments were some distance from the labourers' dwellings. On the Duke's estates in Bedfordshire and Buckinghamshire there were 1,204 allotments, five farms of less than 50 acres and 14 farms under 100 acres. On his estates in Cambridge, Northamptonshire and Huntingdonshire, there were 414 allotments, 17 farms under 50 acres and six farms under 100 acres. On the estates of Mr Charles Magniac MP, every tenant with two or three exceptions had a garden as well as an allotment, and the rent varied from 20 to 33 shillings an acre. At one stage the tenants were gathered together to be informed that they might have as much land as they wished and had means to cultivate. Not one application was made for more land.

In the eastern counties the Commissioners discovered that allotments were extensive and that there was reputedly an ever-growing appetite for additional plots. In the Saffron Walden region of Essex, of three parishes with an acreage of 64,000 acres, there were 232 acres of land devoted to allotments, which was divided into 1,300 allotments ranging in size from one-sixth to half an acre. The rent was 1½d to 4½d per rod. Tithes, rates and the cost of maintaining fences and paths were paid for by the land-owners. In 18 of the 23 parishes nearly all of the land-owners allowed their tenants to cultivate from 10 to 40 rods with potatoes on their farms every year, without charging any ground rent. The tenants were responsible for manuring the ground and keeping the crop clean during the growing season. The employers supplied cartage for the manure, provided the means of tillage and transported the potatoes to the tenant's homes. This privilege extended to the widows of deceased labourers, and in a few cases farmers provided manure free of charge.

In Suffolk Sir Edward Kerrison and Lord Henniker took great pains to give the labourers the opportunity to gain an interest in the cultivation of the soil. On Sir Edward's estate there were more than 500 allotments by 1880, although previously, when growing seasons were bad and prices low, 10 acres of allotment land were ploughed up for want of tenants. Lord Henniker carefully monitored the progress that tenants made on their allotments; if one showed the ability to cultivate a larger space he was given the chance to increase the size of his holding. On the Duke of Grafton's estates there were 820 allotments, which were let at 29 shillings an acre compared to 25 shillings for the adjoining farmland. The Duke also provided every facility that the labourers needed to manage their plots.

In Norfolk allotments were implemented in much the same was as in Suffolk. In 1835 Lord Suffield was convinced that the only method of improving the labourer's lot was to provide him with an area of land to cultivate. The Earl of Kimberley also let allotments on his Norfolk estate, and Colonel Bulwer offered to cut up 40 acres of land in one parish, though there was not a single response from the labouring classes. In some regions of Norfolk allotments were not requested or demanded and ordinary folk went about their daily work and thought little of allotments. The situation in Norfolk was very much an exception, for overall allotments were very popular in the southern counties.

North of the coal-line the Commissioners found a very different picture regarding labourers' living conditions and their attitude toward allotments. Labourers in the majority of Midland and Northern counties were earning 12 to 15 shillings a week, often lodged with their farmer masters and in many cases were hired on an annual basis.

The Commission found that in Warwickshire allotments were highly cherished on the outskirts of the towns. Around Birmingham, Lord Norton gave every able-bodied cottager a quarter of an acre of land, and increased

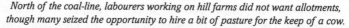

North of the coal-line, labourers working on hill farms did not want allotments, though many seized the opportunity to hire a bit of pasture for the keep of a cow.

the holding to half an acre as the tenant improved his ground. In the Midland counties grazing was the main form of agriculture and the renting out of small plots of land for cultivation in rural areas was almost unknown. In 1873 the Agricultural Department stated that out of the whole of Cheshire and Derbyshire, only 28 acres were let as garden allotments. In Cheshire labourers were provided with spacious three-roomed cottages with large gardens attached, which were let at the rate of £4 10s a year. Some labourers were able to rent cottage farms at £8 to £10 per annum and their earnings, not to mention home comforts, compared favourably to artisans and merchants in the townships. Lord Tollmache allowed his farm workers to hire 3 acres of grassland for the keep of a cow.

In Shropshire the situation was very similar to Cheshire. On Sir Baldwin Leighton's estate the practise of letting land to labourers started in the early part of the century and he advocated the system publicly and in print. On his estate some labouring families had been on the same plot for more than a generation. Throughout the county tenants often occupied holdings of less than 15 acres. On Colonel Edwards's estate there were large farm tenancies consisting of nearly 20 holdings of 13 acres apiece, which were occupied by labourers or village tradesmen who embraced almost every vocation in the countryside.

Throughout Derbyshire allotments were little sought after but pasture for the keep of a cow was much desired and they came to be known as 'Cowleys'. This was partly due to the fact that most cottages had gardens or small plots of ground affixed to them. In rural regions and mining villages, allotments were greatly prized by miners and mechanics. Mr Culley, Assistant Commissioner in the early 1870s, stated:

'I believe it would be impossible to over-estimate the value of such a provision of milk as is within the reach of the families of most Derbyshire labourers. Many labourers in the north of Derbyshire rent with their cottages six or eight acres of grassland with a shippon attached, and are thus enabled to keep two cows during both summer and winter. Others rent a smaller quantity of grassland, which they mow, and graze their cows during summer in one of their master's fields, or more commonly in the nearest nobleman or gentleman's park. Others again, who live near a park where they can enjoy this privilege, and who have no cow of their own, borrow one from a farmer, and so get her milk for the summer months at a cost of from £3 to £4.

Some further examples of the evidence received on this subject will perhaps explain the milk system better, and show how, in the opinion of persons who know both classes, a labourer with his cow-allotment compares with a small farmer.' (Lord Onslow, *Landlords and Allotments*, 1866, p33)

Mr Cottingham, agent to the Duke of Devonshire stated:

'The cottages all have gardens, and most of them have sufficient land to

*A cow provided labourers with a valuable resource,
especially in districts where milk was scarce.*

winter a cow. In summer they pasture their cows in Chatsworth Park, paying £3 for the summer grass, about twenty-one weeks.'

On the subject of cow-allotments versus small farms Mr Cottingham says:

'I think that a man with a small allotment of, say, ten acres, to keep a couple of cows, is better off than the holder of twenty or thirty acres or a farm just big enough to tempt him to do nothing but work on his farm. I reduced one man to ten acres from twenty to compel him to work, and he afterwards told me I had "made a gentleman of him". He now works for the Duke of Devonshire at 14s a week, and has his grass allotment of ten acres. This system works well, bringing up a good class of labourers, and giving their wives an occupation at home.' (Lord Onslow, *Landlords and Allotments*, 1886, p34)

The Reverend J. Hall, Vicar of Edensor, stated:

'I am clearly of the opinion that the small farmers – persons holding from thirty to sixty acres of land – are as a class worse off in this neighbourhood than the labourers, who receive generally from 14 to 18 shillings per week. On the other hand, where a labourer can have, as is common with us, just as much grassland as will enable him to keep one or two cows, which can be managed by his wife, with scarcely any demand upon his own time, his position is undoubtedly much better than that of those to whom this is denied. I am satisfied that these views are shared by nearly all who are acquainted with the district.' (Lord Onslow, *Landlords and Allotments*, 1886, p34)

Samuel Turner, bailiff to the Duke of Devonshire in the district of Bakewell, noted that although the labourers could hardly be called well-off, they were generally of enough substance to be able to keep one or two cows. They invariably fared better than the small farmer who had less than 100 acres and had a great struggle in making a living from the land. The labourers that had no land of their own were usually able to 'ley' a cow for 20 weeks at around £4 a season.

In Nottinghamshire, allotments were very common and in some cases were let free. By contrast labourers that were of a more self-reliant disposition took little advantage of this charitable benefit. Labourers earned on average 2s 6d a day and the wives 1 shilling. There was very little evidence of the gang system and farm workers were more particular about keeping their children at school.

In Leicestershire cow-allotments were much in vogue during the 1860s and 1870s. The cottages were often built close up to the road with little or no garden. A considerable number of allotments existed in the county, though many were left vacant. On Lord Henry Halford's estate tenants grew cereals on their allotments, but by the 1870s the acreage was reduced, owing to the lower price for grain.

In Northumberland, Cumberland, Westmorland, Durham and Lancashire there was very little demand for allotments owing to the higher standard of living. Many labourers were hired by the year and afterwards were free to leave their master and move to another district if they wished; the majority felt less compelled to take up garden allotments. In 1867 Lord Sefton set aside a 25-acre field on his estate on the outskirts of Liverpool, which was conveniently situated near the railway line. He advertised that small plots of land ranging from a quarter of an acre to 1 acre were available for hire, but not one application was received. Some years later the Dukes of Northumberland wished to prevent the yearly emigration of farm labourers to the towns by making tenants hold direct to the landlord instead of the farmer. They established small villages and clumps of four or five cottages on their estate. Each cottage had a stable, a garden and 3 or 4 acres of land attached, which was let at a very low rent. Except for two or three locations, most of the villages and clumps of cottages had been absorbed into neighbouring farms, such was the demand for smallholdings. The labourer clearly preferred the cottage and garden at the farm to the large holding.

Arable allotments were not very popular in Yorkshire, and when Lord Wenlock let land he did not receive a single application for an allotment. Mr Portman told the Commissioners of 1867:

'In one part of the county at least, the advantages enjoyed by the Yorkshire agricultural labourers generally in yearly hirings, high weekly wages, opportunities of piecework and good gardens attached to their cottages, or as allotments in default of them, are, according to the evidence of the Rev S. Surtees, made good use of towards securing provision in old age.' (Lord Onslow, *Landlords and Allotments*, 1886, p42)

In Yorkshire the custom of keeping a cow flourished and almost every labourer had his 'cow and three acres'. On Sir George Wombwell's estate of 12,000 acres, practically all the cottages had not less than 3 acres of meadow or pasture, and to every dwelling was attached a cow-house or piggery. Labourers paid £4 to £5 per annum for meadow grassland and an additional £6 per annum for the run of cowgate or pasture. The system of cow-allotments had been in operation for some years on the Newburgh estates and Sir George Wombwell lost little time in expanding it. Throughout the region 'cow clubs' flourished and they worked well for the labourers. Membership to a cow club did not usually commence until the labourer lost a cow; however, heavy losses of cattle during a murrain left little if any funds to meet the needs of many a club.

In some clubs when a cow died each member paid 7 shillings a month to make up the £11 required. This sum was collected by the pasture master, an office that changed every year. There were no further collections until another member lost a cow. Many other clubs already had a sum in the bank, so that when a member's cow died they paid the bereft member the sum of £10 out of the funds and commenced to collect 1 shilling a month from each member until the full amount was restored to the fund. This system was a distinct advantage to the member who lost the cow as he was spared the indignity of seeking subscriptions from his richer neighbours. One of the most organised of all cow club schemes was conducted on the estate of Mr Heneage, the Chancellor of the Duchy of Lancaster. The entrance fee and monthly subscription to the Hainton Estate Cow Club in Lincolnshire were required before any member suffered a loss. Precautions were also taken, and the cows of labourers to be admitted to the Club were subject to stringent and thorough examination.

The Hainton Club had many rules and regulations, with which the tenants eagerly complied. It was formed for the parishes of Hainton, South Willingham, Benniworth, Six Hills, Legsby, East Barkwith and East Torrington. The Committee consisted of three members from each of the parishes of South Willingham and Benniworth and two each from Hainton and Sixhills, in addition to the President and Treasurer. All members, except the President, were to retire or step down at the annual general meeting, held every April, but they were still eligible for re-election. To become members of the Club, people had to be tenants on the Hainton estate paying less than £50 a year in rent, or cottagers in parishes that the Committee thought desirable to admit. The accounts of the Club were balanced on 31 March every year and subsequently audited by the Club Auditor, who was appointed by the Committee. All book-keeping was conducted within the first two weeks of April.

Each member of the Club paid the sum of 5 shillings for each cow entered and a fee of 2s 6d for every change of a cow. The subscriptions were paid monthly to the person appointed to receive the fees and they were paid on the first Monday in each month. The Committee appointed one member in each district to receive the members' subscriptions and they were responsible for transferring them to the Treasurer before the first week of each month. The Treasurer then deposited the money in a Post Office Savings Bank before the last day of the same month. Any member neglecting to pay his subscriptions for three consecutive months was given a warning by the receiver of subscriptions. If the sum was not paid by the first Monday of the following month, the guilty tenant ceased to be a member of the Club. Any labourer or tenant wishing to enter a cow into the Club had to give notice to the Committee members in the district, who would examine the age, health and value of the proposed cow. No cow older than seven years could be entered, nor could any animal with a value less than a yearly average of £12. The member was not entitled to receive any fund payments if the cow died of milk fever or lung complaint if it was discovered that the tenant had knowledge that the cow was afflicted with the disease beforehand. Marking pincers were provided for the Club to mark each cow to be entered. Each cow passed by the Committee was marked on the ear on the milking side, and no cow was considered entered until it was marked.

When any cow became ill, the owner had to apply to the person who kept the drinks in the district, who was to visit the cow and, if he thought necessary, direct the owner to call in the farrier without loss of time. In cases of emergency the Committee allowed the owner to recoup the cost of any medicine administered to the cow even when the Club farrier had not been called in. Any club member who lost a cow was allowed the sum of £12 from the fund. New members to the Club were not allowed any benefit from the funds until their cow had been in the Club for one month, and the same rule applied to every new cow entered. If the member's cow exceeded 14 years of age, he was not entitled to receive any benefit from the Club funds. Any member who lost his cow and made a claim upon the Club for the same was entitled to the skin, but if value could be gained from other parts of the carcase, the money was ploughed back into the Club funds. The Club appointed a farrier, and a person was also appointed in each district to keep a supply of drinks for the use of the Club. If any dispute arose over any of the rules or regulations, they were to be settled by the members of the Club Committee, whose decision was final. The rules of the Hainton Estate Cow Club were extensive, but it was very much an exception.

Elsewhere in Lincolnshire there were two distinct types of allotment, arable and pasture. With arable allotments labourers were given as much land as they could work in their spare time, which was often of 1 rood if they had a fair-sized garden affixed to their dwelling, and half an acre if they did not. The cultivation of an arable allotment depended upon the family and the help they were able to provide in managing the land. The situations that favoured success were that the ground was in good condition, the rent was a fair sum, the land was not to be more than half a mile from the labourer's dwelling, with a good road for necessary access by cart. The number of allotments on a site needed to be proportionate to the number of labourers seeking them so as to create a little in the way of competition and so keep the ground in a good state of cultivation.

With pasture allotments a different strategy was adopted. Pasture plots varied in accordance with the amount of ground needed, and dimensions varied from enough grassland for a single cow to those adequate for a tiny dairy farm. The general rule was to give the labourer as much grassland with his cottage as he had money to stock. The cottages were often specially selected for such tenancies, since it was desirable for them to have a small cool room for the dairy and an exterior outhouse or shed to house the livestock. Such buildings often became known as 'cow cottages' and there was always a great demand for them. Labourers in service before they were married could often save a considerable sum, and many kept an eye on the possibility of gaining a small cottage or farm dwelling. Many landlords stated that there was much advantage to this system, which provided the labourer with additional income alongside regular wages.

It generally fell to the wife to look after the cow and attend to the dairy while the labourer worked for his master or on neighbouring farms for cash wages. Such tenants paid their rents with the greatest regularity and even during lean times asked for no reduction of them. When grassland near a village became vacant there were often numerous applications for it, which indicated that many labourers had aspirations to invest in a small plot of land without giving up their wage-earning capacity. When a field was too large for one tenant, some land-owners let it to three conjointly, each tenant being entitled to pasture a certain quantity of stock. On one estate in Northamptonshire, the owner provided pasture for ten applicants from the neighbouring village conjointly as a cow-common.

In Wales the system of smallholdings was so extensive that the provision

Many young couples kept their eye on the possibility of getting a 'cow cottage'.

The job of looking after the cow often fell to the wife,
while the labourer was away on his wage-earning chores.

of garden allotments was almost unknown. Lord Sudley, writing of his Welsh property, elaborated:

'On the Gregynog Estate the proportion of small farms is fully maintained, and there are at present no less than 76 smallholdings under 45 acres, and that of those 50 range from two to eleven acres, so that ample scope is given to smaller tenantry to gradually rise to larger-sized farms. This principle of granting in arable districts quarter or half an acre, or instead, where there is pasture available, land under proper conditions sufficient to enable cottagers to keep a cow, is one which I have always been much in favour of, and I am extremely glad to see that there is a wish to have this system more fully carried out. It is not, of course, possible in every case to give sufficient pasture to keep a cow, as due regard must be paid to the conditions and requirements of the neighbouring farms, but, so far as I am concerned, I can only say that I should be extremely pleased to see no exception to the rule, and that in all cases where it is wished industrious and thrifty persons in cottages on the Gregynog Estate should be possessed either of half an acre of garden land, or, wherever possible in pasture districts and where a tenant has the sufficient capital, land enough to keep a cow. It will be clearly quite impossible to extend this system hurriedly, but every consideration will be given to carry it out as soon as possible.' (Lord Onslow, *Landlords and Allotments*, 1886, pp54-55)

Arrangements were made with certain farmers to provide some fields near the principal village on the estate. This district was mainly pasture, and allotments of this class of land were made to eight cottagers. On Lord Sudeley's estate at Toddington in Gloucestershire large tracts of land were devoted to arable, and cottagers were provided with gardens measuring a quarter of an acre, which was considered to be sufficient in most cases. An additional quarter of an acre was supplied to two or three tenants who made such a request.

In Wales the social standard of farmers and labourers was almost equal. Labourers usually boarded at the farmhouse, and many of the farms employed no labourers at all, every member of the family working, often without wages, while the employer was himself a kind of head shepherd. Wages varied tremendously in different parts of Wales. Around the mining districts they ranged from 15 to 18 shillings a week, while in Anglesey the pay was 11 to 12 shillings a week. A large number of imported children were employed and it was not unusual for boys of ten to work as farm servants for eight months of the year, receiving 6d and board.

In spite of the Royal Commission's findings, Liberal MP Charles Shaw-Lefevre caustically implied that the provision of allotment land was, in comparison to that taken during enclosure, insignificant. The forthcoming Enclosure Bill for 1869 proposed to enclose 8,900 acres, and only 6 acres were designated for allotments. Eventually the Bill was stopped, through severe criticism, in the House of Commons.

In a report published in 1867-68, a Nottingham clergyman stated that the provision of allotments delayed wage rises for the labourers, which the Commissioners considered to be well founded. Some years later Mr Herbert Paul wrote:

'The agricultural labourer of 1873, coals and blankets not withstanding, was worse lodged and worse fed than cattle... The wages did not suffice for the decent maintenance of more than a single individual. If he had a family he was dependent either upon aid from outside or at least from his own children.' (Herbert Paul, *History of Modern England*)

In the early 1870s the concept that too much land was owned by too few began to take hold. Critics implied that ownership of the land should be more widely distributed, especially where working folk could benefit. Considerable difficulties remained with provision of allotments in numerous regions. The agricultural labourers often said that members in both Parliamentary parties had made little effort to make it easy for them to gain an allotment. Parliamentary returns for 1873 showed that there were 243,000 allotments across England and Wales, which on average were a quarter of an acre apiece.

Throughout the 1860s and '70s the provision of allotments largely hinged on the goodwill of benevolent land-owners, though the conditions of tenancy (apart from high rents charged) were often trying. During these decades the labourers' outlook was slowly beginning to change. Many read the newspapers and became interested in political events. Opportunities for work in the expanding towns increased and consequently the labourers that remained on the land displayed a new level of belligerence toward the farmers, often striking for higher pay at harvest time.

In 1866 union activity commenced in Kent, and by 1871 had spread to other counties like Hertfordshire, Buckinghamshire and Lincolnshire. The farm labourers had suffered in silence after the revolt of 1830 and were smarting in temper over the low wages, poor housing and lack of land. Social agitation was once again about to trigger a rapid expansion in the development of the Allotment Movement.

4
Victorian Acts and acres

Toward the later part of the Victorian era the Allotment Movement became an increasingly political one. Much recrimination existed between the Tories and Liberals on the subject of providing land for the labouring classes. At the second annual meeting of the Allotments & Smallholdings Association in January 1886, Joseph Chamberlain said:

'The Tories have lied on this subject with a vigour and a pertinacity and a unanimity which had almost elevated mendacity to the rank of a virtue.'
(Lord Onslow, *Landlords and Allotments*, 1886, p1)

After 1884 it was often said that if the labourers voted for the Liberals they would get their 'three acres and a cow', and Jesse Collings, the radical politician, adopted this phrase as his rally cry for liberal reform. At the beginning of the 1880s the Liberals were keen to break the landlords' monopoly and supported the advocates of 'Free Land'. Just as the riots of 50 years earlier had stirred benevolent land-owners into providing plots for the workers, so the Liberals were motivated by further unrest prevalent among rural labourers.

In 1874 the agricultural labourers were agitating for a wage increase once again. Unlike the revolt of 1830, the nature of the dispute was less violent and the behaviour of the labourers was largely exemplary. This time the workers, led by Joseph Arch, had formed the first National Agricultural Labourers' Union, who opted for strike action as opposed to indulging in criminal activity. Instead it was the farmers who got angry and appealed to the landlords for help. The farmers responded to the strike with a massive and almost universal lockout, which eventually threw more than 10,000 labourers out of work. The strike commenced in May and for the first five weeks of the dispute the Union managed to fund its members with 1s 6d a day. Throughout the lockout those who had allotments found them invaluable in eking out their meagre Union payment. Allotments were also used as a tool by unscrupulous farmers and members of the clergy opposed to the strike. They threatened labourers with notice to vacate their plots if they continued with Union action. After five long months the Union lost the battle, though labourers in the Eastern, Midland and Southern counties managed to gain a slight pay rise from 12 shillings a week to 13 or even 14 shillings.

Joseph Arch was the archetypal Methodist lay-preacher, and the book that he quoted from was the one his followers knew. Arch's Union was founded in 1872, when his fellow labourers asked him to deliver them from abject poverty. At the age of 46, Arch deliberated, for he was unsure of his class and knew little of union organisation. It was perhaps his wife, Mary Anne, who inspired him to take up the labourers' cause. Arch knew only too well the predicament of the labourers and often ruminated on the subject while threshing a hedge with a billhook or hiking several miles in search of work. Arch was fortunate – his fame as a hedge-cutter had spread far and wide and had left behind the struggle of living on 9 shillings a week.

Arch had long maintained that the best kind of allotment for the labourer was half an acre behind the back door. Before the inception of compulsory powers, allotments were often far from the village and Arch noted that the tired man with clumps of earth stuck to his boots all day was less eager to turn out after his supper to work on the land once again.

During the dispute some of the Union's middle-class supporters attempted to include the provision of allotments in their programme. Arch was decidedly against this policy and saw allotments as a benefit to those that wanted them, as long as they were not used to lower the wages of the workers. Arch never intended his Union to become a political one, but an economical one, for he was solely motivated by the labourers' rather empty larders. Yet he was too autocratic to pour oil on troubled waters. From a Union membership of more than 80,000 in 1874, it had dwindled to 4,254 by 1889. Suspicion was also rife concerning the maladministering of Union funds. After defeat Arch realised the futility of striking and sought consolation among the ranks of the Liberal Party, which paraded him. Both Joseph Chamberlain and William Gladstone found the labourers' champion an asset to their party, which helped considerably in the passing of the Franchise Act of 1884, which gave the labourer the right to vote. In 1884 Arch stood as candidate for Parliament. However, he carried his union sentiments with him and consequently alienated many potential supporters, which led to the entire Agricultural Trade Union Movement being considered as radical and anti-church. Arch was elected to Parliament in 1885. Initially the Liberals wanted Sir W. Brampton-Gurdon to represent the Norfolk constituency, but the labouring classes supported Arch. At the vote Arch received twice the number of votes that Brampton-Gurdon did.

In January 1886 Arch made his maiden speech in the House of Commons, when he opposed Henry Chaplin's Allotments Bill:

'Honourable gentlemen have said that about a quarter of an acre is sufficient for a working man in a village. There may be some working men such as shepherds and carters who perhaps would be content with a rood of ground: but I venture to say that a very large number of labourers in Norfolk – and I am speaking now from my own experience in that county – would be only too glad if they could rent an acre or two at a fair market price. On the other hand, I do not find any human or Divine law, which would confine me as a skilled labourer to one rood of God's earth. If I have the energy, tact, and skill by which I could cultivate my acre or two, and buy my cow into the bargain, I do not see any just reason why my energies should be crippled and my forces held back, and why I should be content as an agricultural labourer with a rood of ground and my nose to the grindstone all the days of my life.' (Joseph Arch, *The Story of His Life – As Told by Himself*, 1898, pp359-360)

Arch lost his seat in July 1886 when the Liberal Party was split over Gladstone's Home Rule Bill. To the worker on the land, the subject of Home Rule was merely a political hypothesis, which evoked little enthusiasm. Labouring folk wanted bread, better wages and improved living conditions, and did not want to be told that they should get justice in Ireland first.

Arch undoubtedly inspired Jesse Collings to take up the matter of land reform, particularly after the disastrous outcome of the lockout of 1874. Arch recalled the Liberals' enthusiasm for the land question: 'Land, land: that was all we were thinking about and talking about, and the idea of an Allotment Act was in the air.' In December 1881 Arch stated before a Royal Commission:

'If you want the labourer to rise, if you want him to get above being a pauper, if you want to make him self-reliant – we have been too dependant a class – if a man can make a good profit out of his quarter of an acre (and I know some men will make it more than others), let him do so. If that man could take an acre or a couple, and by that means save himself from pauperism, let him. I think it is highly desirable that the labourer should not be limited to a quarter of an acre, but that you should let him have some scope for his ability. A labourer should have a good quarter of an acre attached to his cottage; and if he can cultivate it and get enough out of it to take another half-acre it would be a wise step for any landed proprietor to let thrifty and persevering men have it. Those, of course, who do not properly cultivate their plot should not be allowed to keep it.' (Joseph Arch, *The Story of His Life – As Told by Himself*, 1898, pp342-43)

Jesse Collings favoured the idea of peasant proprietorships, and believed they would essentially redress the existing evils of the land system. The son of a small builder in Birmingham and grandson of a Devonshire labourer, Collings was in the wholesale ironmongery business in Birmingham and became a Town Councillor and later the Mayor. However, he never forgot his rural origins and when he gained entry into Parliament in 1880 he proceeded to bring in a motion practically every year pressing for action on smallholdings. Outside Parliament he created and led the Allotments Extension Association and later the Rural Labourers' League. Collings advocated the establishment of smallholdings from 1 to 50 acres, where a man could work with his family and halt the drift from the land by labourers who saw little future upon it.

'Under a system of land monopoly ... labourers must always be at starvation wages. But could the peasant – with the passionate attachment to the land which leads him now to seek plots for which he is willing to pay enormous rents – have land of his own to cultivate, he would have an object in life, and while securing a modest competence, would have higher aims and increased self-respect.' (*Life of the Rt Hon Jesse Collings*, J. L. Green, 1920, p129)

Prior to 1880, Theodore Dodd, son of an Oxfordshire clergyman, had first stirred up the land question when he discovered that an Act of William IV applied to all charity lands. Howard Evans had then embarked on establishing the facts, and finally drew up a Bill, which Sir Charles Dilke lay before the House. However, the proposal was dropped until after 1880, when Jesse Collings took up the matter once again.

Collings was largely responsible for implementing the Allotment Extension Act of 1882, which enabled labouring folk to gain wider use of charity lands for use as allotments if there was a demand for them. The trustees of charity lands were not always well endowed to let land for allotments, and where they did so the rent was often exorbitant. In some regions the trustees let lands on a lease and so avoided the operation of the Act. The establishment of allotments around urbanised regions, where they were most needed, often fell short of the mark. In rural areas working men were less inclined or too inhibited to exercise their right to gain land for allotments. Under this Act, workers could complain to the Charity Commissioners, who could instruct the trustees to comply. Unfortunately, the validity of the Bill was partially destroyed since the Charity Commissioners were made the final arbitrators and not the County Courts. Lord Carrington took responsibility for this Bill and ensured that it passed through the House of Lords.

Lord Carrington was particularly influential in the development of allotment gardens, and his efforts were followed by many land-owners up and down the country. By the 1880s he had let 754 garden allotments to the labourers around High Wycombe. The plots varied in size from 8 rods to 25 rods each, with rents varying from 3d to 7d per rod, according to the nature of the ground. Few other parishes had such a high volume of allotments. The rents were paid annually at Michaelmas and it became a custom for tenants to receive a rebate of 1 shilling for prompt payment. Naturally this bonus was warmly welcomed by the plot-holders and there was never any grumbling or trouble over rent arrears. Lord Carrington induced his tenants to take pride in their gardens by offering prizes for the best-kept plots. The allotments were divided into various categories in order to make the judging as impartial as possible, for the tenants cultivated their land under different circumstances, and there was an award for each section. By 1883 the prizes were being awarded by the Royal Horticultural Society. The exhibits at the annual show were not only large but often of commendable quality. G. T. Miles, Lord Carrington's own gardener and steward of the allotments, observed that the assigning of prizes greatly enhanced the tenants' efforts in cultivation and cropping. Lord Carrington generously supported the Royal

Horticultural Society and permitted the shows to take place in his parkland, while Lady Carrington distributed the prizes.

In the 1880s many rural labourers still dreamed of the opportunity to keep a cow on a bit of common land, to cut gorse or bracken for the oven or to fashion turfs for firing. While the argument for providing allotments in and around urban areas received much publicity and thoughtful speculation, the Charity Commissioners and certain members of the clergy remained hostile to the use of charity lands. Some of the country clergy were prevented from letting their glebe land for use as allotments. In 1882 Canon Tuckwell, Rector of Stockton in Warwickshire, fought down opposition from his Bishop over this matter and cut his glebe into approximately 200 allotments. After only two years he noted a great improvement in the village and, having visited many labourers, wrote:

> 'Already throughout the village I found corn bags ranged round the walls, potatoes under the beds, hams hanging from the ceilings wrapped in old *Reynolds Weekly* newspapers; the housewives for the first time in their lives facing winter unemploy without alarm.' (Rev W. Tuckwell, *Reminiscences of a Radical Parson*, 1895)

Canon Tuckwell did not regard the provision of allotments as the answer to rural poverty, even though he was a proven land nationaliser. Land that could be used under the Act of 1882 was not inconsiderable and, excluding that allocated to the Church or for educational purposes, the value for purely allotment intentions amounted to £1 million. Among labouring folk there was a strong feeling of injustice over the rent charged, which could be 25% to 500% above the rent charged to farmers.

The Allotment Extension Act of 1885 enabled charity land in the parishes to be let as allotments at the same rate as the adjoining land. However, the Act aroused much consternation among land-owners. Mr J. G. Blomfield of Somerset pointed out (in an irate letter to *The Times*) that land usually let at £5 per acre and let to 80 families could, under the Act, only be let for £2 5s an acre. So for the entire site, the 50 trustees could only ask for £3 7s instead of £7 10s. This Allotment Extension Act was only implemented in areas where the previous Allotment Act of 1882 did not apply.

'T. W.', an allotment society secretary of 20 years, maintained that a well-worked allotment of 15 rods could add from 7% to 10% to a labourer's earnings. He insisted that if cheap prints of the Allotment Extension Act of 1882 were to be circulated among labourers' associations, together with suggestions on how to overcome the difficulties of gaining land for allotments, the Movement would become more widespread and profitable.

'T. W.' was concerned about providing horticultural information for the benefit of the labourers. He declared that it was a naive assumption that the infant labourer was born with a spade in his hands, and somehow miraculously acquired horticultural skills. Since gardening was regarded the highest form of agriculture, how was the labourer to gain the necessary knowledge? 'T. W.' maintained that basic horticulture ought to be an essential educational topic. If every rural school had a plot of garden, pupils could gain practical experience as well as forming extensive theoretical knowledge in horticultural matters. With such tuition the labourer would be able to utilise his skills to earn his living and come to fully appreciate the benefit of his allotment. 'T. W.' added that an activity that should be appealing, diverse and auspicious, all too often ended up becoming a tedious chore on a destitute and uninspiring potato patch.

In 1885 the subject of winter digging was given thoughtful speculation. During the winter months there was often a distinct lack of labour both on the land and in the garden. This situation partially arose through employers wishing to gain as much essential labour as possible during the winter months of short daylight. Basic techniques such as entrenching the land were largely overlooked, and many thousands of labourers were more or less inactive for several weeks during the winter. Critics maintained that thousands of industrious labourers could be employed on a piecework basis to trench and enrich the ground with long manure or other decomposing refuse material.

Since farm workers were not so employed to improve the ground during winter, Mr 'A. D.', a gardening correspondent, suggested that they should work on their own allotments and so make full use of their time and reap the rewards of their effort the following growing season. Many labourers said that such effort would not furnish them with capital to frequent the ale-house come Saturday night. 'A. D.' implied that it would be better for the labourer to work on his allotment during the lean winter months than remain idle. The effort of winter digging would provide a bountiful harvest the following season and thus provide the funding for the labourer to indulge in social activities, though slightly delayed. 'A. D.' claimed that it was best to give the labourer a plot of land and allow him to embark on his struggle to cultivate it, as he thought best.

Jesse Collings quickly realised that without an association to assist labouring folk gain plots, the Allotment Act of 1882 (and later the Act of 1885) would quickly become nullified and virtually useless. In a great many cases the Charity Commissioners were not the least anxious to let the trustees of charity lands do their job and freely dispensed Certificates of Exemption from the Act to the trustees, which was a gross injustice to those applying for allotments. In order to counter such actions, in 1883 Jesse Collings set up and presided over the Allotments & Smallholdings Association (originally the Allotment Extension Association), with Balthazar Walter Foster as Chairman and Frederic Impey acting as Hon Secretary.

'It is unfortunately the case in many instances trustees of charity lands, even though they fully know their duties under the Allotment Act of 1882, refuse to carry them out, or to take steps to let the labourers and others in their districts know anything about the benefits, which they have a right to. The Allotments & Smallholdings Association has been established to help working men who cannot succeed in getting trustees of charity lands to let allotments. The inhabitants of any place where this difficulty exists should apply to the Association at 12 Cherry Street, Birmingham, and they will receive all the help which it is possible to give them. In very many instances, the Association has been completely successful in enabling working men to secure allotments, which had been refused them by trustees.' (Frederic Impey, *Allotments and Smallholdings*, 1886 and 1890)

During the early days of the Allotments Association the Charity Commissioners refused to recognise its efforts. Since the majority of trustees were squires, farmers and members of the clergy, enforcing and getting the law of the land accepted was incredibly difficult. Therefore the Allotments Association added to its programme the securing of a plot of ground for the labourer at a fair market rent. After a few months the Association extended its efforts to include smallholdings as well, since numerous labourers expressed a great desire for larger pieces of land, if they had the chance. By 1886 the work of the Allotments Association became more widely acknowledged, largely through the unstinting efforts of the founder members and supporters. In 1886 the Allotments Extension Association became the Allotments & Smallholdings Association as suggested by Mr Foster. Since the Association agitated for compulsory provision of land and holdings, it was immensely popular with working-class folk and consequently flourished for many decades.

In January 1886 readers of *The Times* were informed about the creation of the Land-owners' Association under the presidency of the Duke of Westminster, for the voluntary extension of allotments. The Vice Presidents included the Duke of Beaufort, the Duke of Manchester, the Earl of Egmont, Lord Tollmache of Cheshire and Lord Mount-Temple. The Land-owners' Association had four main aims:

1 To gain and broadcast information regarding the letting of land to the labourers in the form of allotments, potato grounds, and cow runs.
2 To ascertain and make public the extent to which the allotment system was in operation.
3 To inform other land-owners of the advantages to all parties concerned in agriculture from the practice of letting land to labourers.
4 To draw to the attention of charity land trustees the provisions within the 1882 Allotment Act.

Lord Onslow served as Hon Secretary and was the voice of the Land-owners' Association, which operated from temporary offices at Whitehall.

A correspondent to *The Times* stated that the formation of the Duke of Westminster's Association was a wise and good thing and hoped that many other land-owners would join in the venture. He added that if the labourers wanted allotments, on fair business principles, they should have them, without elevating their own status. The writer also noted that the Allotments

& Smallholdings Association disliked the voluntary provision of allotments but insisted that unless it (the Association) changed its views and made it compulsory upon local authorities to compel labourers to take allotments from them instead of from the landlords, he did not see how the Allotments Association could make any progress. He implied that the public would care little to spend money in doing expensively and defectively what the landlords were achieving simply and cheaply.

Mr Foster responded to the criticism of the Allotments & Smallholdings Association by saying that the voluntary system of supplying allotments might be effective in some districts but not in all, and that a matter of national concern should not be left to the effort of an individual. Mr Foster said that such provision was all too often partial and frequently short-lived, and that that only local authorities, when properly constituted in the counties, could meet the demand for allotments and smallholdings on a national scale. He added that from such authorities the labourer could expect his allotment and home, not as a personal favour on the part of an individual, but as a public right from a national body. Mr Foster recognised that although the compulsory acquisition of land was a great bugbear to many landlords, he believed that this method was consistent with fairness and equity to individuals. Mr Foster finished by saying that when a great and public good had to be accomplished, the greatest of industries (agriculture) had to be revived and the most important class of the population (labourers) had to be lifted from poverty to moderate well-being, the convenience of individuals (landlords) should not weigh too heavy on the opposite scale.

In spite of the controversy, opinions and attitudes were fast changing in favour of the workers. The Duke of Westminster's organisation was a short-lived one. Mr Impey, in his work of 1890 entitled *Three Acres and a Cow*, mentions that the Land-owners' Association was no longer operational. In 1886 he stated:

'Of the administration of charity lands coming under the Act of 1882, although improvement is visible, it is not unjust to state that instances of scandalous mismanagement and favouritism are constantly being brought to light; and, viewed in this aspect, the Act constitutes an additional argument for the control of all such charities by public representative bodies in place of the present irresponsible trustees.' (Frederic Impey, *Allotments and Smallholdings*, 1886 and 1890)

Mr Impey illustrated how co-operation and good management among the labourers prevailed in a successful scheme within the Wellingborough Allotments Association Limited. Some 223 labourers rented a farm of 184 acres, consisting of arable and grassland, and divided up the land into plots varying from 6 acres to an eighth of an acre. Each plot was individually valued for the rent, and the amount included rates, taxes and management expenses. The Wellingborough Association was managed by a Committee of 16 officials. Initially the farm was in a dilapidated condition and the owner was unwilling to risk the rent of £300 a year. Consequently, the Committee had to find guarantors for the rent, which they did by raising and paying in advance on their own account. The original tenant farmer, who eventually gave up, paid an annual sum of 32s 6d per acre, while the Wellingborough tenants were charged at the rate of 35 shillings per acre. The tenants were comprised of artisans, small tradesmen, greengrocers, dairymen, shoemakers and mechanics, with a few farm labourers. In 1886 the annual expenditure amounted to £195 aside from the rent of £299. The Committee was responsible for maintaining the hedges, fences, ditches and drainage of the land. When Mr Impey visited the farm, he found it in an excellent state of cultivation. In the days of the tenant farmer, only four souls were employed on the farm, while under the Association around 40 individuals cultivated the ground. In the previous year the volume of wheat grown had averaged 48 bushels per acre, and one tenant explained that he got more than 56 bushels per acre. Since the responsibility for the rent was divided among the 223 tenants, the Association avoided the risk of having to raise large sums as farming capital and each tenant was left to cultivate his land as best as he could. Mr Impey said that there was seldom more practical business sagacity than that applied to the management of this Association.

By the mid-to-late-Victorian period, forcing pots and frame lights were commonplace on allotments rented by artisans, who could afford to enhance their gardening methods.

He added:

'It will probably be argued that if working men can accomplish so much by themselves, what need is there for the intervention of public bodies in the provision of allotments? But besides the improbability of finding artisans so intelligent and capable as the Wellingborough men in every locality where allotments and smallholdings are needed, the business of finding land, at a fair rent, in suitable positions, would be frequently an insuperable difficulty except for the knowledge that compulsion in the last resort should be applied, and that it would be unjust to resort to, excepting under authority and responsibility of public representative bodies.' (Frederic Impey, *Three Acres and a Cow*, 1890, p18)

The problems faced by the small cultivator around towns were brought to light in 1886 by a Nottingham allotment tenant. Some of the best allotment land in and around the town was let at 2½d per square yard, equivalent to 6 shillings per rod or £48 per acre. Even with such a costly rent the Nottingham

Harvesting the crops at the Wellingborough allotments. The tenants transported their produce to Birmingham by cart and brought back manure for the land.

allotments proved to be extremely profitable. The latent earth-hunger among workers for allotments and holdings enabled tenants to succeed where others had failed. Numerous critics expressed fear that working folk would falter as cultivators. Such criticism proved unfounded, and where the land was of satisfactory quality the allotments became very productive. When other workers saw land falling out of cultivation because large-scale farming had foundered, they asked for the chance to try their hand as small cultivators. Numerous gardeners said that if their venture proved to be futile the problem was resolved, but they implied that in places where the large farmer had failed, it was unjust to prevent them from attempting to gain a profitable income in a more diverse way.

At the time it was often the cry that more allotments were needed, especially around the suburbs of London and the other great cities. Unfortunately, almost every available plot of land was seized for building purposes. Even the remaining commons and open spaces were only spared by the prudent supervision of people directly concerned in their preservation. Any Acts of Parliament that enabled the continual growth of allotment gardens, especially in urbanised areas, were greatly appreciated.

The Allotment Extension Act of 1887 was less directed toward the procurement of allotments in more urban regions as the establishment of

The grim industrial conditions of towns like Nottingham in the mid-to-late-Victorian period are reflected in the workers' desire for an allotment, for which they were prepared to pay enormous rents.

rural allotments for agricultural purposes. The term 'allotment' was added to include gardens since the Act was forged with the welfare of agricultural labourers in mind. The maximum size of the allotments, which could be either arable or pasture, was 1 acre. Joseph Chamberlain proposed that such allotments should consist of 1 acre for arable and 3 acres for pasture. His motion was flatly rejected by the Tory Government.

Under the Act of 1887 any six registered electors who were qualified to vote for Members of Parliament and who resided in the district could appeal to the Sanitary Authority that the needs of the district required that the provisions of the Act be put into force. If the Sanitary Authority was of the opinion that there was a pressing need for allotments, but was unable to obtain land at reasonable rent on a voluntary basis, the Authority was then directed to purchase or rent land that might be available to provide a sufficient number of allotments. The Sanitary Authority was not allowed to obtain land by this method unless all the expenses incurred could be recouped from the rents derived from it.

This Bill amended one other important aspect of allotment gardening. Originally the construction of buildings of any kind was expressly forbidden on allotments, largely through fear of 'shanty towns' springing up. After the Act, tool-stores, sheds, fowl-houses, greenhouses and pigsties could be built.

When local Sanitary Authorities attempted to 'regulate' the village pigsties, it often became necessary for labourers to accommodate their animals on the allotment. The new Act also gave allotment tenants the right to remove any construction on vacating the plot, which extended to trees, bushes and plants. If it was proven that the rent was in arrears or that the tenant had moved more than a mile outside the parish boundaries, the local authority could terminate tenancy with a month's notice. The vacating tenant was entitled to compensation, though to diminish expenditure on the part of the Local Government Board an independent arbitrator was often called in. The arbitrator had the power to disallow expenses claimed by the tenant and to call for his own costs to be met. Special provisions within the Act also allowed for the sub-letting of allotments, although the rent had to be set at a fixed amount and no plot was to exceed 1 acre. No public park, recreation ground or land required for building purposes could be exploited, nor could land belonging to any railway or canal company be utilised for allotments. The Act also forbade the mining of coal or ore on allotment land. Numerous Government supporters thought this Allotment Act was rash, coarse and crudely drawn.

Frederic Impey, Hon Secretary of the Allotments & Smallholdings Association, was one of the sternest critics of the Act. He insisted that various clauses within the Act completely overlooked the 'three acres and a cow' policy and made it no easier for the rural worker to gain an allotment as one of his rights as an Englishman than was the case before the Bill (as introduced by the Tory Government) was brought in. Mr Impey elaborated:

> 'The Act lays down that an allotment may not be more than one acre of arable land, but by this clause, which is the most that could be forced from the Tory Government, the Sanitary Authority may establish a common cow pasture, on which those who have a cow could turn her out to graze by payment of rent as for an arable allotment. It is an unhappy scheme. To have, say, an acre of allotment in one place, a cow pasture in another place, and the working man's home in another place (besides which no cow-house may be put on an allotment), will daily, by its inconvenience and worry, remind a man of the blessings he receives at the hands of the Tory Government, which tries in a hurry to pass an Allotments Bill.' (Frederic Impey, *Three Acres and a Cow*, 1890)

Mr Impey implied that the procedure to acquire land under this Act was so cumbersome and expensive that when the expenditure was to be recouped from the allotment rents, the plots would be so costly as to be worth nothing. He also pointed out that under Section XI of the Act the Sanitary Authority was also given the power to dispose of surplus or unsuitable land.

Allotment schemes under private management fared much better. By the 1870s and 1880s numerous land-owners were contributing articles and features to periodicals and the press highlighting the benefits that their allotment systems had brought to the local working-class communities.

Landlords often expressed their own concept of the ideal allotment and of the rules on which to let it.

The horticulturist John Bennett Lawes founded a thriving allotment club for labourers on his Rothamsted estate near Harpenden, Hertfordshire, in 1852. He gradually increased the number of allotments periodically and occasionally awarded prizes for the best-kept gardens. Every second year a vegetable show was held. Sir John was a staunch supporter of the allotment system but quickly deduced that a 20-rod plot was more than enough for a regular wage-earner to manage during his leisure hours.

In 1857 he added a luxury clubhouse where his tenants could indulge in beer and baccy without resorting to the local ale-houses. Sir John frowned upon such places and assumed over-indulgence in alcohol to be one of the main causes of social deprivation among the working classes. Many of the Harpenden ale-houses had a notorious reputation and the customers were often involved with the police, petty theft and worse offences. Sir John made it abundantly clear to his tenants that the selling of beer to non-members would nullify the private nature of the clubhouse. At one stage he attempted to introduce coffee instead of beer, but this was not popular with his tenants. The labourers said the coffee was good, when supplied gratis, but were loath to purchase it in place of their beloved beer. Two years later Sir John endeavoured to supply the labourers with items at wholesale prices, through a co-operative system. He also started a pig club, a flour club and developed the Harpenden Labourers' Store Society, which failed after a short period through want of support from members. But the allotment gardens became extremely popular.

By the mid-1880s the Rothamsted Allotment Club had more than 170 members. Initially, a certain amount of jealousy existed between labourers in the surrounding area and those employed on Rothamsted Farm. The Allotment Club Secretary, Edwin Grey, recalls:

'The working hours of what one might call the general farm hands were on most farms from 6am to 5pm, from Monday to Saturday night, the wages being 11 to 13 shillings weekly. In the winter months shorter hours were worked, the wage during this shorter period sinking on some farms to 9 shillings or less. Rothamsted Farm was always looked upon as the best round about, for here the wages were a shilling or so in advance of those of the labourers of the surrounding farms, the general hands also ceasing work on Saturday afternoons at 2 o'clock, so they could (as Sir John himself said) spend an hour or two working on their allotment if so disposed, and most of them were.' (Edwin Grey, *Cottage Life in a Hertfordshire Village*)

A committee of 12 members was elected annually to manage the garden allotments and clubhouse – Sir John dubbed them the 'Twelve Apostles'. In the early days of the Club most of the tenants were agricultural labourers, but other members included a butcher, a coal dealer, a platelayer, a shoemaker, a blacksmith, two carpenters and two carters.

As a rule, the majority of labourers were less interested in cultivating large plots. When Sir John displayed a notice in the clubhouse informing tenants that plots of 1 acre adjacent to the original allotments were available for hire, not one labourer applied for a bigger plot, though many enquired after smaller ones.

In 1885 Sir John set aside two fields covering 2 acres, close to a hamlet, to be let in larger allotments. Extensive areas were taken up with plots of one-eighth of an acre; two farm labourers and one butcher took 3½-acre plots, and only six agricultural labourers took up larger plots, while tradesmen rented the remainder. Considerable debate ensued among tenants as to whether they could work their plots in unison, as some labourers were not in full-time employment and other tenants, who were better off, had horses, ponies and other livestock.

On the first Saturday in June, Sir John gave an annual dinner, and had the chance to meet the Allotment Club members and discuss with them matters of mutual interest. Even the delicate subject of strikes was not avoided, but the topic in no way altered the friendliness between Sir John and his tenant gardeners. In the first few years the dinner was held in the clubhouse, but as the membership increased the room became too small and a large frame tent was raised in an adjoining field. The event was always referred to as the Club Feast. Two meals were provided, dinner commencing at 2.30pm and supper at 7.30pm. Usually about 140 members turned up, each contributing 1 shilling toward the expenses.

One of the longest-remembered events in the annals of Rothamsted Allotment Club took place in 1870, when Sir John's only daughter, Caroline, married Walter Pennington Creyke. To celebrate the occasion Sir John arranged for the plot-holders and their wives to visit the Crystal Palace by the Midland Railway. Much talk and excitement circulated around the village as many of the plot-holders had never been on a train before and most had never travelled so far from their home. Sir John had arranged for dinner and tea to be provided at the Palace and had ensured that each member was given a small sum of money to spend there. Apart from the usual meats there was a tremendous array of sweets, including blancmanges, jellies and similar delicacies. Edwin Grey recalls how the waiters at the party were quietly amused at the plot-holders' country talk. One old plot-holder asked the waiter for a second helping of a particular sweet and said, 'I don't know the name of it, but it's that shivery, shakey tackle.' Another old tenant said he would like the Squire's daughter to get married every year. John Pearce, keeper of the paths and roads, vowed that if there was ever another 'excu'sion he was blowed if he wouldn't goo' ag'in.'

In 1893 the plot-holders got that chance. To commemorate the Jubilee of the Rothamsted Experimental Station, Sir John proposed to send the plot-holders and their wives on an evening excursion to see the famous firework display at the Crystal Palace. However, the years had passed and the majority of the plot-holders were advanced in age. They told Sir John they would like to see the display but were worried about the late hours travelling on the

Plot-holders at work on their allotments in the mid-to-late Victorian era.

return journey. Sir John then decided that if the plot-holders could not go to the show, the fireworks would be brought to them. He arranged for the display to be given in one of the meadows belonging to 'Welcome' adjacent to the Experimental Station. Again much talk circulated throughout the district. On the appointed evening a large crowd from the surrounding countryside assembled on the nearby common to watch over the evening's proceedings.

In spite of being treated generously by Sir John, the Allotment Club members had to comply with a series of stringent rules that were rigidly imposed. Every elected member of the Rothamsted Allotment Club had to pay an entrance fee of 1 shilling with an additional halfpenny a week to the Club, and a contribution of 3d upon the death of any Allotment Club member, his wife or offspring. Prospective tenants had their names written on a board and when vacancies occurred candidates were selected in order from the list. New tenants were voted in at Committee meetings.

The rules regarding the beer-drawing duties within the clubhouse were taken very seriously. All the members took turns in the beer-keeping duties according to their number on the allotment. The beer-keeper had to attend the clubhouse from 6pm to 10pm every day; if he failed to show up by 6.15 he was fined 3d, and failure to attend at all incurred a fine of 6d. The beer-keeper was entrusted with half a barrel of beer, an oath book and 16s 6d, which were passed on to the next succeeding member. He was responsible for paying the brewer the sum of 16s 6d and for ordering half a barrel of beer. Any neglect of these duties made the beer-keeper liable to a penalty of 5 shillings, for which he was sued in the County Court and for any deficiency in the amount of money entrusted to him. Members caught selling beer to non-members were immediately expelled from the Club. For giving beer to anyone other than family or relatives a fine of 1 shilling was imposed and the same applied to members drawing beer on a Sunday morning. Members were forbidden to draw beer after 10pm except on a quarter night, when a half-hour extension was permitted. The selling of beer to expelled members resulted in a fine of 3d. When the beer-keeper had drawn the barrel of beer, he asked the next member to take his place; if nobody was present the current beer-keeper was allowed to draw a second barrel. Any members creating or causing others to make a disturbance within the clubhouse were fined 3d. Swearing and repeating an oath in the clubhouse or on the veranda was frowned on and the guilty person was liable to a fine of 2d.

Regulations governing the management of the gardens were equally comprehensive. Members collecting produce after 9am on a Sunday were fined 6d. Fines not paid by 10am resulted in an additional fine of 3d and if unpaid within one month resulted in forfeiture of the garden. Expelled members were eligible to re-enter the Club by way of fresh election. Members not keeping their plots free of weeds or causing damage to their neighbours' land could be turned out of the gardens on recommendation of two-thirds of the Club Committee. Members wishing to give up their plots had to give proper notice to do so. Succeeding members were permitted to enter any part of the allotment that remained un-cropped at the time of notice.

The Committee met four times a year to discuss the Club's transactions, and any Committee member who failed to attend, except through illness, had to pay 3d toward the Club funds. No member was allowed to undertake Committee duties unless they could prove that they were in a position to attend the meetings and take an interest in the proceedings. Upon the death of a member the nearest relative, usually the wife, was paid the sum of £2 out of the funds. Only fully paid up members were entitled to donations from the funds. When Mr Grey took over as Allotment Secretary he looked over the old record book from earlier years and noted:

'I found the maximum fine imposed on a member in any case was the sum of 5 shillings. There are several cases recorded where the Committee had decided to fine a member, this maximum fine for causing disturbances at feast times. Another place records the fact that the wife of a certain member shall be fined 5 shillings for cutting George Smith's cauliflowers; and yet another record wherein after serious discussion it was resolved that a man named Attwood be fined 5 shillings, for calling the Committee an ignorant set of fools.' (*Reminiscences of Edwin Grey*, 1911)

Allotment rents were due on 19 September, and if not paid within a month of that date members forfeited the right to their gardens and legal action was taken by the Committee in the County Court. A fine of 6d was imposed for payment between 19 September and 19 October. Members found to be fighting in the clubhouse or in the gardens were fined 5 shillings for each offence. Members taking tools from another tenant's garden without leave were fined 1 shilling. Anyone laying dung on the gravel paths was fined 1 shillings for the first offence and if repeated was expelled from the Club. Members were allowed to sell their produce but they or a member of their family had to be present. If purchasers of produce were found without a witness in attendance, the tenant was fined 1 shilling.

Rothamsted Allotment Club was remarkably well organised and, though it was not the oldest, it was reputed to be the oldest of its kind. Many observers implied that this garden allotment, democratically governed by 12 elected members, was years ahead of its time and an asset to all that worked upon it.

In Shropshire, Colonel Edwards proudly described his local community as 'A village where there is no poverty', giving this as complete justification for developing a system of labourers' smallholdings (without proprietorship). He had many smallholdings for the labourers on his own modest estate.

Colonel Edwards advocated the expansion of the smallholdings under voluntary means and feared that if irresponsible County Boards were given the power to take land compulsorily, he would be one of the first to suffer. He realised that no labourer could live on 3 acres of land without regular wages and that there would be no employment if such County Boards were to get their way.

Colonel Edwards stated that one of his tenants refused the offer to buy their smallholding, as they lacked the funds for repairs and consequently the holding would soon become run-down. Colonel Edwards knew of many smallholdings that had become mortgaged beyond their value. He added that a labourer with a wife, who was capable of managing a little dairy and a few acres of grassland adjoining their cottage, found his smallholding of immense benefit. Not every labourer was fit to have land and the land-owner often determined the fitness. When a carpenter in the region married the daughter of an old gardener, Colonel Edwards let the couple rent a vacant cottage with around 5 acres of land attached. They were unable to manage on the holding, as the wife was incapable of looking after the cow. After several years they were forced to leave and settle in a cottage with only a garden and had since managed much better. Colonel Edwards concluded that compulsory allotments were not the answer to the labourer's problems. He added that everyone cried out for what they saw others benefiting by, without considering whether they, too, could manage such an enterprise.

Frederic Impey, in *Three Acres and a Cow*, declared that Colonel Edwards was a model landlord but admitted that much could be done by other land-owners to extend the provision of allotments and smallholdings. He stated:

'It will be seen that the value to a working man that a plot of ground on which

A decrepit smallholding in Kent. Many holdings were mortgaged beyond their value and as a result soon became run down.

he could keep pigs and poultry, would be less than £20 per year after he had paid rent and all other expenses, and in indirect ways, if all were reckoned carefully up, it would be found to be a good deal more. The question is, if such things can be provided by the thoughtful kindness of a great landlord in one part of England, why cannot arrangements be made in other parts of England for working men to have an equally good chance?' (Frederic Impey, *Three Acres and a Cow*, 1890, p26)

Mr Impey decreed that a Representative Local Authority should be allowed, by an Act of Parliament, to be able to buy land in suitable locations and hire it out to working men at a fair farm-rent. He added that if land could not be gained from an owner willingly, that there should be a power to appeal to a public authority that would be able to fix a price for the land in the same way as for that gained for a railway or public amenity. He received almost on a daily basis numerous applications and letters from labourers asking for help in gaining land. One such letter read:

'In the village in which I live there are no allotment gardens, only a small plot to each cottage. There are about a dozen labourers and others who would be pleased to obtain some allotment ground at a fair rental, and one or two would like a bit of pasture to keep a cow, for there is no milk to be had in the village.'

Mr Impey said that the labourer feared it would be no use trying to get land from the owners for allotments and asked for their aid. He added that in this state of affairs labourers are powerless, and he forwarded the application to Lord Onslow, who promised to use his influence in getting some land for these people. Another correspondent writing to Mr Impey stated:

> 'I feel certain, as an agricultural labourer, nothing will lift him out of poverty quicker than to have as much land as his means will allow to cultivate for himself, but the greatest difficulty is getting possession of the land.' (Labourer's correspondence to Mr Impey, 1886)

Mr Impey maintained that the labourer's difficulty of gaining land could be overcome by the establishment of a National System of Allotments and Smallholdings. He said a growing unison of opinion was visible in favour of Parliamentary action (within the Liberal Party) toward a great end. He concluded that without some provisions of a universal application, no real settlement could be arrived at.

Mr Goschen was an active supporter of the voluntary extension of allotments, and in opposition to Jesse Collings's motion. In his speech on 26 January 1886 he stated:

> 'I say it is a dangerous experiment, because while you are trying your experiment you may discourage that voluntary movement which is at present going on. A good many landlords who are prepared now with allotments might much prefer that they should sell their land to the community, and that then the community should take all the disagreeable labour of collecting the rents from the tenants of these small allotments. I think you will remove a great part of the duty from the landlords, and you will remove that to which I attach the greatest importance, the sense of duty on the part of the landlords that they ought to give to these allotments. If the State, the community, comes in and says, "On us rests the responsibility of carrying out this movement," will you not discourage the other class? Well, that is a matter of opinion only, Hon Members will say. But I am bound, conscientiously believing that it will discourage the sense of duty on the part of the landlords, to express this opinion in the House.' (Lord Onslow, Landlords and Allotments, 1886, pp67–68)

Dr Gilbert, writing a report on Rothamsted Allotment Club, said that there was little doubt that a garden near or around the labourers' dwellings was a great boon. He said that market gardening schemes and the production of milk and poultry on a small scale might be extended to advantage in some locations. But he was cautious of implementing smallholding ventures by compulsory means, and continues:

'The idea that small farms, with or without proprietorship, and with restricted or borrowed working capital, can compete in general agriculture with moderately sized concerns, large enough to take advantage of machinery and other improved methods for economical production in these days of active foreign competition, is, I believe, quite chimerical, and its advocacy very mischievous.' (Lord Onslow, *Landlords and Allotments*, 1886, pp68-69)

A considerable number of landlords shared Colonel Edwards's opinion, that the establishment of allotments under a compulsory system would allow the letting of land to unwelcome settlers. They asked as to whether the labourers would appreciate compulsory allotments and holdings as opposed to voluntary ones. Under existing legislation voluntary allotments were often within reach of all that wanted them, and in many places they were of considerable advantage, while in others they were a worthless obligation.

Lord Onslow believed that few landlords desired to alienate labourers from the land. He deduced that it was far more probable that the labourers were more than a little reluctant to ask for accommodation with regard to allotments. In 1886 Lord Onslow called to the attention of land-owners, in his book *Landlords and Allotments*, the desire among labouring folk to possess an allotment. He added that nothing could be more damaging to the interests of the labourer than to endanger their regular wages of 13 or 15 shillings and that allotment cultivation was to be regarded solely as a leisure-time recreation.

Lord Onslow did not regard the upkeep of pasture allotments in the same way, where the wife was able attend to the dairy work and that only at haymaking time was any serious demand made on the labourer's time. He decided that it was unwise to assume that the labourer's wives in every part of the country were competent to manage a dairy allotment, and that in arable counties the keeping of a cow would be the perfect white elephant. Lord Onslow said that it would make an interesting experiment if a number of landlords would endeavour to educate the labourers' wives and daughters in the ways of dairy work, with a view to establishing them on their estates. Cottagers would quickly learn from each other and, in a county that was predominantly devoted to grazing, this might be easily implemented. The building of cow-byres could be relatively inexpensive if made from materials readily available on the estate, and that any cost would soon be recouped from the rental.

Rather like Joseph Arch, Jesse Collings and countless others, Lord Onslow thought the best kind of allotment was the garden plot affixed to the labourer's cottage. The regulating of fields for steam-powered cultivation could render additional bits of ground for use as 'cottage' allotments. Where cottages already existed such methods were not possible and the next best course of action was to establish allotments in centrally situated fields adjacent to the high road, and easily reached by carts and horses. However, no allotment should be more than half a mile from the labourer's dwelling.

Lord Onslow believed that the landlords should be entirely responsible for all the rates, tithes, taxes and outgoings, and for maintaining the fences, gates and allotment boundaries. Where cowgates were not established, two pasture fields would suffice, one for grazing and the other for the mowing of hay, which could be held in common by the labourers. Wherever possible the labourer was to be given the option and amenities to keep a pig, for the manure was of the greatest value to allotment cultivation. Earlier, Lord Winchelsea had estimated that 50 rods of land would keep an average family supplied with vegetables, and fodder sufficient for the keep of a pig, fowl or ducks. Lord Onslow said the matter of allotment rent was of paramount importance and one that should be exercised with extreme caution. Although many labourers would pay a high rent for an allotment, he thought that asking for a higher rent than that of the surrounding land was unwise. The situation near a town was slightly different for this was regarded as accommodation land where a higher rent might be asked for. In agricultural districts not a penny more should be asked above the rate let to an adjoining farm.

Lord Onslow said that it was equally undesirable to let land free or below its proper value. He noted that in general the labourer rarely valued that for which he paid nothing. If the labourer felt there was anything of a gratuitous nature to his tenancy, he would never be quite sure of whether he would be dispossessed of his plot of land at some stage in the future. This should never be done, except in cases where the land was required for building purposes. Lord Onslow felt there should be something of a clause that would bind the landlord to make the fullest compensation, such as a tenant might expect, if compulsorily expelled from land for the development of a railway or similar. Such a provision was not to extend to tenants convicted of a crime or those guilty of non-payment of the rent, but even under these circumstances, the tenant should not be dispossessed of his crops without some form of compensation.

Lord Onslow stipulated that no landlord should be afraid of accepting a tenant of idle or dissolute habits. He said that the cultivation of an allotment could well be the salvation of him, with the necessity of complying with the rules and keeping his bit of land in a fair state of cultivation. He added that there should be a committee of allotment-holders to judge on the amount of compensation between outgoing and incoming tenants.

In spite of the landlords' reluctance to accept peasant proprietorships, a number of successful enterprises flourished in different parts of the country. Toward the later part of the Victorian era, the parish of Epworth in Lincolnshire was well endowed with smallholdings of between 5 and 15 acres. One small farmer, who held 10 acres of land there, and who was also the rate-collector of the parish, strongly advocated the system of smallholdings. When asked about the provision of allotments of more than 1 acre or more for the rural workers, he told Mr Impey:

'I can without hesitation say that farm labourers here who have from half-acre to two acres are in fact in a far better position than those not holding land; they and their families doing the necessary work at times when they would be at their ordinary work, the result being, as a rule, bread, bacon and potatoes for the family consumption for the greater part of the year. I have been told by several of such that oft in the winter months, before having such holdings, they were on the point of starvation; now they feel in a better position to face a cold winter fearless of hunger. Men farming from five to twelve acres are, as a rule, better situated here than those farming from twenty to fifty, one class being able to do all the labour, the other not, and often short of money to employ labour sufficient.' (Frederic Impey, *Three Acres and a Cow*, 1890, p39)

These peasant holdings were situated in 'open parishes', as the rural folk described them – that is, land not the property of one great land-owner under whose authority and influence such schemes would be an unheard of circumstance. Mr Impey added that if land-owners in the future could keep their property in the same manner as those at present, peasant smallholdings, such as those at Epworth, would continue to be almost impossible to establish, as they were during the 1880s in the majority of English rural parishes.

5
Appetite for allotments

In 1889 all the various governmental departments connected with cultivation of the land were formed into one immense committee, which became known as the new Board of Agriculture. This huge achievement was directly attributable to the efforts of Henry Chaplin, the first President of the new Board. By now a large majority of townsfolk had developed an appetite for a bit of garden and took advantage of the legislation provided. Thousands of mill and factory workers, together with mechanics and machiners, took up the spade as a means of relaxation and a health-giver at eventide, as long as there was light. Writers and influential people stated that there could be little better exercise than gardening, quite apart from the financial advantages. In rural areas the once vast migration of labouring folk from the country districts began to cease. This was very evident in regions where the acquisition of land for allotments was made comparatively easy.

Mr Chaplin produced an extensive 600-page report on the allotments in 1890, largely with the aim of developing further sites. He wished to eradicate the numerous blank spots where no allotments of any kind existed, and thought that this problem should be addressed. In 1873 the number of allotments in Great Britain was 245,398, but by 1886 this figure had increased to 357,795 and by 1890 stood at 445,005. It was estimated that there was roughly one allotment for every two labourers. As the Commission of 1867 found out, the number of allotments varied considerably in different counties: in Lincolnshire there were 16,000 allotments, in Norfolk 28,000, Leicestershire 23,000, and Northamptonshire 49,000. The figures did not take into account large gardens attached to cottages or any of the 320,000 smallholdings of less than 20 acres or the 17,000 potato plots or railway allotments.

In some counties the provision of allotments in rural regions was sparse, while in urbanised districts they were numerous, especially those below a quarter of an acre. In Kent the greatest number of plots were to be found in the vicinity of the major towns. The 1890 census showed that Maidstone had 544 allotments of less than a quarter of an acre, Tonbridge 256, Ashford 242 and Folkestone 458. In Sussex allotments also prevailed in towns; Littlehampton alone had a staggering 327 allotments, while the village of Wivelsfield only had two plots of less than a quarter of an acre. In the regions surrounding London, allotments (below a quarter of an acre) were in some locations very abundant: Ealing had 294 plots, Edmonton 354, Enfield 276,

A railway worker's neat allotment garden, circa 1895. By the 1890s
allotments were becoming increasingly popular among the artisan classes.

Finchley 197, Twickenham 142 and Willesden 187. At the time of the census, no plots were recorded for the inner districts such as Islington, Kensington, Paddington or Hammersmith, nor were there evidence of allotments in the Bethnal Green or Whitechapel districts of East London.

In Surrey allotments were more evident in urban regions. Croydon had 278 plots (below a quarter of an acre), Kingston-upon-Thames 153 and Wandsworth 142. In Hampshire allotments were fairly evenly distributed, though Andover had 426 (under a quarter of an acre) and Basingstoke had 385.

In Wiltshire the distribution of plots was extremely varied, and in many regions plots of between a quarter and 1 acre prevailed. In Dorset the occurrence of allotments was very patchy, while in Devon the number of plots around the major towns and larger villages (not all) was fairly consistent. Hertfordshire was well endowed with the smaller quarter-acre plots. In Leicestershire the principal towns often had in excess of 200 quarter-acre plots, the exceptions being Belgrave with 1,464 and Bromkinsthorpe with 1,372.

In the North and the Midlands, allotments were much more popular around industrial districts. For instance, in Derbyshire Ilkeston had 771 allotments of less than a quarter of an acre but Matlock had none at all. Similar discrepancies occurred in Nottinghamshire and Lancashire. In Warwickshire smaller allotments tended to be slightly more evenly distributed, though the highest figures recorded (in the 1890 report) were around the larger towns. In the *Gardeners' Chronicle* a correspondent stated that in the mining districts gardens would be a great boon to the miners, and where they occurred they were warmly cherished by those that tended them. He implied that this kind of labour was the most humanising of all the labour in the land.

General dissatisfaction with the Allotment Act of 1887 eventually led to the passing of a new Allotment Act in 1890. Under this Act the County Council had to have a Standing Committee on allotments, and if and when the Sanitary Authority failed to gain land for plots by voluntary agreement, it became the duty of the Allotments Committee to hold a public inquiry. If the Committee found that there was a demand for allotments, but the conditions for the sale or letting of the land were deemed unreasonable, the County Council could then put into effect the compulsory clauses of the Land Clauses Consolidation Acts. After the passing of the Parish Council Bill in 1894, if the County Council refused to act, then the Parish or District Council could then appeal to the Local Government Board for an order. However, any such order over-riding the decision of the County Council had to have authorisation from Parliament. In spite of the improved legislation, no Allotment Act could reduce the amount of labour required to maintain a plot or the hours that a worker chose to spend upon it.

In many instances throughout the Victorian era numerous labourers overworked themselves on their allotments. One old labourer said that every hour spent on a field allotment meant one day off a man's life. The labourers that worked in this way felt that they were making the sacrifice for the benefit of their families.

During the 1890s the advent of the plough on large field allotments had done away with the necessity for overwork. Originally the ground was worked with a spade or, more commonly, a fork, and horses were only used to haul carts. The 'breast plough' was the only kind in use, which was used to clear bean-brush stubble in the autumn months; wheat was then planted without further cultivation. Subsequent to 1880, when field plots became larger and more numerous, the horse and plough became more common. Small plots of only a rood or two were not usually worked with horses, and manure was wheeled in by barrow from the village. Potatoes and other produce harvested were conveyed in the same manner.

By the late 1890s fewer labourers were employed on a casual basis throughout the winter months, and those that were could afford to hire the village haulier to plough the field allotment. Labourers in winter employment were less inclined to make a long slog of it by digging the land with hand tools. Before 1900 it was not unusual to see several hired workers digging a field allotment. In a few villages two or more men would be continuously employed in digging an allotment for an artisan, stockman or someone in regular employment. Digging alone in the fields was a monotonous and dreary task, but by combining forces the labourers overcame two problems at once with a method that was of mutual benefit: two men would go and dig half an acre of one man's plot, then go and dig half an acre on the other's, or they would spend half a day on each other's plot. Even this strategy did not entirely kill the boredom, and when the opportunity for alternative employment arose they would not stay and dig.

On heavy clay ground the demise of field allotments was due to the lack of digging and the inclination to dig. In regions where the soil was lighter and sandy the compulsion to work the land was very much stronger. Digging by hand still had a great advantage over ploughing, since work could be carried out at times when it was considered unwise to put a horse and plough to the land. The development of the small plough (which could be drawn by two horses) made turning the soil on a field allotment much easier, and they were often referred to as 'allotment ploughs'. A patent for one such type of plough was taken out in 1894, but they did not come into general use in the Midland districts until ten years later. During the late 1890s the improvement of tracks and roads in the sub-division of allotment land led to the popularity of ploughing instead of digging. Wide roads enabled easier access to the land and only left one headland, which avoided trespass on a neighbour's plot. Horses were used for drilling and harrowing and for this reason the dibber more or less vanished from the large field allotments to be replaced by the drill for the sowing of beans, when planted in quantity. Wheat and barley were sown with a five- or three-furrow drill. Potatoes were still set by hand, occasionally dibbed and rarely trenched or dug in.

The crops cultivated on field allotments usually conformed to those grown on surrounding farmland, due to the nature of the soil. In regions with light soil the plot-holder frequently divided his plot, one half for wheat and the other for potatoes and barley. In some regions root crops (carrots, swedes and parsnip) were also grown. On heavy soils beans replaced barley as the rotational crop. Wheat remained the most profitable cereal crop, even if sold or merely fed to a pig. Mangolds and swedes were favourite crops with holders as they provided feed for pigs.

During the late 19th century the connection between pig-rearing and allotment gardening was very close. In Warwickshire the closing of the pigsties in one of the larger villages nearly put the all the local allotments out of cultivation. With pig manure the fertility of the soil was assured, and with a pig in the sty all the waste vegetation from the allotment was put to good use. Without a pig, few labourers could afford to maintain the fertility of an allotment. The necessity of sustaining productiveness and the difficulty of doing so was one of the main reasons why labouring folk found it difficult to cultivate more than half an acre of land.

In the late 19th century the possession of an allotment was, in rural areas, still regarded as the first rung up the social ladder toward achieving a smallholding and independence. The argument for self-advancement could not apply to everyone, especially when working conditions and pay were slowly beginning to improve. Every labourer or worker of the land could not become a smallholder or farmer.

When asked about the doings of younger workers in the village, one old labourer complained bitterly that the adolescent generations only wanted Sunday clothes, a cigarette and a bike. He said the young men had forgotten what drove their forefathers to take up an allotment, and they felt less obliged to spend their leisure hours growing vegetables. When young men were asked why they did not choose to cultivate allotments they usually replied with comments like 'Why should we?' In the absence of economic necessity there was no answer, and the Board of Agriculture found that the majority of younger men belonged to some kind of benefit society.

From 1870 the wives and daughters of farmer classes felt less compelled to engage in agricultural tasks, especially in the field. By the 1890s this notion had spread to the wives of labourers. Town culture and refinement appealed to all classes of women, even when many lacked the finances to pursue them. The restricted scope of fieldwork for women was no drawback to them, though at the time there was little degradation attached to a short spell of light gardening.

While some rural dwellers were less enthusiastic about allotments, a different picture was emerging in urban regions. By 1892 Windsor was a rapidly expanding town and, as the majority of working-class dwellings lacked a garden, there was tremendous enthusiasm among townsfolk to take an allotment. The tenants had to contend with a rent of 1 shilling per rod or £8 per acre. One farmer was reputed to have rented land at 50 shillings an acre and let the land to plot-holders at £8 per acre. Much of the allotment land was located on low-lying terrain and subject to flooding during the winter months, resulting in serious loss of crops. Mr E. B. Foster, the County Councillor representing the district, promised to look into the matter of flooding and of the prohibitively high rents charged.

By 1893 some town workers were going to extraordinary lengths to ensure that their battle with the land would become a success. A working man residing in Bethnal Green took an allotment of ground under the jurisdiction of London County Council at West Ham, which was a considerable distance from his dwelling. His 16-rod plot at Millmeads was initially swamped with long coarse grass and he asked for guidance on how to proceed, as his experience was rather limited. Although the task of converting a rank, weed-infested wasteland into a productive garden was arduous and the allotment far from home, he finally did well.

A correspondent writing to the *Gardeners' Chronicle* in 1893 stated that:

'The "Poor Artisan" shut daily in dismal city surroundings would become a hero with a few roods of land. Although initial clearance might be a daunting prospect, uncompromising ground could become a green paradise, if only for the cultivation of potatoes and cabbages. It might be crude horticulture, but for the townsman it was a pleasing and useful occupation.'

Although the allotments provided by local authorities were less bound by arbitrary regulations than those under the jurisdiction of landlords, the matter of tenure was less than secure. At Kingston in Surrey plot-holders had long been provided with allotments for several years by a land-owner. There were more than 100 plots within divers fields and all were taken and well cultivated and cropped. Conditions of tenure were subject to six months notice. The rent was 1 shilling per rod or £8 per acre, which was double the rent paid for nearby agricultural land; not surprisingly, the land-owner gained a considerable profit. When this land-owner died, the plot-holders became very anxious and hoped that the local authorities would step in so that their tenancy would be secure. On seeing the plight of these tenants, even the gentlemen of the district expressed a desire for the forthcoming Parish Councils Bill to become law so that local authorities would then be empowered to acquire land for allotments.

In 1893 a scheme to introduce allotments in the recently formed Borough of Richmond in Surrey seemed like a forlorn dream when the original plan to gain some plots in the Old Deer Park foundered. In spite of severe criticism, 20 acres of capital land were finally secured next to Mr Kingston's nursery. The land was marked out and divided into 196 plots of different dimensions. All were immediately taken up at 1 shilling per rod and were cultivated very efficiently. The rent of 20 shillings for a 20-rod plot was regarded as rather steep, but at Richmond the sum was cheerfully paid. Tenants came from all occupations that were very different from that of gardening. Few of the

The allotment gardens at Richmond. The tenants'
results for the first year surpassed all expectations.

tenants had any previous knowledge or experience of gardening – many had never even handled a spade before. Originally the land had been cultivated as a market garden, but the ground had never been dug more than 12 inches deep and the unbroken subsoil was, at first, difficult to work. During the first growing season the shallow soil was adversely affected by drought, but the tenants' results surpassed all anticipation. By late autumn of that year all of the 20-rod plots yielded approximately 40 shillings worth of winter crops. The tenants made a supreme effort to store manure for use the next season. As the ground was cleared, trenching and manuring work was undertaken. Numerous observers stated that these gardeners reaped a rich reward for their efforts. So successful were the allotments at Richmond that interest spread to nearby Kingston, where more than 100 workers signed a petition asking the Corporation to supply land for allotments. Apparently, more than 500 signatures could have been obtained with little effort. Overall, the demand for plots in urban areas steadily increased. One gardening correspondent stated that in 20 years' time the allotment garden would become a major factor in the country's welfare.

Throughout 1893 the forthcoming Parish Councils Bill created considerable excitement among rural folk, especially with the section pertaining to the supplying of allotments. Many people suggested that where allotments did not exist, they should be provided on a compulsory basis and that they should be able to help the most expedient workers gain larger holdings if they made such a request.

In many rural parishes workers became very anxious over the continual antagonism instigated by some members of the clergy upon the matter of allotments, but gradually the hostility petered out as the nature of the Parish Councils Bill became better recognised. In 1893 a most earnest hardworking vicar in Surrey was particularly worried that the term 'compulsory' should remain in the Bill because he felt that without such power the clause would be useless. This warm-hearted vicar was particularly troubled on the matter of allotments, as the plot-holders' right to tenancy was unsubstantial. Even in the late 1890s allotment land could be seized in an instant, and this situation was far from satisfactory. This vicar was deeply concerned about the wellbeing of local labourers and saw this Bill as a way to make the matter of gaining further allotments very much easier while ensuring security of tenure for the holders.

Under the Local Government Act of 1894, the newly established Parish and Urban District Councils were given the power to provide land for allotments as long as it was through voluntary agreement. If unable to hire land they had to apply to the County Council to make an order, which was liable to authorisation of the Local Government Board. Hired land gained through voluntary agreement could be let in allotments but not exceeding 1 acre to each individual. When land was hired compulsorily, no more than 1 acre of arable and 3 acres of pasture could be let to one tenant. On voluntary hired land the tenant was free to construct a cow house, barn or stable, but on compulsorily gained land the construction of any buildings was expressly forbidden. Allotments gained under compulsory means could not be secured at a rent less than 1 shilling per rod, whereas those gained by the voluntary arrangement could be let for half the rate. Parish Councils achieved their greatest success through the acquisition of allotments by voluntary means. After 1894 more than 40,000 working men held land directly from the Parish Councils.

The most interesting settlements were carried out by Parish Councils at Belbroughton in Worcestershire and Moulton in Lincolnshire. Worcestershire County Council was the first to apply the powers provided to it by the 1892 Smallholdings Act, which attempted to establish peasant proprietorship in England as a permanent feature of land settlement. In 1892 the County Council agreed to buy a farm of 147 acres near Catshill at £33 an acre. When the manufacture of hob-nails became mechanised, numerous workmen at Catshill were thrown out of work and the poor rate went up in leaps and bounds. After 1894 the penniless workers seized the opportunity, through their Parish Council, to apply for land and in 1895 the Council provided an 18-acre field that accommodated 30 nailers. The following year a further 16 acres were added, and in 1903 another 34 acres were included. The 177 acres enabled 112 men to obtain a living by market gardening. The paupers of Catshill 'grew their own poor rate' and elevated themselves from destitution to comparative independence. The holders used no fewer than 26 horses in ploughing, carting and transporting vegetable produce into Birmingham and bringing manure back to the land.

By 1894 the social outlook for the agricultural labourer had improved considerably over the previous 20 years, though Assistant Commissioner W. C. Little maintained that this was largely due to the cheaper cost of the prime commodities of life. He estimated that 16 shillings enabled the labourer (in 1894) to purchase the same volume of principal goods as 20 shillings would have done in 1871. In his Parliamentary Report on the agricultural labourer for 1894, Mr Little said:

'In the opinion of several observers the labourer has also advanced morally: he is said to be more sober, more provident, and less dependent upon charity or poor relief. But, not withstanding the improvement which has taken place in every part of the country, there are, it is feared, too many of the class who, partly by their own fault and partly by misfortune, are in a chronic state of poverty and distress; but in this respect it is considered that the agricultural labourer will compare favourably with those of any other class; and the lot of the least fortunate is in many respects better than that of many dwellers in towns.' (W. C. Little, Royal Commission on Labour, 1894, C6894-XXIV, p99)

On the subject of allotments, Mr Little stated:

'As regards allotments it appears that there is little evidence of an unsatisfied demand in England; labourers complain that allotments are let at a much higher rate than the rent paid by farmers, and it is observed in the report that in many cases the rents of allotments are apparently very high. Allotments are reported to be unpopular in Wales; potato grounds, however, are to be found everywhere and gardens are very commonly attached to cottages.' (W. C. Little, Royal Commission on Labour, 1894, C6894-XXIV, pp97-98)

In 1894 a 'Rural Dweller' noticed much opposition to the taking of ground for allotments, even though the farmers were finding it difficult to make their land pay. He offered to take some land and pay twice as much rent to create garden plots for schoolchildren. Even though the children would get their gardens rent-free, none of the school managers, which included four farmers, were interested in the motion. They implied that if the children were instructed in farming technique, they would end up telling them how to run the farm instead of following orders. The local landlord was of the same opinion, even though he was offered double the rent a year in advance. The County Council had spent a considerable sum of money in educating people how to cultivate fruit and vegetables even though many did not own so much as a back yard. The 'Rural Dweller' said that it was far better to provide people with allotments first and instruct them afterwards, than to speculate on educating prospective plot-holders, who may never be able to gain a plot. The writer was concerned that labourers should be able to gain benefit from their cottage gardens and allotments by the sale of produce. He advocated a cheap form of conveyance in order to ensure that the crops cultivated by the tenants would reach the towns. In Sussex, large chicken farms had made specific agreements with the railway companies for the transit of produce; a man with a horse and cart went round all the farms and collection points to gather the stock, which was then delivered by rail to London and other cities at the ton rate. The senders got their money returned by the next day's post and the whole venture amounted to roughly 2½d per head. If a similar system could be implemented for the transport of allotment produce, the plot-holder would have a considerable source of income and there would be a benefit to the occupants of the towns. Such a scheme would also wipe out any worry that land would cease to remain in a state of cultivation.

Even in the 1890s the motion to acquire land for allotments was a long-winded and cumbersome process. Six or more ratepayers seeking allotments had to petition their District Council or Sanitary Authority in order to hire or purchase land on a compulsory term. If the District Authority failed to comply with the petition, the applicants had to appeal to the County Council. The Parish Council also had the power to petition the District Council, and the County Council, if the Sanitary Authority refused to act. In the event of the District Council conforming, they were at liberty to hire the land voluntarily or purchase it compulsorily. Working men living in urban districts could apply to the Urban District Council to hire land voluntarily or purchase it compulsorily. If the Urban District Council failed to acquire the land, the working men could then appeal to the County Council, under the Allotment

Act of 1890. Residents in County Boroughs containing a population of more than 50,000 inhabitants had to apply to the Sanitary Authority to hire land voluntarily for allotments. To acquire the land compulsorily, it was necessary for the Sanitary Authority to apply to the Local Government Board for its authorisation. If the Sanitary Authority refused to act, the petitioners could not appeal to a higher authority. Municipal Boroughs had no power to hire or purchase land compulsorily, unless the Council of the Borough appealed to the Local Government Board to invest them with the power, duties and liabilities of a Parish Council.

Within the neighbourhood surrounding London some gardens were gained by favourable means and were carried on very successfully. Many of the allotments were divided into 25-rod plots and land-owners let them direct to the tenants, usually at the rate of 1 shilling per rod on an annual basis. Such was the case of allotments on Lord Northbrook's estate at Lee near Blackheath. In another instance a city gentleman hired land near the Borough of Catford, and sub-let small plots to needy and worthy prospective tenants. This gentleman only made a marginal profit out of the venture, most of which was ploughed back into funding for repairs to fences, roads and other maintenance. From the profits came prize money in order to encourage tenants to keep their plots well-cultivated and tidy.

In the mid-1890s London County Council acquired an extensive tract of land at Forest Hill, which was once a disused brickfield, for the purpose of providing allotments. London County Council was most unwilling to let the land out in small plots and would only let the ground in 1-acre plots to trustworthy persons; the tenants of these 1-acre plots were permitted to sub-let to honest working men of integrity. The plots were not to be sub-let at a profit and the rent was generally 1 shilling per rod each year. The reason the LCC would not lease land of less than an acre was largely due to the time and trouble involved in collecting numerous small rents from individuals. The arrangement worked well without any major hitches, since various philanthropic gentlemen undertook the obligation of leasing the ground and collecting the rents.

A similar scheme was put into operation on swampy waste ground at the Isle of Dogs. Under the control of Mr John MacDougal, the LCC and a company of enthusiastic workers, a patch of waste ground once used as a sanitary dumping ground was converted to a large garden of small plots, which were cultivated by local residents and working folk. In the early days local stable-keepers in the locality used to pay the Allotment Committee 6d per load for the privilege of dumping manure from their stables. Subsequently the gardeners had a bountiful supply of free manure as well as the means of collecting a fund toward the cost of the annual rent. Although this case was exceptional, it clearly displayed what could be achieved under the voluntary system of gaining land for allotments.

The Ladywell & District Horticultural Society ran another very successful scheme in south London, which mostly consisted of working men. Many of the members were able to gain small plots of land and raised excellent produce, which often graced the show tables, not to mention winning prizes, at the Society's exhibitions. Such achievements and events prompted less fortunate members to hanker after plots, and as a result the Society Executive was induced to take measures to obtain further land.

In 1891 the chance arose in the form of 4 acres of land at Lewisham Park. The land belonged to the Rt Hon the Earl of Dartmouth, the Lord of the Manor at Lewisham. On being approached, his lordship freely consented to the land being leased to the Society at the annual rent of 3d per rod. The Earl even undertook to see that an unclimbable iron fence was installed around the gardens, together with a sturdy gate; such measures were often necessary precautions. The terms of the lease were as follows:

'We, T. W. Sanders, T. White, W. Bennet, C. Green, and A. Pratt, being respectively Chairman, Vice-Chairman, Treasurer, Trustee, and Secretary of the Ladywell & District Horticultural Society, hereby propose to rent and take of the Earl of Dartmouth, from Lady Day, 1891, all those four pieces or plots of ground more particularly set out on the plan endorsed hereon, and containing in the aggregate four acres more or less, situate in Lewisham Park, Kent, and now unoccupied, at the yearly rent of six pounds, free from any deductions for rates, taxes or other outgoings, payable quarterly.

And we further undertake and agree that land shall be used only for the purpose of cottage allotments, and that the rent charged to the tenants shall not exceed the sum of sixpence per rod of land. To uphold and keep the fences in good repair. To keep off trespassers, and to prevent any nuisance or annoyance to adjoining occupiers from the user of the land.

And we further agree to hold the same as a yearly tenancy from Lady Day aforesaid, and to quit at any Lady Day, on having three months' notice, without claiming compensation. It being understood and agreed that should any portion of the land be required for building purposes, the same may be taken at any time, upon compensation being given, such compensation to be first assessed by a valuer to be mutually agreed upon. In witness whereof we have this 23rd day of March, 1891, set our hands.' (T. W. Sanders, *Allotments*, One & All Garden Books, 1907, pp13-14)

The agreement was a plain and simple one, which gave the tenant security of tenure for a year, together with fair settlement for any undue disturbance to crops. Most of the plots were of 10 rods, though some tenants could not manage these portions, so a number of the plots were sub-divided into 5 rods.

The Lewisham Park tenants holding a 10-rod plot had to allow for the creation of 24-inch wide pathways between their plots, while each tenant had to consent to 12 inches of his plot being utilised for the pathways. Every plot-holder was supplied with a key to the gate and held responsible for its safekeeping and ensuring that the gates were locked on leaving. Tenants who lost their keys had to pay for new ones at the rate of 3d each. A series of rules were also laid down to safeguard the terms of tenancy and the management of the site.

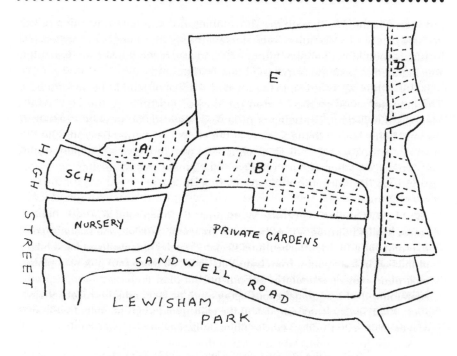

A map showing the allotments at Lewisham Park.
(After One & All Garden Books, 1907)

Every tenant had to be an elected a member of the Society and his subscriptions fully paid before being eligible to undertake any cultivation of the ground. The rent of 6d per rod was to be paid in advance at Midsummer (Lady Day) and every tenant was provided with a free rent book. Any tenant who lost his rent book was liable to a fine of 3d as well as paying for a new one.

The sub-letting of plots was forbidden and no work was to be conducted at the site on Sundays after 10am. No constructions of any kind could be built on plots and no fruit trees or shrubs were to be planted less than 3 feet from the pathways. The removal of fencing was prohibited unless by consent of the Allotment Committee. Dogs, perambulators and children of minor years were not to be admitted unless under full control. No rubbish could be dumped on the public road or footpaths. All tenants were to keep their ground in a state of proper cultivation, protect fences, mend pathways and safeguard their neighbours' produce as well as their own. Surrender of tenancy had to be provided with three months' notice in writing to the Secretary, to expire at Lady Day. Every rule was to be strictly adhered to and the Society had the right of repossession of the ground without notice or refunding. If a plot-holder found himself unable to pay the rent either through illness or lack of employment, his case was assessed before the Committee and, if found to be worthy, the rent was absolved. Any imbalance was made up from the reserve of funds.

A sub-committee of plot-holders managed the gardens and it was the Secretary's duty to make frequent summaries to the General Committee, to ensure that rents were collected, and that the rules were adhered to. During the spring and summer the plots were inspected at intervals and judges awarded points for tidiness, orderliness and sensible cropping. The tenants with the most points won the prizes. The Committee thought a 10-rod plot was quite adequate for the wage-earner to manage in his spare time. Many of the Lewisham Park tenants grew flowers as well as vegetables, though the cultivation of orchard fruit (apples, plums and pears) was forbidden and restricted to the usual soft fruit associated with allotments.

After 1895 the local authority insisted that the Society pay rates for the site, which amounted to £9 per acre. Eventually, after much discussion and a call for help to the Assessment Committee, the rate was reduced to 30 shillings per acre, but this completely swallowed the 6d rent money from the tenants and the remainder had to come from the Association funds. The Society stated that it was grossly unfair that the small cultivator, growing for his own consumption, should be asked to pay rates.

Although a number of other horticultural societies around the London region endeavoured to set up voluntary allotment schemes, they concluded that there was little point in approaching land-owners for single plots – they

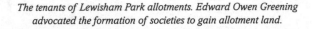

The tenants of Lewisham Park allotments. Edward Owen Greening advocated the formation of societies to gain allotment land.

Preparing for the One & All Garden Show, circa 1907.

did not care to be troubled by a handful of prospective tenants seeking individual plots. When it came to letting land to a small society, formed of co-operative workers, the venture was much more assured. Societies were in a better position to secure manure, seeds and tools as well as to lay on a water supply.

> 'How can a land-owner, who is probably a busy man, be expected to let 300 acres to 1,200 different people, when he can let the whole to one good responsible tenant respecting whom he knows everything to be satisfactory?
>
> There is one way out of the difficulty, and one way only. The men who want allotments, whether they be few or many, must form themselves into societies with which landlords can deal just like dealing with a single reliable tenant. To expect anything else is to be unreasonable.' (Edward Owen Greening, One & All Garden Books, 1907, p24)

Tradesmen and people with a position in society were, in nine cases out of ten, only too willing to help with innovations that would counteract idleness and drunkenness. Horticultural societies were heralded as a great sympathiser for the call to establish allotments, in regions where there were none. They often had little other work to do, as the annual flower shows did not exhaust their powers to conduct the good works. Edward Owen Greening was of the opinion that a mutual co-operative society could establish allotment schemes with great ease at little cost. Even a small society consisting of seven members could form a society by subscribing a share each, and each member would only have a liability of 5 shillings or £1 or a similar amount. Shares could be paid at the rate of 3d a week. Mr Greening offered advice on the forming of societies:

> 'The Association of which I am Managing Director has helped to form and register a great many societies of many kinds in its forty year existence. It is always open to do what it can. I recommend the pioneers of allotment work to make themselves Associates of our Association, subscribing 5 shillings per year, and receiving all our many helpful publications as they are issued. Whether they do this or not, I shall be glad to hear from them if I can by any means be of use in helping forward their work.' (Edward Owen Greening, *Allotments*, One & All Garden Books, 1907, p24)

Before 1908 both Parish and District Councils that provided allotments, with the consent of the Local Government Board, could issue customary regulations for their use. There were generally four conditions, which formed the rules for allotments governed both privately and publicly.

1 The tenant should keep the allotment free of weeds, manure it, and otherwise maintain it in a proper state of cultivation.
2 He should not plant any trees or shrubs so as to be injurious to any adjacent allotment.
3 He should keep every hedge that shall form part of the allotment properly cut and trimmed.
4 He shall not deposit weeds, manure, or any other obstruction upon any road or path, nor cause any nuisance or annoyance to the holder of any other allotment.
(A. Ashby, *Allotments & Smallholdings in Oxfordshire*, 1917, p20)

In many cases it was necessary for the public authority, allotment society or land-owner to take charge of maintaining fences and to ensure that plot-holders were spared grievance caused by one tenant's failure to take proper care in managing his garden. The care of fencing was divided among the tenants that gardened upon the site, which proved to be favourable to both land-owner and tenants alike.

By 1897 Lord Carrington had more than 1,200 plots on his High Wycombe estate ranging in size from 16 to 20 rods. The annual rent paid by the tenants varied from 2d to 4½d per rod, in accordance with the soil quality and location of the plot. A contract was drawn up between the tenant and Lord Carrington. Tenants were responsible for ensuring that the land remained free of weeds, crops were kept clean and the land well manured. If the tenant constructed a building such as a sty or shed, he was at liberty to remove it on vacating the allotment or to sell it to the subsequent plot-holder. Although Lord Carrington undertook to maintain the boundary fences, if tenants wished to fence in their plot they had to do so at their own cost. Lord Carrington also let tenants till their plots as they pleased, and therefore some were better cultivated than others. No tenant was allowed to sub-let any part of his allotment to another gardener. At High Wycombe, if a patch of allotment land near the town was required for building purposes, he supplied an alternative plot of land for use as gardens.

Lord Carrington had allotments on all of his estates. In 1892 he established 35 acres of land for plots for the labour-force at Spalding in Lincolnshire: 32 acres were divided into plots of 1 acre, which was let at 33 shillings an acre, clear of other charges, and seven plots of half an acre were also let at 21 shillings. Around 28 acres were taken by an Allotments Club formed by labourers of the Spalding region. During the 1890s demand for allotments at Spalding exceeded the amount of ground available, for the allotment system across south Lincolnshire was fast spreading. After the space of just one year it was estimated that the net profit from the 35-acre field on Lord Carrington's estate amounted to £211 (after the cost of seed and hired labour had been deducted); the highest profit of £8 15s 3d was derived from an acre of potatoes, while the lowest profit of £3 9s 9d came from an acre of barley. By 1898 Lord Carrington provided no less than 400 acres of land in the Spalding region for use as allotments. He stated that the predicted failure of the allotment system (originating in Buckinghamshire) proved unfounded. He was convinced that if one in ten of the farms in the region were devoted to smallholdings, the labour threat to the rural landscape would be vastly diminished. Richard Winfrey added that the movement, which started in 1890, incorporated 19 parishes around the Spalding region with more than 2,000 acres of high-quality plots.

The following year Lord Carrington presided over the distribution of prizes at Richmond Allotment Holders' Association on 12 July, and was full of praise for the efforts and work conducted there. However, he considered the annual rent of £8 an acre (charged by the Crown) to be exorbitant and thought that a reduction might possibly be obtained.

By 1898 the Technical Education Committee of Surrey County Council was taking a considerable interest in allotment cultivation. Horticultural teachers were authorised to call upon allotments assemblies when invited by local committees. The Technical Education Committee occasionally awarded Certificates of Merit to plot-holders with the best-kept ground, though never twice to the same tenant. The Committee dispensed rudimentary, though practical, books on gardening. Such prizes were much treasured. Mr E. J. Halsey, Chairman of the County Council, was very eager to see all the various allotment groups in the county assembled under one authority, believing that a considerable surge forward in the cultivation and expansion of allotments would result. Mr Halsey hoped to develop a federation of district or parochial cottage garden societies and to have an annual county exhibition of allotment and cottage garden produce.

The Smallholdings & Allotments Act of 1907 made various amendments to the previous Acts of 1887 and 1890. Where land could be gained reasonably through voluntary hiring, it became the duty of Local Councils to provide allotments to persons who belonged to the working population of the borough, district or parish. All expenses had to be recovered through the rents charged. The Council was at liberty to construct and adapt buildings, provided there was not more than one house on each allotment nor any house on less than 1 acre of land. Local Councils could not provide more than 5 acres of land in one or several allotments for the benefit of one tenant, without consent from the County Council, and were not bound to provide more than 1 acre per person. Although they were able to let to co-operative societies, no individual tenant was allowed to sub-let his plot. If the Council failed to let all the land held for allotments, it was allowed to let it in an alternative manner to generate the best rent possible.

Under the Smallholdings & Allotments Act of 1908, the Board of Agriculture became the central authority for all allotment legislation except for financial matters, which remained under the jurisdiction of the Local Government Board, while the Board of Agriculture authorised the regulations regarding allotments. The 1908 Act stipulated that:

'No land may be acquired for allotments except at such a price or rent as will, in the opinion of the Council, permit of all expenses being recouped out of the rents to be obtained from the allotments. The rents to be charged for the allotments must, therefore, be sufficient to cover all the expenses to which

Late-19th-century smallholdings in urbanised districts brought the need for regulation.

Workers digging a drainage channel on agricultural land. (After R. Haggard, 1899)

the Council are put in acquiring and adapting the land. with sufficient margin to cover bad debts and the cost of collection. The land may be improved and adapted by draining. and fencing. and cottages and buildings may be erected or existing buildings adapted. but not more than one cottage may be erected for occupation with any allotment of less than one acre. Councils will be well advised to satisfy themselves before erecting cottages on small allotments that it will be possible to let them readily at sufficient rents to cover the cost of their erection.' (Smallholdings & Allotments Act. 1908)

Local Councils were permitted, with consent of the Board of Agriculture and Fisheries, to let allotments to co-operative societies for the purpose of promoting the creation of allotments. Councils were given jurisdiction to make regulations regarding the terms and conditions on which to let the allotments, subject to confirmation from the Board of Agriculture. Councils were permitted to apply to the County Council requesting for the provision of communal pastureland. However, sufficient charge had to be made for the use of such pasture to cover the cost of acquisition. The Act also gave the Council the power to acquire land or grazing rights for the purpose of providing grazing rights to be attached to allotments provided by the Council.

'Councils can acquire land for allotments outside their borough. district or parish. If suitable land cannot be acquired by agreement. a Parish Council may represent the case to the County Council who may. on behalf of the Parish Council. exercise powers of compulsory acquisition under an Order of the Board of Agriculture and Fisheries. No part of any holding of fifty acres or less can be compulsorily acquired. Borough and Urban District Councils are themselves empowered to acquire land compulsorily for allotments under an Order of the Board of Agriculture and Fisheries. Regulations dealing with the compulsory purchase and hiring of land have been prepared by the Board and may be purchased, either directly or through any bookseller, from Messrs Wyman and Sons Ltd, Fetter Lane, Fleet Street, London EC4 price 1d per copy or post free 1½d.' (Smallholdings & Allotments Act, 1908)

By the early 1900s small garden allotments in urban areas were usually cultivated entirely by hand tools. Tenants who employed a small haulier to plough their land were regarded as decadent, since the rate was 1s 6d per job. The plot-holder who adopted this strategy was rarely successful or a permanent cultivator. Crops raised on urban allotments usually included potatoes, green vegetables and soft fruit, especially strawberries. Flowers were also grown, which included herbaceous perennials, roses and sweet peas. Mr Ashby elaborated on the tenancy of urban allotments:

'The real value of urban allotments is not to be tested in the economic sphere; it must be treated on a broader basis. Nor can urban garden allotments be regarded as a device to provide an important addition to the labourer's income; for as a matter of fact, in some districts artisans and small tradesmen are more numerous as allotment gardeners. While the demand for allotments from these classes is to some extent economic it is more definitely sentimental. And that labourers are not more numerous as cultivators is partly due to their lack of friends who can introduce them to persons who have allotments to let. The membership of mutual societies for the provision of allotments is very largely confined to highly respectable artisans and to a few workers of good standing.' (A. Ashby, *Allotments & Smallholdings in Oxfordshire*, 1917, p57)

Few tenants in urban areas could evaluate the worth of their plots (usually of 20 rods), though some thought the value of their produce, based on the purchase price in shops, was between 3 and 4 shillings a week, all year round. In urban areas the annual rent varied between 15 shillings and £1. Plot-holders rarely cultivated produce specifically for selling and those that did sold direct to the consumer.

Although urban plot-holders were able to work on their land during Saturday afternoons (or half-day closing day) as well as Sunday morning, few endeavoured to carry out winter work such as entrenching the ground or cultivate green crops; often the ground remained untouched once the potato crop had been lifted in the autumn. Townies were less advantaged than rural dwellers with regard to supplies of manure. The advent of the motor car curtailed the use of street clearings to manure the ground. Many plot-holders insisted that traces of oil and tar introduced poisonous elements that would damage their crops. Consequently, the cost of fertilising the ground increased and in some cases manure costs matched that of the annual rent.

Rural garden plots were cultivated in much the same manner as urban ones, although few farm workers bothered with the cultivation flowers or fruit. Large gardens were usually reserved for staple crops like potato, swede, parsnips and carrot, with onions and greens where care and vigilance were required. Villagers were much more dependent on bulk supplies of vegetables than townsfolk, who were frequently able to obtain cheap fresh meat.

However, villagers were more fortunate than town workers with respect to supplies of manure, but they were at a distinct disadvantage with regard to leisure time. Cultivation of the plot was confined to the evening hours after 5 o'clock. Whereas townsfolk were free to garden on the Sabbath, country dwellers were far too conscious of public opinion to work on their allotments on Sunday. The value of a 20-rod plot to the rural labourer varied between 1s 6d and 2s 6d per week.

On urban allotments home-made sheds and tool-stores were usually much in evidence, though the quality of craftsmanship was never very high. In some cases rickety sheds were patched up with faded advertisements. On rural and field allotments constructions of any kind were rare, largely due to the distance from the village.

Arthur Ashby commented on the state of urban allotment sheds:

'They rarely fail to be a blot on the precincts of any town, and, although restrictions would never raise the aesthetic quality very high, the worst abuses might be abolished by prescribing some range of colours which would suit the locality.' (A. Ashby, *Allotments & Smallholdings in Oxfordshire*, 1917, p58)

At the beginning of the 20th century allotment land became increasingly difficult to find due to the expansion of industry and the need for more housing. The increasing number of prospective tenants in urban regions often necessitated the dividing of existing allotments into smaller ones. After 1900 there was much confusion between smallholdings where small tenant farmers raised livestock as well as crops, and garden allotments that were solely cultivated with hand tools. The Local Government Board decided that there was a pressing need for some kind of regulation, and under the Smallholdings & Allotments Act of 1908 the greatest majority of allotments became garden-sized, not exceeding a quarter of an acre (40 rods). The smallest plots were usually of 10 rods.

The Land Enquiry Committee was set up in 1912 by the Liberals, who argued that insecurity of tenure had prevented tenants from investing their own capital in more intensive farming. This also applied to the cultivation of allotments. The Land Division of the Board of Agriculture provided an illuminating account of the provision of allotments in the second part of their report of 1912. The information was supplied by Town Councils, Urban District Councils and Parish Councils, and 7,906 of the 8,300 local authorities responded to the Board's request for details. The returns indicated that in a great number of cases no land was held for use as allotments and that no applications had been made. Around 1,999 local authorities reported some action, of which 1,557 were Parish Councils, 287 Urban District Councils, 154 Town Councils and one from London County Council.

The total quantity of land let for the purpose of allotments by various local authorities in England and Wales stood at 31,089 acres, of which 7,143 were the property of the Councils and 23,946 acres were leased. This land was let to 117,562 individual tenants and 21 associations. Figures for 1912 show that 1,259 acres were acquired for use as allotments, compared with 1,267 in the previous year, when 8,523 individuals and three associations were provided with plots. In 1912 there was still a great unsatisfied demand, with 11,789 applications from individuals and four associations, amounting to 4,522 acres in all.

In 1913 the Land Enquiry Committee set about addressing the great land problem. Investigators were dispatched to all parts of the country and enquired into the wages of farm workers, their housing, the provision of allotments or smallholdings and the matter surrounding security of tenure. The Land Enquiry Committee found that in rural districts only one-sixth of cottages had a garden exceeding an eighth of an acre. Rural folk preferred a large garden affixed to the house than an allotment at a distance from the village. Only two-thirds of all villages surveyed had allotments and most were fully utilised. Where allotments remained uncultivated, the rent was too high, the ground too poor to warrant cultivation, or the site was too far from the village. In some cases the long hours the labourer spent in employment prevented cultivation. The Land Enquiry Committee also discovered that there was still a great unsatisfied demand from the labourers for allotments. In places where there was a demand for plots but applications were lacking, this was largely due to apathy on the part of the Council, hostility from the farmers, high rents demanded, or the reluctance of the Council to apply compulsory powers of purchase. The Committee suggested that the Parish Council should be able to acquire not only allotments but also village greens and common pasture. The Committee also implied that Parish Councils should be given the power to obtain compulsory orders for the purchase of land at a fixed rate set by a Land Court. Legal costs could be borne by the Exchequer or, in the case of smallholdings, by the Parish Council concerned.

The Land Enquiry Committee revealed a keen thirst for allotments in urban areas, though by this time the majority of plots were usually of 10 rods (300 square yards). The Committee suggested that the provision of allotments on the outskirts of towns would reduce further requests for land, but it did not, and in most towns demand exceeded supply. By the end of 1913 there were 600,000 allotments across the UK, and the pace was finally set for the development of the 20th century urban allotment that would prove to be vital in the welfare of townsfolk in the coming years.

6
Digging for Dora

When Kaiser Wilhelm unleashed his troops upon Belgium in August 1914, Europe was plunged into a terrifying new war, on a scale previously unknown. As enemy submarines slipped into British waters, the nation awoke to a world of dwindling provisions. Unsure of its agricultural policy, Herbert Asquith's Government dithered while the impending food crisis deepened. The idea that amateur gardeners could grow vegetables on scraps of waste ground never entered the minds of Government officials.

A year into the war a Royal Commission, the Government's own Agricultural Consultative Committee, enlightened people and even the press questioned the Government's tardy response to food production. On 12 August 1915 Sir Charles Bathurst, Chairman of the Central Chamber of Agriculture, called on the Government to act without further delay.

From the start of the war, most high-ranking officials and authorities assumed that after a few swift, vigorous battles the conflict would be over by the spring of 1915. It was also the considered opinion of many that the end of the war would result in mass demobilisation leading to severe unemployment, which would rupture the labour market from one end of the country to the other.

The concept of cultivating vacant land had developed long before the outbreak of war. In America during the pre-war years Mr Joseph Fels had realised the connection between idle land and idle labour. On 8 November 1907 he had formed the Vacant Land Cultivation Society (VLCS), with the aim of addressing two great social ills of the time.

Between 1907 and 1914 the London branch of the VLCS made a considerable effort to get useless waste ground put into cultivation by the unemployed. These well-meaning efforts met with a lukewarm response, largely through the apathy of land-owners and the customary formalities of local authorities. At the start of the war the VLCS had only 140 plot-holders cultivating roughly 17 acres. With the urgency of wartime, the Society re-organised its constitution and renewed the campaign to convert derelict wasteland and prospective building sites into productive vegetable gardens.

In spite of the uncertainty, from the onset of war to the end of 1916 numerous inspectors undertook detailed surveys of building sites and waste ground in and around London with the possible view of creating allotment gardens. Hundreds of acres were examined, the findings registered in a handbook and scores of letters dispatched to land-owners asking for help

Plot-holders clearing unpromising land on a derelict site in Battersea.

Such waste ground was converted to well-tended and productive plots by the efforts of the VLCS.

and co-operation. Prior to 1916 only a handful of enthusiastic gardeners and voluntary societies recognised the potential of using waste ground to grow food.

On 11 January 1916 Lord Selborne, President of the Board of Agriculture, impressed on the Mayors of Boroughs and County Boroughs the need to produce as much food as possible from allotments and gardens. He stipulated that local authorities should ascertain whether there was an unsatisfied demand for allotments in the region, if the absence of men away on military service or those working in the munitions factories had affected the number of allotments in cultivation, and whether shortages of manure were likely to dissuade tenants from fully cropping their plots. He added that his Department would endeavour to address the matter and thought that the formation of a 'War Food Society' would assist in attracting a wider interest in allotment cultivation. Lord Selborne added:

> 'It would greatly aid the Movement if a small fund were raised for the purpose of giving prizes for the best cultivated allotments, or for the best crops produced. I am aware that the general level of cultivation in many borough allotments in this country is already high, but I am convinced that a good deal more can be done to increase the production of food from them in this time when the nation needs every pound of food, which can be produced within its borders.' (*Board of Agriculture Journal*, 1916, p1012)

By 1916 the Borough of Stafford was well endowed with allotments. Exclusive of vacant sites that were being cultivated, some 90 acres of allotments were let on various estates. The Stafford Allotments Group was by far the largest, comprising 70 acres and situated near Coton Hill. The land was divided into 401 plots cultivated by 650 plot-holders, who were resident Freemen. The administration of the allotments lay in the hands of 12 elected trustees, who were empowered to grant the plots to the Freemen only, the annual rent being 2s 6d, including rates and tithes. If a Freeman decided not to cultivate all his allotment, he was at liberty to sub-let or sell off part of his plot. However, the sub-tenants were not recognised by the trustees, nor were they entitled to any form of compensation. As a result, the sub-tenants, of whom there were a considerable number, were less inclined to expend time and effort on their plots and no lasting or permanent improvements were installed. If a Freeman allowed his plot to fall into a state of neglect, he was liable to forfeit his right to tenancy. Even so, the system of giving one tenant notice to quit, then establishing another in his place, was a slow process and invariably the land became infested with weeds, which did harm to the surrounding plots. Ploughing of the land was forbidden on the estate.

The Borough of Croydon was particularly allotment-minded and quickly endorsed Lord Selborne's request to grow food. Miss E. L. Hudson, Hon Secretary of the Croydon branch of the VLCS, provided an illuminating account of the Society's efforts, which gained momentum during the autumn of 1915. A Garden Sub-Committee had been formed to carry out the important work of inspecting land, marking out plots and letting land to applicants, while supervising and providing advice on cultivation. The Sub-Committee was fortunate, for its Chairman was a keen gardener, who threw himself into the work with ardent enthusiasm. In order to advertise its existence the Society placed notices on all the vacant plots, but by December 1915 this had become unnecessary as there was a waiting list of 150 prospective holders. Although some of the plots varied in size, the majority were of 10 rods. The sub-letting of plots was supposedly forbidden, but this rule was frequently broken; tenants that sub-let still had to pay their full subscription before retaining only part of their plot. In the Garden Sub-Committee's report for September 1915, it was stated that:

'The plots are receiving good cultivation in each instance. Where tenancy began last autumn, the cultivator is now getting good returns for his labour. Some excellent crops have been gathered, and the ground, after being properly treated, has been replanted. Other grounds let at a later date have been well trenched, and are mostly cropped with vegetables, which will yield produce in the coming winter and early spring. Neatness and tidy appearance are found on each plot, and it is a pleasure to walk round these grounds and observe the welcome change made in the last few months from barren wilderness to a productive piece of land.' (Croydon Garden Sub-Committee, *Board of Agriculture Journal*, 1916, pp965–966)

On a plot of 9 rods, produce to the value of £6 12s 9d had been harvested at the end of 1915. On a 5-rod plot, where the ground was so poor that it was nearly refused, one tenant raised a staggering 5½cwt of potatoes. At the end of 1915 another tenant, who gardened on a 10-rod plot, wrote of the produce he cultivated:

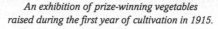

An exhibition of prize-winning vegetables
raised during the first year of cultivation in 1915.

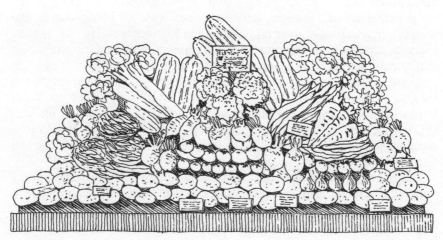

'About 200 spring cabbages, 100 cauliflowers, 1 row of broad beans, 2 rows of runner beans, 1 bed of shallots, 1 bed of turnips, 1 bed of beet, 2 rows of parsnips, 1 bed of onions, 1 bed of shorthorn carrots, 3 rows of intermediate carrots, 1 bed of vegetable marrows, 3 beds of lettuces, several crops of radishes, 4lb of tomatoes, and 18 bushels of potatoes. The ground is now well cropped with winter things, such as Brussels sprouts, savoys, broccoli and curly kale. Enough vegetables have been grown on this plot to keep my wife and family through the winter.' (*Board of Agriculture Journal*, 1916, p966)

The Croydon branch of the VLCS was fortunate to have invaluable assistance from the Guild of Help, together with the members of the Garden Sub-Committee, which made their work comparatively easy. Tentative enquiries were made in another suburban area, where conditions were less favourable, and the provision of land for allotments made little progress. The Board of Agriculture stated that the formation of the Parliamentary War Savings Committee might be able to assist with other similar schemes. Overall, the outlook for the VLCS remained as daunting as ever.

By the end of 1916 the Society's plot-holders had only increased to 800, and they gardened upon 50 acres of land. As the food shortages worsened, the demand for land increased, while the waiting list of prospective plot-holders grew ever longer. By 1916 a multitude of unsatisfied applicants outnumbered the plot-holders by three to one. Previously, needy families had always been given priority with plots, but by 1916 applications were so numerous they were dealt with in the order that they were received. The steady demand for allotments over the past few years had rapidly advanced into a frantic scramble.

In December 1916 David Lloyd George was swept to power at the head of the Coalition Government. Asquith had resigned and was largely discredited through his indecision. The new Prime Minister was extremely enthusiastic about extending the provision of allotments; he himself gardened on an allotment and was anxious that no opportunity to grow food should be overlooked:

'If you can use a spade, if you are good at gardening – go on to the land at once. Go to help replenish our dangerously low stocks. Go now while there is still time for the spring sowings to yield you summer and winter food. In a few weeks it will be too late. It is essential for the safety of the nation, for the life of the nation, that we should put forth immediately every effort to increase production for this year's harvest and the next.' (Lloyd George, 'National Service' Industrial Army leaflet, 1917)

The 'National Service' Industrial Army crest as depicted on numerous leaflets. (After HMSO)

Railway authorities, colliery proprietors and private companies were asked to dedicate land around their works to enable their employees to grow vegetables during their leisure time.

In early November 1916 the VLCS gained wider recognition and was asked to send a delegation to interview Lord Crawford, now President of the Board of Agriculture. At last the VLCS was able to explain the difficulties encountered in acquiring land for allotments in order to combat the crippling food shortages. The meeting with Lord Crawford lasted for over an hour and afterwards the greatest land reform for years was about to take place. The privilege of the few was about to become the right of the many. In line with the Defence of the Realm Act (DORA), the Government intended to seize certain lands so that allotments could be provided on a grand scale. Two weeks later the Cultivation of Lands Order of 1916 was passed. Through this Order all unoccupied (un-rated) land in the boroughs and urban districts in England and Wales could be secured by the Board of Agriculture or by those acting on behalf of the Board. Almost at once the VLCS was informed of the jurisdiction granted to London County Council under the Cultivation of Lands Order, and the VLCS Secretary promptly attended a meeting with the LCC Parks Committee to discuss their reclamation projects.

The Society asked if it could start work on the Furzedown Estate in Tooting, where hundreds of prospective allotment tenants had been waiting for several weeks. Astonishingly, instead of providing co-operative assistance, the LCC began to raise one bureaucratic obstruction after another. One LCC official declared that he was not prepared to take part in appropriating land without consent from the owner. When the applicants at Furzedown Estate had to wait further for their allotments and gardens they were barely able to restrain their anger and impatience. After vigorous protest over the LCC's inaction, half the designated land was eventually (and rather reluctantly) handed over, and hundreds of plot-holders prepared the ground over the Christmas holidays. After the holiday period further applications were made to the LCC asking for authorisation to take over other plots of ground in the London region, which amounted to 650 acres. This time the LCC granted permission for the VLCS to take possession of the land, which included the remaining 25 acres at Furzedown Estate. The LCC retained 2 acres at Plumstead for the playing of football. No further land was allocated to the VLCS by the LCC, and the latter constantly rebuffed attempts to acquire further un-rated (derelict) land and invented a variety of half-baked excuses. All land that the VLCS applied for had previously been inspected by practical horticulturists and pronounced as suitable for cultivation. So while the LCC raised many objections to taking over of un-rated land, the Government extended the Cultivation of Lands Order to allow Metropolitan Councils to acquire rated land as well. Naturally the LCC remained unyielding and insisted that it was right.

The obstinate and unpatriotic spirit of the LCC did not go un-noticed. Many condemned its extraordinary blocking policy, and not even the press would justify the Council's stand on gaining land for allotments. On 2 January

1917 the *London Evening News* summed up the feelings of the population with a cynical comment on the LCC:

THE GREAT BODY AND THE COMMON PEOPLE

A Fable of Today

Once upon a time, long, long ago – in fact, before the war – there was a great body called the LCC, which modelled itself upon the lines of the Mother of Parliaments. It had members and parties and much internecine strife, and red tape and officials – especially the officials – and it moved with the slowness and deliberation, which is characteristic of a Great Body.

And then war came upon the land, and slowly at first but more and more rapidly as time went on the face of things were altered. Many differences began to be noticed by the people in their daily lives, and even the Mother of Parliaments received a severe shaking up, but there was one thing which the war could not alter, and that was the LCC. It still retained its committees and its red tape and its officials, and when anyone asked whether it knew that there was a war on it would reply, "We understand that this is the case, but our organisation being already perfect, and it being clear that any change must be for the worse, we do not propose to take any steps in the matter."

Now during the war there came a year of bad harvests, and what with small crops and the lack of means to carry what corn there was, and the fact that many men had forsaken tilling for fighting, there was a shortage of food in the land, and the State called upon all its citizens earnestly to cultivate such soil as lay ready to their hands. To this end the Local Bodies were urged to make a record of all vacant land under their respective jurisdictions and to parcel it out among those who were willing to help in making it bear the crops which were so desperately needed.

Many bodies at this word fell upon the task, so that in quite a short space of time there were men digging with spades and enthusiasm to prepare the soil for the harvest. But the LCC, being a Great Body, merely referred the matter to a Committee, which discussed it with another Committee, which disagreed with everything the first Committee had said, so that in the end the only crop which was raised was a crop of objections.

The common ordinary people to the number of 6,000 cried aloud for land to cultivate, that later on they might have bread and potatoes to eat, but the LCC absolutely declined to be hurried. The fact that so many stalwart men were willing to serve their country in their spare time had no interest for it. It wanted additional information and statistics, and as for the patriotic cultivators who had nothing to cultivate, if they grew weary of waiting they could lean upon their spades, which were admirably adapted for this purpose.

Now there was a Society for the Cultivation of Vacant Land, which not being a Great Body had got to work, and scheduled the vacant land and the applications therefor, and demanded of the LCC some 600 acres to fill the present needs of the patriotic cultivators. The Great Body replied, "Go away: can't you see that we are busy raising objections? Do you not know that it is the first maxim of officialdom that what has never been done before cannot be done at all?"

Thus were the glorious traditions of officialdom upheld before the face of the enemy. Nevertheless, at the end of three weeks, out of 14,000 vacant acres no less than 23 had been allotted, and it was calculated that this phenomenal rate of progress all the land would be under crops in another thirty years or so, if the war would last that long.

But the patriotic cultivators murmured among themselves, saying, "Who are these officials who stand between us and the duty laid upon us by the State? Do we not pay the salaries of these men in order that they may order our business and aid us to win the war? Why, then, should we stick this sort of thing any longer? There is a time for digging, and a time for planting, and a time for gathering in the crops, and if the time for digging be spent all in waiting then we can neither plant nor gather in. Get a move on, ye children of Red Tape, or make way for them that will."

But the LCC merely smiled in a superior way, and answered, "It is plain, O common people, that ye know nothing of the art of government, which is Wait-and-See!"

But Wait-and-See was dead and his successor Do-it-Now reigned in his stead, and when Do-it-Now heard of these things he was wrath, for he cared nothing for Great Bodies but only for the people, and he sent messages to the LCC, saying, "Get on with your task, and let the people have land, or..."

The end of the story is not yet written.

(*London Evening News*, 1917)

Early in February 1917 the LCC responded by stating to the press that the land coming within the terms of the Cultivation of Lands Order was not to exceed 500 acres. Three of the Metropolitan Boroughs, Wandsworth, Woolwich and Lambeth, obtained direct powers under the Order, and within a matter of weeks 386 acres were allocated to the VLCS. The LCC claimed that left just 114 acres of available land in the other 25 boroughs, less than 5 acres for each Metropolitan Borough. The other Metropolitan Boroughs allotted hundreds of acres in spite of opposition from the LCC, since they too were given powers as allotment authorities.

Wandsworth was one of the first Metropolitan Boroughs to exert its new-found control bestowed by the Board of Agriculture. Numerous other boroughs had asked the LCC for land and received the same treatment as the VLCS, so they applied to the Board of Agriculture for jurisdiction to provide allotments. The obstinacy of the LCC seriously delayed the Cultivation of Lands Order from 5 December 1916 to 22 January 1917, and save for the intervention of the Board of Agriculture the delays would have been much longer.

The Defence of the Realm Act (DORA) enabled local Councils and

Metropolitan Boroughs to press ahead with providing allotments. But like many laws, DORA was riddled with loopholes and the worst aspect was the lack of a clause making it compulsory for local allotment authorities to put the Cultivation of Lands Order into operation. The Board of Agriculture found that numerous civic organisations were reluctant to seize land, while others took land without the owners' consent and let it at very high rentals, thus profiting from the venture.

By the spring of 1917 a mighty tidal wave of 'allotmentitis' swept across the country. Day and night unceasingly, allotment authorities and provincial societies were inundated by an increasing swell of prospective plot-holders who wanted to join the great adventure. It became the Englishman's goal to give the Germans a hearty thrashing and to till the land. The wave of enthusiasm for land cultivation resulted in an abundant supply of potatoes, cabbages, turnips, beans, peas and salad crops, which greatly eased the dire food crisis. Special thanksgiving services were even held in the open air on allotments. At the weekends, in order to save time, afternoon tea on allotments became a regular Sunday event. For the first time DORA was really popular. The New Order in Progress enabled plot-holders and patriotic citizens to shout down selfish individuals and dismissive public institutions that hindered the nation's needs in wartime. Incredibly, the supply of plots still never satisfied the demand. Every reference in the newspapers informing of land to be let was immediately followed by a flood of letters from people anxious to gain an allotment. For every successful candidate there were at least three disgruntled complainers.

Just six months after the Cultivation of Lands Order of 1916, membership of the VLCS had swelled to 8,000. Previously it had taken nine years of arduous striving to find allotments for 80 citizens, but once the land was unlocked through DORA, ten times as many tenants were provided for in less than six months. Even in this time of national emergency, some land that had been applied for more than six times over still could not be obtained. This was due to the fact that local authorities were only permitted to ask land-owners for accommodation instead of being able to commandeer the land.

The unexpected rush for allotments saw the VLCS expand. Every day its postbag grew heavier as letters arrived from all parts of the country with requests for advice on land management and horticultural matters. A very large volume of work was conducted by voluntary helpers, who quickly recognised the patriotic nature of their efforts. Many citizens devoted much time and effort both in the office and to the marking out of new plots.

Every week hundreds of additional plot-holders were established on emergency wartime plots, and in most cases maximum supervision was required to ensure that each tenant made a good start. The plot-holders received notification to attend the site at the time of marking-out and to bring a spade and plenty of string. In many instances plots were already marked out and each tenant was shown his particular patch. Due to much planning and organisation by the volunteers, large tracts of land were quickly allocated to the patriotic diggers. During weekends the appointing of plots invariably took place on Saturday afternoons. Almost overnight, offensive patches of rubbish-strewn waste ground were magically transformed into hotbeds of industrious activity. A new species, the woman war-worker in the raincoat, conducted a great deal of the initial marking-out of allotments.

By early March 1917 the eagerness for cultivating land reached fever pitch and the lighter evenings and warmer weather brought thousands of extra recruits to the ranks of the 'spade and hoe' army. Even city gents dashed home to change into working clothes to toil like agricultural labourers on their allotments. Not surprisingly, garden tools started to become a scarce and precious commodity. The spate of activity spurred lethargic and indifferent District Councils into action, egged on by the constant requests of local residents. In some regions most of the available land had been taken up without reducing the demand from prospective plot-holders. Across the country meetings were held to gain yet more land for allotments. The Government urged citizens to secure land for growing food through their Local Councils. In regions where all the land was taken, Local Councils urged the Board of Agriculture to extend their powers.

The main difficulty encountered by the VLCS and those aiming to cultivate derelict land lay with the bitter cynicism of land-owners and their agents, together with stuffy public institutions that depended heavily on guidance from the so-called experts. In many cases, when an application was made for the temporary loan of a piece of land, the expert would often decide that the ground was unsuitable for gardening. In a few instances the specialist advice was genuine, but in the majority of cases this was a subterfuge to avoid further difficulty. An application for land at Putney resulted in a furore over its suitability for cultivation. The VLCS advisors found the land to be ideal, while Mr Prothero of the Board of Agriculture disagreed. Numerous would-be plot-holders were discouraged and refused to take up any of the ground. Eventually the Board was pressed to re-assess the decision, and within weeks all 5 acres at Putney were taken.

Some incredibly rough ground was converted into gardens of high productivity. In 1915 a great deal of attention was focused on a desolate site at Battersea that was smothered with rubbish, which in parts extended to a depth of several feet. Previously the Local Council had used the site as a tip for the dustcarts. Although the Council had been approached, a number of councillors thought the plan to grow vegetables on this former rubbish dump was utter foolishness. Mr John Burns, a local MP, stated that any land in London would not be fit for growing a consumptive cabbage. In spite of such remarks, by January 1916 the site was assigned to the VLCS and volunteers commenced clearance work. By the first week of March around 80 tons of rubbish, rubble and hardcore had been hauled away by hand using barrows and baskets. Even after clearance, the resulting landscape appeared as unpromising as ever. As the work of trenching proceeded the number of critics swelled and their acidic comments became more outspoken with each day that passed. On some parts of the Battersea site it was necessary to trench to a depth of 10 feet in order to reach decent soil. In the face of constant ridicule, the volunteers persevered and after several weeks the entire site was neatly divided into plots of well-dug soil. By May the plots were flushed with green as new vegetation started to burgeon. At the end of the growing season the venture at Battersea was regarded as an unqualified success and the critics had vanished, only to be heard of periodically when new applications arose.

Numerous sites with similar difficulties sprang up all around London. Before the war patches of derelict land were only a miserable waste that lowered the tone of the district and provided little joy to those living nearby. Through the sheer hard work of countless volunteers it was shown that desolate landscapes could be retrieved. However, many of the volunteers had to tolerate a barrage of scathing comments on their efforts to get the land productive. One gardener wrote of his efforts:

'Two years ago, our plots were the scene of a fair, and a roundabout stood on the bit of land I have been working. When I began to dig, I found the soil rich with iron bolts, sheet iron, brickbats, broken bottles, china, old boots, oyster shells and rags. But I hacked my way through, and now, with winter coming on, I thank God for the abundance He has given me.' (G. W. Butcher, *Allotments for All*, 1918, p29)

Another plot-holder, attempting to reclaim swampy land in south-west London recalled:

'Owing to the apparently practical impossibility of ever making anything of this plot, I believe two previous holders threw it up as unworkable, and when I took it over, which was not until last Easter, I found it to consist of an absolute swamp at the end of the next road. About a quarter of its full extent was completely covered with water, varying in depth from three inches to over a foot, whilst the greater part of the remainder was covered with accumulations of builder's rubbish, some of the heaps being over five feet high. I often had nasty remarks thrown at my head as to whether I intended to grow watercress, go in for trout fishing, or let out pleasure boats on my allotment, so you can perhaps judge what a terrible fight I had to make it a practical garden. However, I think I may be excused for saying I feel quite proud of the fact that, in spite of what I have been repeatedly told was an impossibility, by dint of sheer hard work I have conquered its drawbacks.

I have trenched all my ground to a depth of 3 to 3½ feet, and have been rewarded by a splendid crop of turnips, a good supply of potatoes, and a fairly decent crop of other vegetables. I may also mention I have grown some sugar beet, and some of my roots have been sent out to a soldier in France who has a craving for some but wrote that there was none to be had in that country. I have a very promising supply of green crops on the land for winter and spring, and am looking forward to being able to work on my allotment next season without such heart-breaking trials and hard labour as I have been through this season.' (G. W. Butcher, *Allotments for All*, 1918, pp29-30)

Mr Butcher, who was Superintendent of the VLCS, dismissed claims that the Society was trying to turn the country into a vast cabbage patch. He stated that if every man in the UK were to be given a 10-rod plot to tend in his leisure hours, only one-ninety-sixth of the surface area of Britain would be under allotment cultivation. He also decreed that the allotment-holder had improved the landscape, not defaced it. Before the grim winter of 1916 the majority of urban areas were blemished with scraps of derelict land that over the years had degenerated to become eyesores of the most demoralising aspect. Mr Butcher elaborated:

'Strewn with filth and rubbish, a general depository for refuse of every description, the absence of fencing provided access to children by day and loafers by night, the typical building site presented a grave indictment of our atrocious "land system". It was usual for such places to be frequented on Sundays by youths and men playing football or pitch and toss, while it was quite common for them to become clubhouses, as it were, of rowdyism, with resultant manifestations which formed a constant source of annoyance to those living near. In a number of cases known to us where land of this description adjoined workshops or factories, it was practically impossible, owing to the causes mentioned, to keep a pane of glass unbroken. And meanwhile the land produced nothing – not even rates – though in nine cases out of ten it was capable of yielding, at pre-war retail prices, wholesome food to the value of £80 an acre.

Now these sores are in process of being healed. The unsightly, unhealthy, uncared-for building plot has become a trim, neat, well-cropped vegetable garden. It is no longer a plague-spot to be shunned but a centre of attraction to be visited. A novelty in sight-seeing has, indeed, been provided, for visitors to the plots are more numerous even than the plot-holders themselves, who, men, women and children alike, may be observed every day and evening in the summer busily and happily engaged in a task that is beneficial to themselves and to their fellow-citizens.' (G. W. Butcher, *Allotments for All*, 1918, pp30-31)

Allotment sites were not entirely free from threat (even in wartime) and, as in the 1890s, urban plots had to be made secure against damage and theft, not to mention acts of malicious vandalism. Numerous allotment holders called upon the Home Secretary to tackle the issue of safe-guarding allotment sites in and around the Metropolis. Although the problem was being addressed under the Cultivation of Lands Order, the Food Production Department suggested that tenants set up voluntary patrols, and that possibly the custodians might be paid a small fee from the association funds. The majority of allotments in and around London fell under the jurisdiction of the LCC, which reluctantly set up special notice boards to inform would-be miscreants of the consequences of damage or theft to allotments in wartime. The penalty for unlawful trespass was six months' imprisonment together with a heavy fine not exceeding £100 in accordance with the Defence of the Realm Act.

In the spring of 1917 the topic of school gardens arose as a way of educating the young in the importance of cultivating food. Much heated discussion over this issue raged on in different parts of the country and numerous educational authorities decided that children lacked the skill to grow food plants. Mr Prothero, President of the Board of Agriculture, was not of this opinion and gave authorisation for sections of playing-fields to be dug up for wartime gardening, so great was the demand for food.

In September 1917 the Food Production Department urged economy in the use of vegetable seed in order to make cultivation and weeding less laborious, save seed and so reduce labour:

'Many people habitually sow seeds extravagantly, thus increasing expense and labour. In ordinary times this may not matter greatly, but now it may mean that by doing so they would deprive their neighbours of a fair share of the restricted supplies available.

For such crops as parsnips, beets and beans, which have to stand singly at certain distances apart, do not sow in a continuous line of seeds. Instead, sow, from one seed in the case of beans, to eight or ten in the case of parsnips, at intervals corresponding to the distances apart at which the plants are ultimately to stand.' ('Economy in the use of Vegetable Seed', Food Production Department leaflet, 1917)

Before the war it was common practise for lowly paid railway employees, especially porters at stations in rural regions, to work on their plots between the arrival of trains. In the process of acquiring land for new tracks, the private railway companies were often obliged to purchase more land than was needed. The excess ground was allocated to employees, who could grow vegetables as a supplement in much the same way as the agricultural labourers had in the previous century. Broad embankments that bordered the tracks were ideal for use as plots. In a number of cases these lineside plots were some considerable distance from the station and it required an excellent sense of timing for station personnel to conduct stints of gardening between train services. Under emergency wartime measures the railway companies came under increasing pressure to let people from outside cultivate the lineside plots. Permission was granted, since in the age of steam locomotion the danger from a live rail did not exist. Rules and regulations pertaining to railway plots were not all that strict – all the prospective tenant had to do was apply to the nearest station master for a plot.

As well as managing to run a railway, the employees were particularly industrious when it came to raising crops, and they were offered incentives to cultivate food on waste ground alongside the line. Staff of the London & South Western Railway established their own Garden Plots Committee and held exhibitions every year at the Brunswick Institute at Vauxhall. At the beginning of 1917 around 5,300 plot-holders tilled the earth on land belonging to the railway companies, and throughout the course of the year their number expanded by another 600. The companies helped their tenants

Allotments on railway land belonging to the London & South Western Railway,
which held its own horticultural shows at Vauxhall.

in many ways such as obtaining supplies of seed potatoes at 6s 10d a bushel (normally £1), by offering the use of spraying machines, and supplying sugar beet seed free of charge. Sir William Portal, Deputy Chairman of the LSWR, opened the exhibition for 1917, the first show to be officially recognised by the railway company. The exhibits included every kind of vegetable and fruit and even extended to apples and plums. The quality of produce was very high and illustrated the viability of cultivating waste ground in wartime. Mr Portal stated that the exhibition would not be the last of its kind. D. H. Jenkins, the judge, warned gardeners against the notion that the biggest vegetables were the best. The judge was particularly awe-struck by the high quality of potatoes and carrots, and was enthralled by the class for collections of vegetables. Proceeds from the show were donated to the London & South Western Railway Company Servants' Orphanage Fund. A year later, following the second show, Mr W. Buckmaster, Chairman of the Railway Garden Plots Committee, received a glowing letter from the Board of Agriculture, praising the efforts of the railway staff.

Exhibitions and shows helped bolster the mood of patriotism among the plot-holders, though few needed encouragement. At the Hackney & District Plot-holders Association's 6th annual show, prize-winning exhibits included a cabbage that weighed in at 17lb, a marrow at 26lb and a pumpkin at 17lb. The exhibits were sold off at auction and the £2 16s raised was used to purchase cigarettes for the war wounded. Surplus and unwanted vegetables were supplied to local hospitals.

At the quarterly meeting of the affiliated branch of the VLCS, the Chairman, Frank Smith, stated that the war had created a desire for gardening on a scale previously unknown. He stated that foodstuff to the value of £4,000 had been raised during the year from Christmas Eve 1916 to Christmas 1917 on 24 acres of derelict land in a district of south-west London.

Before the passing of the Cultivation of Lands Order, the Croydon branch of the VLCS relied entirely on the goodwill of land-owners for access to vacant land. After 1916 Croydon Corporation appointed an Allotments & Smallholdings Committee, chaired by Councillor Adams, and entered upon 61 acres of land, which was divided into 790 plots and leased at 5 shillings for a 10-rod plot. Shortly afterwards the Croydon VLCS added a further 65 acres in 850 plots, paying up to £3 per acre. All the land was quickly taken and by the end of 1917 the Croydon branch of the VLCS was responsible for 176 acres, which were secured through voluntary agreement.

After January 1918 Croydon Corporation resumed possession of the land, including that held by the VLCS, in order to establish and consolidate land for various plot-holders' associations. Small fragments of land too small for associations remained in the hands of the VLCS, which amounted to 630 plots on 70 holdings, and these had increased to 745 by the autumn of that year.

'The excellence of crops raised was manifest in many vegetable shows in the Borough, both those promoted by the great horticultural societies and many others arranged by the plot-holders' associations. Great industry and no little skill were shown on all sides by the cultivators; lectures and practical demonstrations were frequently given and well attended. Further, much good will and many kindly offices existed among the plot-holders. When the local sweep went abroad to fight, his wife's allotment was kept going at full strength by her neighbours. There will be heartburnings when the owners of the "valuable building-sites", which have for these last years been feeding us with cabbages and potatoes, desire to replace those crops with indigestible bricks and mortar.' (H. Keatley Moore BA BMus JP, *Croydon and the Great War*, 1920, pp215-16)

It wasn't only around London and the suburbs that gardening took a hold on the population. In Britain's second city considerable effort was made to put waste land into cultivation.

After the passing of the first Cultivation of Lands Order of 1916, Birmingham's City Council delegated the task to the Parks Department, under the watchful eye of the Chief Officer, Mr W. H. Morter. The new powers were conferred in February 1917, and afterwards the development of putting the Order into force was rapid and continuous.

'From the outset, the requests for land were received in overwhelming numbers, and the issue of application forms, together with rules and regulations, ran into several thousands. As it was evident that many of the intending cultivators were undertaking the work for the first time, it was deemed advisable to divide the city into areas and to appoint a man in each to look after the plots and assist the allotees with advice and instruction when necessary. The plan was successful and the good crops produced by this means encouraged others to try.' (R. H. Brazier & E. Sanford, *Birmingham and the Great War*, 1921, p331)

Even though the applications were numerous, by the spring of 1917 the demand in most districts had been met. The seized lands were divided into plots of 400 square yards each and after four months no less than 650 acres had been secured for cultivation by 6,250 applicants at the rate of 10 shillings per annum. The Birmingham Parks Department also made arrangements with the principal seedsmen in the city for the supply of seed at reduced rates to the plot-holders, and similar concessions were made with ironmongers with regard to tools. The scarcity of seed potatoes created many difficulties for the plot-holders, but this was met by the distribution in two years of 2,000 tons at cost price. Further assistance was rendered by the purchase of a number of spraying machines, which were hired out to tenants, and other items were sold at a reduced price.

In 1918 all the tenants were ready to take up their plots once again, together with an additional number of prospective plot-holders. Since the cost of labour and materials had increased by 40% above the previous year, the size of the plots was reduced from 400 square yards to 300. By 1918 the wartime plots covered more than 1,000 acres and were divided among 12,000 tenants.

The cost of running the enterprise was not small. Rents received from 6,250 plot-holders amounted to £3,118 17s 3d. The approximate expenditure on salaries and wages for the year amounted to £752 12s 3d. Rent, rates and taxes were in the region of £1,451 4s 0d; outlay for fencing and pegs came to £796 3s 10d; printing, stationery and advertising charges amounted to £116 15s 0d; and miscellaneous expenses came to £203 15s 3d. Law and professional fees came to £79 7s 6d, and the stamp duty was around £116 15s 0d. Compensation costs rose from £234 11s 11d to £3,751 4s 9d.

In order to bolster the plot-holders, an exhibition was held in the Town Hall on 6-7 November and was regarded as a tremendous accomplishment. Mr F. D. Acland, formerly the Parliamentary Secretary to the Board of Agriculture, expressed misgivings at rising costs and urged plot-holders to form societies or associations for the joint purchase of their requirements, the sale of their surplus produce and for the co-operative hiring of land.

The Agricultural Organisation Society created a special Allotments & Smallholdings Department under the jurisdiction of a committee chaired by Mr Acland, to help plot-holders organise their activities on a business footing. The Society also published a booklet to illustrate the best way to set up and run an allotment society or association, with a set of sample regulations and many tips on the management of societies. A range of pamphlets covering the various aspects of renting co-operative land was also available from the Society's headquarters in London SW1. The Allotments Department of the Society even issued a special leaflet giving full details on the successful management of co-operative piggeries.

The Agricultural Organisation Society was the officially recognised association for the improvement of co-operative food production and worked in close communication with all the government departments concerned; it dispensed its services to plot-holders for free. By March 1918 more than 400 allotment societies were affiliated to the Society with a membership of more than 60,000. Mr Acland said it was difficult to over-estimate the value of co-operative schemes in food production, which was of benefit to individuals as well as the country as a whole.

In January 1918 Sir Charles Bathurst made a dramatic statement:

'It is my confident belief that food will prove to be the deciding factor in the war. It is unlikely that the ordinary farmhand of Great Britain will do much more (by augmenting its arable area) than make good the loss of productivity resulting from the growing foulness of the land normally under the plough. If so, the issue will rest mainly with the wartime allotment holder and cottage gardener, whose unselfish patriotic efforts have my unstinted admiration, and whose potatoes, beans, peas, onions, and parsnips will be of untold value in saving the nation from starvation and humiliation in the very critical year which lies before us.' (Sir Charles Bathurst, 'Allotments and Gardens', 1918)

Mild weather in the spring of 1918 saw an upsurge in allotment popularity. With the war now in its fourth year there was an ever-increasing demand for allotments in urban areas, especially in and around London. Both the Food Production Department and the Board of Agriculture pressed to have compulsory powers to acquire unoccupied private gardens in order to cultivate food. Paddington Borough Council insisted that there was enough spare land in the district without resorting to such drastic measures. Once again, an independent expert decreed that the local recreation ground was virtually useless for growing vegetables. It was suggested that Kensington Council should be asked to provide extra ground for allotments within Kensington Gardens. However, a model allotment site already existed in the Gardens near the east side of the Albert Memorial. Each of the four plots measured 10 rods, which aimed to show local people the range of vegetables that could be raised in London without undue problems. A similar model garden was laid out for the benefit of the enquiring public in Regent's Park at the Broad Walk near the Zoological Gardens. This site was split into four plots of 16 rods, which was considered to be ideal for the labourer's garden. The site was maintained by an experienced workman under the command of the park superintendent, who was very happy to answer questions from the

The demonstration allotments at Regent's Park: citizens were shown the range of vegetables that could be raised in London without due complications.

general public about vegetable gardening. So successful was the scheme that half a dozen parks under the jurisdiction of the LCC were utilised as model allotments, which was a considerable achievement considering the Council's initial opposition to the allocation of land.

Vegetable crops to the value of £146 were raised on the model allotments. In addition, nearly 3½ tons of tomatoes with a value of £153 were grown in nine of the London Parks. The Food Production Department stated that around 200,000 acres were under cultivation in 1,109 districts. Vegetable cultivation was one thing, but the keeping of pigs was expressly forbidden in the park grounds, especially at the model sites. In spite of the success of allotments in parks, in West London and South Kensington in particular, an extraordinary amount of land in the form of semi-public squares and gardens remained uncultivated – the custodians would not allow their amenities to be defaced by rows of potatoes and cabbages, wartime or not. A considerable number of local residents expressed their disgust and implied that the gardeners' time would be better spent cultivating vegetables rather than sweeping up leaves and trimming lawns. Others claimed such motives to be selfish and unpatriotic.

The majority of allotment-holders needed very little in the way of encouragement, but they got it nevertheless, from Royalty. King George V was a keen allotment gardener and, after lunch, the assemblage of Royal guests would divide into two parties, one to work in the munitions factories and the other to work on the allotment gardens. In April 1918 the King insisted that the flowerbed surrounding the Victoria Memorial be planted with vegetables instead of the usual scarlet geraniums. A photograph of the King and Queen Mary digging on an allotment, and the King's enthusiasm for allotment cultivation, only popularised the Allotment Movement further.

On 20 July 1918 the King and Queen, accompanied by Mr Prothero, President of the Board of Agriculture, Colonel Clive Wigram and Captain Brian Godfrey Fausett, embarked on a long-promised tour of allotment sites around south London. At Putney Lower Common the plot-holders were out in force together with their wives and children. As the Royal party passed down the central path, they admired the rows of excellent vegetables and stopped to chat with the plot-holders, who were very eager to show off their produce. Wimbledon Park Piggeries and Allotments were the second stop for the Royal party. The vegetable plots were cultivated on intensive lines and were surrounded with outbuildings where pigs and rabbits were housed and fed on waste vegetation.

The London & South Western Railway's power station was the next stage on the tour. The company's Chairman, together with the Chairman of the Allotments Committee, warmly welcomed Their Majesties and guided them around the allotments, which were tended by the employees in their leisure time. The Royal couple were full of praise for the tenant who had won first prize, and he later presented a gift of carrots and peas to Queen Mary, which she warmly accepted.

Their Majesties next toured around Ridgeway Place Allotments at Wimbledon. This site was earmarked for building purposes, but had been appropriated through private means. It was largely through the efforts of Mr G. W. Dampney, Chairman of the Surrey Horticultural Sub-Committee, and Dr Rideout, Secretary of the Wimbledon Home Produce Society, that the entire hillside was covered in productive vegetable plots. At Merton Park Allotments the Royal party were addressed by the Chairman of the Urban District Council and members of the newly formed Horticultural Committee for Surrey. Mr R. W. Johnson, Master of Merton School, escorted the King and Queen around the school allotments, which covered half an acre and were cultivated on a commercial system by five different classes, each consisting of 14 boys from the nearby school.

Tooting and Battersea Rise on the north side of Clapham Common were the last points on the tour, and the King and Queen met the Mayor of Battersea together with the Town Clerk and members of the various allotments associations. The King and Queen chatted with the tenants and their wives and children, and King George noted the cultivation of vegetable marrows and underlined their usefulness in the production of jam, when other fruit was scarce. With the tour over, the greatest day in the history of the Allotment Movement had come to a close. R. E. Prothero was full of praise for London's wartime gardeners, and said that plot-holders had raised cabbages from concrete and broad beans from brickbats.

A woman war-worker gathers in the fruit crop for preserving or jam-making.

Less than four months later, the war in Europe came to an abrupt end, when the German army surrendered at 11am on 11 November. Even before the end of the war there was a certain amount of anxiety over the future of allotments gained under DORA. The Board of Agriculture insisted that, under the Cultivation of Lands Order, tenancies on land acquired under DORA would be extended until after the growing season of 1920. In some cases this was extended until 1923.

Many writers of garden books were anxious that the cultivation of allotments should continue:

'The motto of every patriot must still be "Cultivate", "Cultivate", "Cultivate" every available patch of land, since the need for producing all the vegetable food we can will remain a potent factor in our daily lives for some time to come.' (T. W. Sanders FLS FRHS, *Allotment and Kitchen Garden*, 1919)

In 1918 Frederick Ernest Green said that the enthusiasm among some of the urban allotment societies was an indication of a newly awakened interest in 'The Land'. Allotment holders formed themselves into associations,

associations into federations, and the federations grouped together to form the National Union of Allotment Holders, which came into being in London in October 1917. Linked up with the National Union of Allotment Holders was the Co-operative Union and the Distributive Union of Co-operative Stores, which agreed to aid not only the supply of tools, seeds and fertilisers but also the sale of surplus produce, thus establishing a link between the rural plot-holder and the market centres. Mr Green insisted that the nation owed an immense debt to the plot-holder and hoped that Lloyd George would ensure further legislation to regulate the price of seed and assure security of tenure for the holders.

Even though the war had ceased, the demand for allotments escalated dramatically. In December 1918, 26 local authorities provided 5,000 new allotments; throughout 1919 the enthusiasm for cultivating the land continued to flourish and 7,000 new applications for allotments were received each week. The desire for plots was triggered by various factors. First, the free advice and assistance offered during the course of the war generated interest in cultivation. Immediately after the war there was a steep rise in the price of vegetables, while the closure of munitions factories and a general ban on overtime left countless workers without any profitable way of filling their newfound leisure time. Large-scale demobilisation from the forces and the provision of allotments for ex-servicemen added to the process. The reclamation of emergency wartime plots also created further demand, especially when alternative sites were not provided for displaced tenants. Mr T. W. Sanders insisted that the provision of allotments should be a matter of national concern:

'We are sorry to learn from information published in the press that certain public authorities, the LCC in particular, have come to the decision to withdraw the privilege of continuing the cultivation of allotments in their parks and recreation grounds at the end of 1919. This step is much to be regretted, as it will deprive hundreds if not thousands of citizens from carrying out their patriotic efforts to grow food crops for the sustenance of themselves as well as their families.' (T. W. Sanders FLS FRHS, *Allotment and Kitchen Garden*, 1919)

As greater numbers of soldiers were demobilised, the feeling of relief on being discharged quickly evaporated as they sought their cottage with an orchard and found them not. The Government was quick to point to the 60,000 acres that it was trying to obtain for settling the soldiers. However, only 6,000 could be accommodated, if each man were allocated 10 acres, and the County Councils were finding it difficult to provide homes. As a result, in 1919 the Land Settlement Facilities Act was passed to make further provision of land for use as smallholdings, to reclaim and drain ground, as well as to amend enactments relating to allotments and otherwise facilitate land. Besides permitting the acquisition of holdings below an acre (usually half an acre) the Act contained a useful clause:

'The Council of any borough, urban district or parish may purchase fruit trees, seeds, plants, fertilisers or implements required for the purposes of allotments cultivated as gardens, whether provided by the Council or otherwise, and sell any article so purchased to the cultivators, or, in the case of the implements, allow their use, at a price or charge sufficient to cover the cost of purchase.' (Land Settlement Facilities Act, 1919)

No official census was taken of the number of allotments during the height of the war, but the Board of Agriculture estimated the nationwide figure to be around 1.5 million. By 1920 there were approximately 1,330,000 allotments across the British Isles. Wartime gardening had given the nation's workers a taste for cultivating the land, and within the next few years allotments would be used to combat an overwhelming new peacetime enemy – the Great Depression.

7
The inter-war gardeners

The extraordinary measures taken under the Defence of the Realm Act (DORA) created an insatiable thirst for allotments. During the 'long hot summer' of the inter-war years the majority of working-class families struggled on low incomes, so the provision of an allotment was greatly desired in urban areas. While demand for allotments continually rose, the number of plots fell, due to reclamation of wartime sites.

In the early 1920s an increasing number of tenants saw their allotments as a new money-making venture and cultivated flowers for selling at local markets. This enterprise flourished in north-west Surrey, and Hampton District Council received numerous complaints about this activity. The Council's Vice-Chairman claimed that the plot-holders' flower-marketing

The illicit flower-growers of 1920: the blooms raised were destined for shops and markets.

strategy was no more harmful than selling off excess vegetables, but local opinion differed. Hampton Council appointed borough surveyors to ascertain the extent of flower cultivation on allotments; tenants who were found to be growing more flowers than vegetables could, under certain conditions, be dispossessed of their allotments, which would be re-let to prospective tenants on the ever-growing waiting lists.

By April 1920 the demand for allotment gardens had become so intense that in some regions it was necessary to sub-divide existing plots to accommodate an increasing number of prospective tenants. Fortunate applicants were given plots almost immediately, so that they could reap the benefits of spring plantings. Sir Daniel Hall, Scientific Advisor to the Ministry of Agriculture, stated that out of 141,000 acres held for use as allotments, only 86,000 were in private ownership. The remainder were under the jurisdiction of local authorities. The rent was roughly 18d per rod for the first 12 months, which excluded the supply of water. On average a 10-rod plot produced vegetable crops to the value of £9, although £3 had to be deducted to cover the initial cost of rent, manure, seeds and tools. The remainder contributed a substantial saving within the household budget and overall was of major economic value in the national food bill. Sir Daniel continued:

'There is no more deeply seated desire or delight than that which men associate with growing things, and this, with the quickened interest of competition with their fellow cultivators, makes life very real and vivid, and lends a glimpse of poetry and nature worship to men whose lot is otherwise cast in grey, and even sordid surroundings.' (Sir Daniel Hall, Report of the Departmental Committee, Ministry of Agriculture, 1922)

In the early 1920s many Borough Councils were experiencing considerable difficulties in acquiring further land for allotments. This problem was aggravated by private land-owners who were unwilling to let prospective building land with a high value be taken for allotments. The Ministry of Agriculture insisted that allotments were still of national importance and was not satisfied with existing legislation. Any Borough or Urban District Council could still hire land compulsorily for a term of 14-35 years, but if the land-owner did not agree with the Council on the matter of rent, an independent arbitrator had to be called in. Allotment rents were generally based on the value of the overall lease; prospective mining or building values were not allowed (in theory) to influence the arbitrators' rental evaluations, but this was often not the case.

A year on and the spirit of wartime gardening remained strong among the population, and in some regions there was a cry to establish permanent allotments. Many local authorities were receptive to the benefits that allotments provided to the community, appreciating both the economic usefulness and the healthy recreational value. A considerable number of councils took advantage of the Allotments & Smallholdings Act (1908) to provide appropriate land for allotments.

In stark contrast, other local councils were directly opposed to the Movement and adopted various subterfuges to nullify and invalidate the Act. Some councils said that the creation of permanent allotments would add a charge to the rates, and this assertion was generally enough to dispel any further notion of acquiring suitable land. Ratepayers were told that a special allotment department would have to be set up, which would result in additional establishment charges. But if the scheme were handed over to a responsible society operating outside the jurisdiction of the corporation or council, then there would be little or no charge to the ratepayers.

At one large town the plan to acquire land for permanent plots was rendered inert since the whole borough had been mapped out for extensive development under a town-planning scheme. The Town Council argued that expensive building land could not be secured at a low enough price to make the allotments a financially viable enterprise. The Town's Councillors firmly opposed a motion to obtain land for permanent allotments, and made the excuse that there was no demand. When the local allotment committees chaired a public meeting it was discovered that more than 500 applications for allotments existed. The hand of the Town Council was forced and eventually several acres of vacant land were secured for the plot-holders. The Ministry of Agriculture was fully aware of the conflict surrounding provision of allotments and closely monitored the situation.

'It has hitherto been one of the chief grievances of allotment holders that they were liable to be dispossessed of their plots on short notice, and although the existing legislation provided that the allotment holders should be entitled to compensation for their crops etc, this did not altogether meet their contention that, after putting a considerable amount of time and labour into the cultivation of their plots, they were liable to be dispossessed without being able to reap the full rewards of their labours.' (*Ministry of Agriculture Journal*, 1922, p545)

Continual demand for allotments in urban regions raised the importance of providing allotments, and to secure protection for tenants the Government passed the Allotment Act of 1922, which had a much wider application than previous allotment legislation. Under the Allotment Act of 1922 an allotment garden was defined as:

'An allotment of land not exceeding 40 rods in extent, which is wholly or mainly cultivated by the occupier for the production of vegetables or fruit crops for consumption by himself or his family.' (Ministry of Agriculture, the Allotment Act, 1922)

This Act stipulated that notice to quit the land should not be less than six months, except in cases where the land was needed urgently for building purposes; under these circumstances the notice period was reduced to three months. If the tenant quit his land before that period, he was not entitled to any form of compensation for loss of crops or the value of manure that had been applied to the land. There was an exception to this rule in cases where land was required urgently:

'Where land is required for building, mining, or any other industrial purpose, or for roads or sewers necessary in connection with any of these purposes, or where the land is required by the owners or lessees of a railway, dock, canal, water or other public undertaking for the purpose (not being the use of land for agriculture) for which it was acquired, or held by the corporation or company, or in the case of land let by a local authority (other than land acquired by the local authority before 4 August 1922 under the Housing Acts) on account of the land being required by the local authority for the purpose not being the use of land for agriculture for which it was acquired, the landlord can re-enter under a power of re-entry contained in or affecting the contract of tenancy after three months' previous notice in writing to the tenant of the allotment garden.' (*Ministry of Agriculture Journal*, 1922, p546)

In 1922 Mr F. Forbes, General Secretary of the National Union of Allotment Holders, stated that there were 1,250,000 plot-holders across England and Wales. He estimated that on average the annual total volume of produce from all allotments in the UK amounted to 700,000 tons of vegetables (including 200,000 tons of potatoes). There was still a growing demand for plots and no fewer than 50,000 applications had been received. At the time almost 250,000 gardeners were cultivating land acquired under DORA and it was suggested to implement extensions into 1923 under the Allotment Act of 1922.

By 1922 there were many cases where plot-holders working on land acquired under DORA were dispossessed by local councils, as the land was supposedly required for building purposes. However, in a growing number of cases construction projects had not taken place and the land reverted to a state of wilderness once again. The Ministry of Agriculture insisted that it was then up to the local authorities to re-acquire the land for allotments using their special powers. When builders issued notices to vacate, they were to be ignored as only the Ministry of Agriculture or the local authority had the legal right to serve notice to quit.

Allotments within public parks were in a different category and could only be held by the local authority until 1 September 1921. The local authority concerned was left to decide on whether the allotments should remain as such for the full period or not. The Ministry of Agriculture had no jurisdiction over these allotments in peacetime, but suggested that local authorities should endeavour to provide alternative sites when reclaiming allotment land in parks.

The Departmental Committee appointed by the Ministry of Agriculture published its report on the provision of allotments in 1922. The Committee spoke highly of allotments, both from a national and social perspective. In

1920 it was estimated that there were more than a million allotments occupying 157,620 acres. The Departmental Committee recognised that security of tenure was an important issue for plot-holders and recommended that local authorities should adopt a long-term strategy and continue to purchase land for allotments when practical. The Committee also insisted that local authorities should be empowered to provide special transport facilities for plot-holders to allotment sites that were located on the outskirts of towns. The Departmental Committee further recommended that, under the Public Health Act, loans for the purchase of allotment land should be excluded from the debt of the local authority in order to avoid diminishing the borrowing power of the authority for different purposes. The report continues:

'While we are of the opinion that security of tenure can only be obtained if land is purchased for allotments, it is clear that it would be quite impossible for any large proportion of land at present under allotments to be purchased, as the capital sum involved would impose a burden on the financial resources of the country, which at the present time would not be justified. It will be necessary, therefore, for local authorities to continue to use their present powers of leasing land, subject (in the case of land having a present or prospective building value) to resumption of the land by the owner if he requires it for building, mining, or other industrial purposes or for roads necessary therefor.' (Report of the Departmental Committee, Ministry of Agriculture, 1922)

The Departmental Committee also made recommendations on the length of notice to terminate tenancy and suggested that notice given between Lady Day and Michaelmas should be rendered invalid. It added that tenants should not be entitled to any form of compensation for disturbance or loss of crops, providing the proper six months' notice period had been served. The Committee stated:

'It must not be forgotten that the main object of the provision of allotments in an urban district is to supply plots for cultivation by the holders in their spare time and are not intended to provide whole-time occupation. The evidence we have received appears to indicate that 20 rods is, normally, the largest area, which, if used for the production of vegetables, &c. can be cultivated properly by an individual part-time. We consider, therefore, that a local authority of an urban district should not be under a statutory obligation to supply allotments exceeding 20 rods in extent. If there are no applicants wishing to take plots, the local authority would still, apparently, have the power, under section 27 of the Smallholding Act, 1908, to let, temporarily, a larger area than 20 rods to any person who was capable of cultivating such an area properly.' (Report of the Departmental Committee, Ministry of Agriculture, 1922)

It was suggested to the Departmental Committee that an Allotments Advisory Committee be set up in connection with the Ministry of Agriculture, on the lines prevalent with the Agriculture Advisory Committee and the Horticultural Advisory Committee. The Departmental Committee felt that such an organisation would be of practical benefit and hoped this suggestion would be adopted.

Under existing legislation there was no obligation imposed on any local authority to appoint a special committee to attend to allotment matters arising within the region under its jurisdiction. In many cases allotment undertakings were dealt with by municipal committees that were involved with more general matters, such as parks and open spaces, and as a result allotment questions did not receive adequate consideration. The Departmental Committee was of the opinion that every Borough, Urban and District Council should be under obligation to set up Allotment Committees to which all matters regarding allotments should be referred.

In 1923, in accordance with the suggestions made to the Departmental Committee on allotments, the Allotments Advisory Committee was established to advise and assist the Ministry of Agriculture on matters relating to allotments (although this only applied to allotments in England and Wales). The Allotments Advisory Committee comprised the following persons: the Rt Hon The Earl of Ancaster, Parliamentary Under Secretary to the Ministry of Agriculture, Chairman; the Rt Hon The Earl of Stanhope, representing the Central Land-owners' Association; Sir Kingsley Wood MP, representing the Parliamentary Allotments Committee; Francis Dent Esq, representing the County Councils' Association; H. A. Learoyd Esq, Town Clerk of Hull, representing the Association of Municipal Corporations; Reginald C. Graves Esq LLB, Clerk and Solicitor to the Tottenham Urban District Councils' Association; and C. Crofton Black Esq, Barrister at Law, representing the Land Union. The Rt Hon F. D. Acland, George Nicholls Esq OBE and Walter West Esq represented the Agricultural Organisation Society, and Robert Norman Esq, Alderman H. Berry and J. Forbes Esq represented the National Union of Allotment Holders. Mr Lawrence E. Mitchell acted as Secretary of the Committee and could be contacted through the Ministry of Agriculture at Whitehall Place, London. The Association was incredibly astute in its operations and was still dispensing assistance and advice some 30 years later.

While the Ministry of Agriculture commended itself on the establishment of the AAC, the majority of plot-holders faced a new menace in the form of Potato Wart Disease. The affliction was so serious that the Ministry of Agriculture passed the Wart Disease of Potatoes Order in 1923. The Ministry stated:

'In land on which Wart Disease has been known to exist at any time, the only potatoes which may be planted are those stocks of approved immune varieties which have been inspected while growing and officially certified as being true to type. A grower may, however, plant on infected land

potatoes of immune varieties which have been saved from the crop grown
on that land in the previous year.' (Wart Disease of Potatoes Order, Ministry
of Agriculture, 1923)

The main areas infected included the whole of Wales, and the regions of
Monmouth, Stafford, Chester, Lancaster (south of the Ribble), Preston, North
Salop, Birmingham and Sutton Coldfield, and certain parishes within
Derbyshire and Worcestershire. Smaller infected areas occurred in Berkshire,
Leicestershire, Nottinghamshire, Westmorland and Surrey. The provision of
this Order applied to allotments and other premises within affected areas.
The Ministry added that:

'No potatoes grown in an Infected Area may be moved or consigned to any
place in England or Wales which is not in an Infected Area. An exception to
the rule is, however, made in the case of ware potatoes of approved immune
varieties, provided that a statement is made on the invoice or sale note
relating to each consignment, or in a label or ticket inserted in or attached to
the package containing the potatoes, to the effect that the potatoes are of an
approved immune variety, that they were grown in an Infected Area, and
that they are not intended for planting. Any person receiving potatoes
consigned from an Infected Area without this statement must notify the
Ministry of the fact within seven days, and must not part with or plant the
potatoes without permission of the Ministry.' (Wart Disease of Potatoes
Order, Ministry of Agriculture, 1923)

The emergence of the potato disease may have swayed potential holders and
gardeners from taking allotments. By 1924, according to the Ministry of
Agriculture, the number of allotments dropped slightly to 1,170,000 as
opposed to 1,190,000 in 1923.

Under the Allotment Act of 1925, Urban District and Borough Councils
were obliged to consider, at least once a year, the need for allotment land.
Councils were no longer required to make allotments self-supporting, being
able to spend a penny in every pound for allotment purposes. Having
purchased land for use as allotments, local Councils were forbidden to sell or
dispose of such land for any other purpose without consent from the
Ministry of Agriculture. The Ministry urged urban authorities to do
everything in their power to extend the area used for allotments in order to
foster a movement that had a definite economic and social value. Parish
Councils were not permitted to acquire land for allotments unless it was
assured that the expenses could be offset from the rents accrued.

In its annual report, the Allotments Organisation Society and Smallholders
Limited stated that 1926 had been a difficult year for the Society. The rapid
expansion of building was reputed to be co-extensive, resulting in a decline
in the number of allotments across England and Wales, which were
numbered at 64,000, a decrease of three times as many as the figure given
by the Ministry of Agriculture in the previous year. The Allotments

Organisation Society realised that the increasing popularity of sports had taken a toll on the Allotment Movement. The Society also recognised that in some districts persons responsible for the administration of allotments placed them at the bottom of the list of public utility services, the result being that they did not receive the attention that they merited. In one large County Borough, the Allotments Committee was nothing less than a sub-committee of the Cemeteries Committee, which explained why the town failed as an allotment provider, until great pressure was brought to bear on it. In another instance where the Allotment Movement was on the verge of extinction, the local administration was extravagant. However, a district association was formed and the property that it purchased came to be worth thousands of pounds. The Society added that allotment associations should bear in mind their responsibility toward each other, and that the more united they became as a national movement, the greater and more prosperous they would become.

The Allotments Organisation Society found that enlightened authorities used every means possible to gain large tracts of land for allotment usage. Some cities like Birmingham, Liverpool and Bristol endeavoured to take care of their plot-holders. Birmingham owned one of the largest allotment estates in the country, the Wyrley Birch Estate, consisting of almost 100 acres that accommodated more than 1,000 tenants. The Corporation in Leicester also adopted a progressive policy by purchasing land for permanent allotments.

The Society reported a steady increase in the number of allotments associations in affiliation with it, which was regarded as a good sign, for as long as plot-holders could speak through a corporate voice, their needs were more likely to be attended to since public authorities preferred to deal with representative bodies rather than individuals.

With regard to the future outlook for allotments, the Society implied that far too many relied on help from outside and looked to Parliament and local authorities for support. The Society implied that cultivators were allowed to fall out of the Movement far too easily and that little effort was made to retain allotments or help tenants find new ones. Although there were just a little over 1 million allotments left, the Society estimated that the national wealth of the Movement was increasing to the extent of £10 million each year. In its report, the Allotments Organisation Society stated that employers realised the potential benefit of allotments in keeping their workers fit and alert, resulting in better craftsmanship and increased output. Many factories and industrial works had allotments affixed to their land. Where such allotments did not exist, employers and managers encouraged the formation of horticultural and allotment societies.

In 1927 the National Homecroft Association highlighted its scheme to supply workers with allotments affixed to their dwellings. The Association recognised that insecurity of tenure and the distance from the tenant's home could be overcome by its scheme. The Homecroft Association's aim was to provide every working man who desired it with a plot of land at his very door, sufficient for the cultivation of food for himself and his family. At

Cheltenham the Association had purchased 10 acres of ground that was to be divided into 25 'homecrofts' (cottages on 2-5 acres). Ten of the cottages were built and shortly to be let. Interested persons were to apply to the Secretary of the Homecroft Association at Charles Street, Cardiff.

In 1929 the Local Government Act ensured that agricultural land was exempt from assessment for local rates, and since allotments fell in this category they also benefited. Under the Act the general term 'for the labouring poor' was also dropped from the definition of an allotment or allotment garden. The slight drop in allotment cultivation was quickly reversed due to high unemployment. However, overall the number of allotments (for 1928) stood at 1,028000. Part of the discrepancy in the figures lay in the fact that larger allotments were sub-divided among the tenants. It was at this time that the 10-rod allotment came into more general use. By the end of the decade the provision of allotments was thought to be of immense importance to unemployed men, who faced a bleak and unpromising future where hope was a far-away dream.

In 1929 thousands of unemployed miners in South Wales and in parts of Yorkshire were in fear of losing their unemployment allowance due to the fact that they had been gardening during the day. In some districts the men had previously been warned by inspectors that they would forfeit their right to unemployment pay if they continued to garden in daytime instead of looking for work. This incident created a certain amount of anxiety among allotment tenants. Eventually, the National Union of Allotment Holders took the matter up with the Minister of Labour, who managed to obtain assurance that, provided the tenant lost no opportunity to seek work, his efforts on the allotment would not jeopardise his claim to unemployment pay.

In more salubrious districts it was not the amount of activity on allotments that was causing consternation but rather the lack of it. In the same year Richmond Allotment Committee in Surrey experienced considerable difficulty in letting allotments. On the site at Manor Road in Richmond, 63 plots were vacant out of 173. The loss of rent amounted to £161 per annum and further expense was incurred by attempting to keep the land free of weeds, which was estimated to cost £45 a year. Although eager to acquire allotment land, potential plot-holders in Richmond insisted that the Town Council's annual rent of 52 shillings a year for a 10-rod plot was simply too high. The Allotments Committee was authorised to re-consider the question of rents and submit a report to the Council.

The Lord Mayor's Fund for the relief of distressed mining areas was highly approved and enabled the provision of allotment sites with reduced rates, together with seed, seed potatoes, fertiliser and, in some cases, fencing at cost price. Due to this scheme a very large number of allotments were kept in cultivation. There were between 60,000 and 70,000 plot-holders in South Wales, Durham and Yorkshire, and the total cost of providing this service amounted to £15,000. The Allotments Committee noted a definite improvement in the morale of unemployed miners and allotment tenants.

At the 10th annual meeting of the Yorkshire County Allotments Federation at Huddersfield, Mr N. Buxton, Minister of Agriculture, stated that the Allotment Movement was deserving of every encouragement, by individuals, local authorities and the State. Before the Great War only a quarter of the allotment area provided by the State lay in urban districts, but by 1929 the figure had risen to half. Urban plot-holders outnumbered those in rural districts by two to one, for there was still much demand for fresh vegetables, although 30,000 allotments had disappeared since the end of the war. This was due to the acquisition of land for building, and reclamation of wartime sites for their previous usage. However, the total volume of land owned or leased by local authorities remained much higher than before the war: in 1928 they held 57,021 acres compared to 33,523 in 1914, representing an increase of 23,498 acres. There was still a large and unsatisfied demand for plots and Mr Buxton urged local authorities to attend to the matter of providing more allotments immediately. In 1929 one-ninth of all the allotments in England and Wales lay inside the three ridings of Yorkshire, and five-sixths of these were located in urban areas.

In 1930 the National Union of Allotment Holders and the Agricultural Organisation Society amalgamated to form the National Allotments Society, which secured the co-operative organisation of allotment, village produce, small livestock and welfare societies. The National Allotments Society's branch in Hull deplored the decline of 335,000 allotments over the previous 10 years, and called on the Government to halt any further decrease; the Government was urged to give allotments the same degree of status as that granted to parks, pleasure gardens and recreation grounds. Sir Francis D. Acland, President of the National Allotments Society, stated that although the decline was heavy, it was remarkable that there were still nearly a million plot-holders across the country, a figure that was six times the number before the war. Mr R. Norman, Joint President, suggested that the Government should tighten up allotment legislation to ensure the security of tenure for present gardeners and for those of the future.

In 1931 the Ministry of Agriculture appointed a Central Executive Committee to promote the cultivation of allotment gardens by the unemployed or those not in full-time employment. It became the Ministry's aim to stimulate the formation of voluntary committees to further the Allotment Movement and to provide seed and tools for any person requiring them. Mr G. W. Giles was appointed Secretary and Sir William Waterlow Bart KBE was Chairman. The Ministry noted the benefits:

'The idea has received support from all political parties, and there is no question of the beneficial results obtained, both morally and physically, and the displays at various horticultural shows testify to the excellent results that can be obtained by unemployed miners and other industrial workers; while as regards the material results, the abundance of fresh vegetables that may be produced from an allotment garden must have a marked effect on the health of the family, who would in most cases, but for the allotment, have to go short of such food.' (*Ministry of Agriculture Journal*, 1933, p1007)

During the 1930s the problem surrounding security of tenure was, for plot-holders, a major one. The Ministry noted that the only way to gain absolute security was to purchase the land, either individually or through an association. However, relative security could be obtained by a long lease without a resumption clause or by purchase of land by the local authority for use as allotments. In 1931 the Agricultural Land Utilization Act, though mainly concerned with farmland, amended Section 8 of the 1925 Allotment Act, which improved legislation in cases where the local authority had purchased or appropriated land for use as allotments:

'The local authority shall not sell, appropriate, use or dispose of the land for any other purpose other than for the use for allotments without the consent of the Ministry of Agriculture and Fisheries, after consultation with the Minister of Health, and such consent shall not be given unless the Minister is satisfied that adequate provision will be made for allotment holders displaced by the action of the local authority or that such provision is unnecessary or not reasonably practicable.' (*Ministry of Agriculture Journal,* 1933, p1005)

By 1933 the Central Executive Committee, working in conjunction with the Society of Friends Allotment Committee and the National Allotments Committee, enabled 100,000 unemployed men to gain and work allotments. They hoped to increase the number of allotment tenants if funding could be obtained. All the prospective tenant had to do was apply to the Town Clerk for an allotment. The managers of Labour Exchanges were also willing to help unemployed applicants gain plots. By now the number of benevolent societies operating allotment schemes had increased from 1,291 in 1931 to 2,240 in 1933. The overall number of men who benefited from an allotment during this period rose from 62,527 to 100,035. By 1933 around 27,000 new allotments had been established, and the total expenditure on the venture during the previous year amounted to £44,331. Tenants were helped to procure supplies of seed, fertiliser and tools and they showed their appreciation by contributing small sums (as much as they could afford) on a weekly basis. These donations, collected by more than 2,000 association secretaries, amounted to £26,259 by 1933. Government grants and personal donations provided the balance required to carry out the scheme.

In 1934 the Land Settlement Association took over from the Society of Friends. Some 23 schemes had been set up in the North of England and were known collectively as group holdings, and plots of half an acre enabled the unemployed to rear pigs and poultry; more than 2,000 tenants were keeping livestock on plots. Tenants paid small instalments on a weekly basis to cover the Land Settlement Association's costs.

By 1936 there were four times as many plots in urban areas as in rural locations. Naturally the need for fresh vegetables was greater in more heavily populated areas. Since plot-holders in urban areas often needed more assistance with hints on gardening than their rural counterparts, the Ministry

145

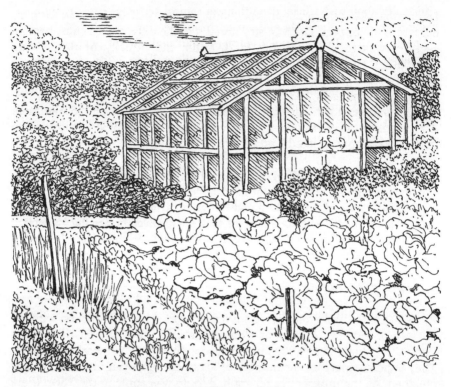

A well-cultivated model allotment site, as recommended
by Mr John Stoney, Parks Superintendent of Staffordshire.

of Agriculture published a special bulletin for novice plot-holders. The author, John Stoney FRHS, Horticultural Superintendent for Staffordshire, gave specialist advice relating to gardening on problem soils, using manure, liming, earthing up and the best varieties of vegetables to cultivate. A special section dealt with techniques such as forcing and inter-cropping. This bulletin (Number 90) was available from HM Stationery Office at Adastral House, London WC2, priced at 1 shilling net.

Winnigstat cabbage was incredibly popular in the 1930s.

In 1936 the Ministry of Agriculture gave approval to demonstration plots:

'If, on every block of allotments or in the local park, an allotment could be set aside to be cultivated under supervision of the county or local horticultural expert, there can be little doubt that the result would be very beneficial to the local plot-holders. For, in place of each and every allotment holder experimenting with many varieties, and determining their suitability

for cultivation under local conditions, a central series of trials could be undertaken and the wide and varied re-duplications avoided. As with varieties, so with manurial treatments and methods of pest control.'
(Bulletin 90, 'Allotments', Ministry of Agriculture, 1936, p43)

Mr Stoney stated that the more specialised operations such as fruit-pruning, cordon-training, inter-cropping and cultivation with cold frames could be illustrated. At the Walsall Arboretum, the Park Superintendent put these ideas into operation and supervised the work; the small cost involved was fully warranted and the scheme was regarded as a success. During the summer months a beginners' class was held, and throughout the winter special indoor lessons took place; the Local Education Authority funded the lectures. Four years earlier a similar demonstration plot had been established at Newcastle-under-Lyme and was a major achievement. Mr Stoney added that public parks were the best locations for demonstration plots as they were well equipped, had expert advice and assistance at their disposal, and commanded more attention from the general public as opposed to those on allotment sites.

The Ministry maintained that the economic value of allotments could not be overlooked, although there was much variation in different parts of the country owing to the climate, soil quality and other factors such as the use of a greenhouse. On average a well-cropped plot could yield produce to the value of £6 10s a year. On a 10-rod plot in Durham the total volume of produce raised for a year had a value of £15 5s 8d. The outlay was minimal, with seeds valued at £1 9s 1d, seed potatoes at 4s 6d, farmyard manure at 10s 6d, other fertilisers at 2s 6d, lime and soot at 6d, and the annual rent of 7 shillings, making a total of £2 14s 1d. These figures did not take into account produce raised in cold frames or greenhouses. In Glamorganshire the total volume of produce grown on a 10-rod plot gave a return of £13 9s 9d. Again, the annual expenditure was very small, amounting to £2 7s 0d, which covered seeds at 14s 6d, seed potatoes at 7s 0d, farmyard manure at 15s 0d, other fertilisers at 3s 0d, and the annual rent of 7s 6d.

Even in the 1930s the social problems surrounding allotments were often all too prevalent. Urban, District and Metropolitan Councils habitually attached little importance to control or management of the municipal allotment. Officials hurriedly inspected sites, provided scanty reports to the corporation concerned and left it at that. Consequently, many gardens slid into a state of dishevelled chaos and ceased to be a credit to the local authority.

In 1935 Alexander Cameron stated (in the *Gardener's Chronicle*, p27) that:

'Year in and year out the allotment is expected to look after itself and rapidly degenerates into a public eyesore. Many sites have badly neglected pathways, indistinct boundaries between plots, and an array of shacks, sheds and huts in every colour, shape and size are situated where they are not supposed to be, which gives the impression that the tenants can do exactly as they please.'

A squalid allotment site of the 1930s. Such sites were
much criticised by Alexander Cameron in 1935.

Mr Cameron maintained that plots should be something the tenant could be proud of and that there should be a power to require that land vested within a local corporation should be subject to regulations for the efficient management of sites. He saw no reason why allotments should not have fruit trees, attractive shelters and seating, and stressed that it was not enough for a local council to temporarily fence off a tatty tract of land and call it an allotment, which invariably ended up being held as offensive by the non-gardening public.

In many regions allotment paths were left to develop naturally over a lengthy period and were often topped up with old pots, broken crockery and other household refuse. Communal huts together with accommodation for hens, pigs and goats were generally regarded as a nuisance and the cause of much strife between plot-holders and local residents. Stand-pipes were a general feature, but they had been improved upon as watering places when placed at pathway junctions. Many officials requested the replacement of the assemblage of unsightly shacks with those of a uniform design.

Lady Marjorie Allen FILA, of Hurtwood, had aspirations to elevate the role of the allotment to the same status as parks and sports grounds, thus assuring security of tenure for plot-holders. Her inspiration came from a trip to Sweden, where she saw highly ornate communal gardens with neat hedges, colourful shrubs and, at the centre, a little pavilion or 'magic house'. Swedish people recognised gardening as a leisure activity and their pleasure grounds reflected this idea. On returning to England, Lady Allen noted the unkempt character of allotments and saw little reason why they should not be improved upon.

In 1936 her ideas were published in a little 22-page booklet entitled *How Allotment Gardens could be made an Amenity Asset to the Community*. As far as Lady Allen was concerned, the allotment could alleviate the problems of malnourishment that prevailed in smoky industrialised regions, where debilitating afflictions among the young were still commonplace. The League of Nations addressed the importance of a healthy diet in its report 'The Problem of Nutrition', which emphasised the need for fresh fruit, leafy greens, potatoes, tomatoes and onions. Excluding potatoes, under-consumption of vegetables prevailed in towns. Sir John Orr, in his booklet 'Food, Health & Income', stated that a 25% rise in the volume of fruit and vegetables would be required to feed the distressed half of the population. Lady Allen maintained that there could be no better way to accomplish this end than to advance the husbandry of allotments.

Although only the foolish few questioned the value of allotments, it was equally impossible to dismiss the fact that the majority of sites were a blemish on the local landscape. The age-old problem surrounding security of tenure lay at the heart of the trouble. After serving three months' notice to quit, private land-owners were legally entitled to sell their land to a builder or property speculator. Allotment associations or societies often had little in the way of resources, and consequently tenancy remained precarious. During the 1930s working-class people had little money to spend and allotment tenants simply opted to utilise cheap or free materials for their allotments.

Even farmers were reduced to scouring the pages of second-hand newspapers for sources of cheap cement and corrugated iron sheeting to patch up their dilapidated barns. Plot-holders, with flimsy tenancies, adopted the same strategy. Although the National Allotments Society made a brave attempt to encourage the construction of presentable sheds, it only needed a few shabby sheds and untidy plots to spoil the whole appearance of a site.

Lady Allen insisted that if allotments were linked to open spaces like sports fields, the problem of security of tenure would be overcome and make possible a proper planning scheme; the allotment could then become both beautiful and productive and the centre of community life in towns and villages. The provision of school gardens was often connected to allotment garden schemes, and she thought that they could be regarded as an extension to allotments and used for evening classes and to retain interest in young people until they were old enough to apply for a 10-rod plot. The plan to create a communal centre with allotments included the provision of football and cricket pitches, bowling greens and tennis courts. If a social club were established on site, tenants and their families would be able to enjoy group activities.

Lady Allen's plans were put into practise on a site organised by Nuneaton

Allotment Association. There were more than 2,000 members and, with ancillary activities, the association soon became self-supporting. A dividend of 5% was paid to the enterprising members who put up the original capital. Although the support of local authorities was essential for such ventures, the best results were gained when organisation and development was entrusted to the enterprising allotment associations, consisting of plot-holders.

Lady Allen maintained that the design of well-laid-out gardens needed to be implemented at the start and not piecemeal. Playing-fields should be on level ground and the area for allotment gardens situated on gentle slopes, preferably facing south or south-west. Steep or boggy ground was to be avoided. An adequate water supply was required and, if funds permitted, could be made into a decorative feature.

Belts of trees around the perimeter would serve as a windbreak and thick hedges would keep out unwanted visitors and prevent destruction by animals; in North Wales mountain sheep had repeatedly broken into allotments and caused extensive damage to crops during severe winters and periods of drought. Entrances should be made welcoming, and one plan involved the creation of a semi-circular hedge around the gates, providing seating areas by the side of the road.

For economy of space plots were to be rectangular but not necessarily of a uniform dimension. The minimum size for plots was to be 10 rods, and those in more rural areas could be larger. Allowing for space, there could be 15 plots per acre, but the majority could be larger if possible.

A hardcore drive of not less than 10 feet would provide easy access, if possible located down the centre of the site. This main avenue could be made decorative with large flower beds 6 feet wide on either side with standard or half standard fruit trees planted behind. This would make the plots adjoining the drive very popular and they could be slightly larger. Cordon, espalier or pyramidal fruit trees could be grown along the side of barrow-ways, which would be at right angles to the main avenue.

According to Lady Allen, presentable communal huts should be located at the centre of the allotment and large enough to hold meetings and lectures, with additional storage space for tools, seeds and fertiliser together with a lavatory and a veranda, where men could go to sit and smoke. Lady Allen proposed to replace the much-hated, improvised shack with a system of lockers (of a cheering design) that could be sub-divided for every four, six or eight plots. An alternative idea was to have one partitioned locker for every two plots. Only the largest plots were to have individual sheds, and then only when located with due care. Lady Allen noted the tenant's desire for his own shed, and that if the holder could afford it the hut should be in the form of a pleasing summerhouse, with a small veranda. In urban areas, where plots were small, individual huts were not to be recommended.

Since a great majority of townsfolk were unused to gardening, Lady Allen suggested setting aside a plot for demonstration purposes under the guidance of a park superintendent or horticultural expert. As this facility would be classed as educational, the scheme would qualify for a grant from the Local Education Authority. Classes for beginners could commence in spring with demonstrations on planting, sowing and manuring the land. More experienced gardeners could gain advice on the best varieties to grow and the best methods of cultivation. The demonstration plot could also have a glasshouse, cold frames and cloches. Winter months could be occupied with lectures in the community hut.

Lady Allen concluded her booklet by stating that if enterprising local authorities were willing to incorporate allotment gardens into a wider comprehensive scheme and lay out areas as a model group, the propaganda value would prove inestimable. She said it was unfortunate that most people, including local councils, were wrong to think that allotments could not be made elegant or attractive. She maintained that this error was best refuted by practical demonstration.

In 1937 Sussex was selected as the area with the best-kept allotments, which may well have made Lady Allen quite proud. In Lewes most of the allotments were under municipal control and their tidy, presentable appearance formed a stark contrast to the few remaining plots where little or no regulation was exercised. A special correspondent for *The Times* stated that the untidiest allotments were often swamped with a jumble of ugly sheds, tin cans, baths and iron bedsteads in their last stage of decay. Not even the tall growth of scarlet runners could hide the unkempt character of these items, and in winter the bare ground added to the melancholy of such objects.

However, in Lewes, both extremes were visible within the town. A well-ordered group of allotments alongside the road to the nearby village of Kingston was presentable and let to tenants at a very reasonable rate. A broad path ran for the length of the site, and each plot had one shed, and one only, prescribed to a uniform pattern that was painted in an unassuming shade of green. Plot-holders were forbidden to install receptacles to catch water, unless they were sunk to ground level so as to be unobtrusive. There was no uniform scheme to separate the plots, though many tenants achieved this by planting privet hedges.

Lewes Council also acquired another tract of land alongside the Brighton Road in a region known locally as Hope-in-the-Valley. The plots were laid out in an orderly manner and the same regulations applied. The land contained a small orchard, which the Town Council decided to leave standing separately; however, due to the large number of rabbits, it was necessary to fence off the site with wire netting. The other allotments in Lewes, adorned with all the undesirable features, were about to become part of a municipal housing scheme. Arrangements were made to compensate the tenants with a new site on the outskirts of the estate, where their plots would be subject to reasonable regulations. While a certain amount of controversy arose over the appearance of allotments, they were still regarded as of immense importance to unemployed folk.

The question of allotment tenure was raised in the House of Commons. Mr W. S. Morrison, Minister for Agriculture, implied that while he had no authority to make regulations giving security of tenure to plot-holders, he remained eager to exercise to the full his existing powers for the maintenance and extension of the Allotment Movement. The Minister had in mind some new form of legislation. However, Parliament was already under heavy commitment with other programmes and he implied that it would be unlikely that anything could be done to introduce a Bill to deal with allotment matters that season. Mr Morrison promised to consider issuing a circular to local authorities, asking them to give plot-holders the maximum amount of security possible. Mr Morrison implied that it might once again be necessary to regard plot-holders as major contributors to food production, should the nation's seaborne supplies become threatened once again.

In 1938 the Society of Friends Allotment Committee and the Central Allotments Committee were highly commended on the splendid work in assisting the unemployed to cultivate plots. Their report for the year ending 31 August 1938 stated that 112,264 unemployed men were cultivating plots, and produced fresh vegetables to the value of £600,000. Evidence of the help that the Central Allotments Committee was able to provide was depicted through the medium of 2,623 local secretaries. Commitments throughout the course of a year came to £50,659. Donations of pennies were collected weekly from the tenants by the local secretaries, which amounted to £26,540, which covered half the cost of supplies to the Allotment Committees. The remainder was made up by a Government grant and from private donations. Administration costs, which included the secretaries' salaries, printing, stationery and a grant to the Society of Friends Allotment Committee, amounted to £7,481 11s 6d. Around £42,813 13s 1d was spent on seeds, seed potatoes and tools. However, there was a large reserve of funds, and the interest on deposits came to £391 4s 9d. The Government provided a grant on the usual 50/50 basis: for every penny collected from private subscribers, the Government gave the same amount. Hence, the greater the sum amassed, the greater the assistance for the unemployed. The Society of Friends Allotment Committee operated from its headquarters at Friends House in Euston Road, London NW1.

By 1938, in spite of the good work conducted by the societies and organisations, the majority of urban allotments were often regarded as a necessary evil, instead of being held of great importance and of benefit to the local community. One Allotment Committee reported that the number of allotments under its control had decreased by 50% in recent years, though there was sympathy for tenants dispossessed of their plots. By this time the general enthusiasm for allotment gardening had started to wane, and by 1937 there were only 907,000 allotments in England and Wales. This figure fell even further, and by 1939 there were roughly 815,000 allotments left.

The decline in allotments was causing consternation among various organisations and societies connected with small-scale cultivation. Mr G. W. Giles, Secretary of the National Allotments Society, stated that the number of allotment-holders in the country had decreased from 1,600,000 to less than 1,000,000 over the previous 18 years. In the London area the number of plot-holders had dropped from 14,000 to 7,000 in the space of 10 years. At the annual conference of the London & Home Counties Area Allotments Organisation, held at Ilford, Essex, the assembly passed a resolution calling to the attention of the Minister of Agriculture the dispossession of plot-holders in the London area.

Earlier in the year Mr Ellis Smith had asked the Minister of Agriculture what steps had been taken to implement the considerations given in leaflet N, issued by the National Allotment Society – namely the cultivation of vacant land. Mr W. S. Morrison, representing Cirencester and Tewkesbury, stated that while he was not aware of the official estimate of the annual produce of allotments, he recognised that they were an important source of food, while at the same time providing a healthy and useful recreation. At the time it was estimated that the total number of plot-holders across England and Wales in urban regions numbered 611,900 in 1935 and 606,000 in 1936; by 1937 the figure had fallen to 592,500. The decline was attributed to the demand of land for housing. Local Councils still had the power to possess land for allotments through purchase. Mr Morrison impressed on local authorities the importance that the Government attached to the provision of permanent allotments. However, he realised that the National Allotment Society's proposals regarding the acquisition of further land and the provision of greater security of tenure for the plot-holders would require legislation.

During the late 1930s allotment tenants were highly co-operative, spread their experience and knowledge, and often exchanged plants and seedlings. Plot-holders also expressed a strong desire for territorial division, which resulted in the fabrication of unsightly barriers around their plots; such constructions were often made from old bedsteads, sheets of corrugated iron or asbestos and discarded timbers. Many associations and societies resorted to asking for notices requesting the unsightly objects to be removed in order to tidy up their allotment sites. Unsightly huts and shacks were considered to be another main reason why local authorities had become lethargic towards the provision of allotments. One progressive allotment committee built 200 uniform sheds of a pleasing design on one of its sites, and they were hired out for a small extra fee alongside the annual rent. No other construction was permitted on this particular site, which was surrounded by a well-trimmed hedge and became the source of much pride among the tenants, as well as the community, and a joy to the townsfolk who passed by. Mr Stoney took stock of the widespread criticism directed towards the ill-favoured sheds and added:

'The chief cause of unsightliness is that huts are not often built to a pre-arranged plan or idea but are "thrown together" and repaired with any odd scrap of waste material. With a little forethought and care a quite presentable hut can be contrived from cheap, even waste material. The ugliness of existing huts can be modified or hidden in many ways. A few posts and lattice work, with very little other wood, will provide a small veranda, but the greatest improvement might be effected by the growing of climbing plants to cover the structure. The most speedy plants for this purpose belong to the clematis family.' (K. Stoney, Bulletin 90, Ministry of Agriculture, 1936, p48)

Mr Stoney also recommended one large communal hut instead of a multitude of individual ones. On a few sites several such community huts had been built through the Society of Friends Assisted Scheme for the Unemployed. The Society suggested that shrubs and flower borders could provide a surround for huts, and wherever possible straight lines should be avoided. Communal huts needed to be large enough to hold meetings, lectures and for the exhibitions of produce. But it was not just the matter of sheds and huts that influenced the appearance of allotments.

In the 1930s numerous allotment tenants adopted their own unique gardening methods, which were little heard of. On one site a tenant was observed planting seedling potatoes during late November. When asked about the late (and unusual) sowing, the tenant stated that they were 'chancers', since there was a high risk of them being cut by frosts during the early spring. Apparently three out of four of the plants escaped frost damage and the tubers could be dug up several weeks before those from a spring planting.

On another occasion an old plot-holder was seen creating a seed bed for cabbages, but the tenant implied that he couldn't sow the seed yet as the

This tenant could now plant his cabbages since the moon was in the full phase.

lunar phase was not yet in full. The cabbages from the previous season, which had been planted according to the lunar phase, looked very healthy.

A scruffy tenant, who was mildly rebuked for cultivating an untidy, weedy-looking plot, expressed disinterest in growing conventional vegetables that could be bought at the market. He insisted that his speciality was the cultivation of unusual vegetables such as Chinese artichokes, Australian cress, celeriac, salsify and eggplants. On being told that it was better to raise ordinary vegetables well instead of uncommon vegetables badly, he became very agitated and appeared to be surprised by the suggestion that eggplants required the warmth of a cold frame or glasshouse.

During the late 1930s a larger number of tenants were devoting their entire plots to the cultivation of flowers, especially dahlias, lupins, asters, delphiniums and chrysanthemums. Most of the blooms raised ended up on the horticultural show table, but in some cases the flowers were for selling, and the authorities (having failed to stamp out the practise in the 1920s) decided that this was not an activity to be encouraged. Even at horticultural shows some tenants were rather devious; in one incident the carrots on display had their cracks filled in with coloured soap, but the strange scent implied that the exhibits had been doctored!

The carrots on display had their cracks filled with coloured soap.

During the late 1930s outdoor tomatoes were very popular on allotments and plants bearing heavy crops were a commonplace sight. Unlike later decades, pilfering of produce was rarely heard of. While various allotment association and committee officials stated that it was sad that there were too few to champion the allotment cause, storm clouds were gathering over Europe. The 'long hot summer' finally came to an end in the autumn of 1939, when hostilities with Germany were renewed. At 11 o'clock on 3 September, the nation listened to the Prime Minister's grim radio broadcast of the declaration of war. Everyone knew what that meant.

Allotment gardening was about to peak once more.

8
The victory diggers

O n 4 October 1939 the Ministry of Agriculture launched the 'Dig for Victory' campaign; the priority was to get half a million new allotments productive as soon as possible. Experts at the Ministry of Agriculture had estimated that 500,000 plots of well-worked land could support one million adults and one and a half million children for eight months of the year. The new drive for allotments was not aimed at competing with commercial growers or farmers, but simply to avoid famine in fresh vegetables. The nationwide cultivation of vegetables on allotments released thousands of acres of farmland for the production of additional grain crops and sugar beet.

The famous 'Dig for Victory' logo. (After HMSO)

Sir Reginald Dorman Smith, Minister for Agriculture, reinforced the new campaign in a special radio broadcast on 8 October. Just weeks after the outbreak of war the Ministry published the first *Growmore Bulletin*, price 3d, and Sir Reginald Dorman Smith stated:

'Everyone possessing a garden or allotment will wish to produce as many vegetables as possible during a period of emergency and especially to arrange the cropping in such a way that supplies from the garden may be continuous throughout the year. It is important to produce those kinds of vegetables that have nutritional value – viewed in its widest aspect. The medical view is strongly in favour of fresh green vegetables that contain vitamins and minerals, and it is especially important to have adequate supplies of these during the winter and spring months.' (Sir Reginald Dorman Smith, *Food From the Garden*, Bulletin No 1, 1939)

A correspondent to the *Gardeners' Chronicle* ('Mr P.') expressed his dismay at the apparent demise of allotments during the late 1930s and apportioned blame upon local authorities for their lack of foresight on the matter. He added that people who continually advocated the extension of allotments rarely had a fair deal, since all too frequently the sites allocated for the

156

purpose were of little use for anything else. Also very little thought was given to the suitability of the land in question, for the cultivation of vegetable crops. 'Mr P.' insisted that it was necessary for allotments to be located on as fertile land as possible, while at the same time provide them near to the homes of potential cultivators.

With regard to storage for the tools required 'Mr P.' insisted that this need not be of undue concern. Since the wartime plots were of a transitory nature the construction of hideous huts and shacks was to be prohibited. He claimed that on urban allotments, a low-lying tool box constructed of timber, measuring 4 to 5 feet in length, 2 feet wide and 2 feet deep, would be quite adequate. Since timber was in short supply a layer of corrugated iron could be used for the lid of the box, and by making the lid of oversize dimensions the woodwork below would be protected from the elements. He added that it was necessary to place brick-bats below the box in order to allow air to circulate underneath. Apparently, tests made on such boxes showed that they remained in good condition for several years. If constructed in a uniform size many boxes could be situated within a small area. 'Mr P.' suggested a small additional rent for the use of such a tool box and no hesitation was made in recommending them for general use. He implied that they were vastly preferable to the nondescript huts that were all too prevalent on many a site, which usually engendered opposition to allotments.

In October 1939 Lady Marjorie Allen requested, in a letter to *The Times* newspaper, that allotments should be carefully laid out with due consideration to the planning before the sites were handed over to the tenants. She pointed out that all too frequently allotment sites were not places of great beauty. Lady Allen also stated that the seemly placing of tool-huts was important. She asked if it was too much to hope for that local authorities might give some thought to preparing a comprehensive layout, so that the new gardens (as she called them) would become cheerful places for recreation as well as centres of food production.

The first major difficulty experienced by the plot-holders was the scarcity of fertiliser, especially stable manure. Some citizens suggested that the Government should open up local depots so that those plot-holders could obtain manure at cost price. The Government was quick to point out the various alternatives to manure, which included leaf mould, leaf soil, basic slag, burnt earth, wood ashes, and chemical manures. In *Growmore Leaflet No 1* the Ministry urged gardeners to consider composting refuse:

'A properly managed compost heap should provide compost ready for digging in at the expiration of about 6 months. Those with no previous experience in composting will find the making of good compost from garden waste to be a simple matter, and no one should hesitate to adopt the practise through lack of experience.' (*Growmore Leaflet No 1*, Ministry of Agriculture, 1939)

Experts from the Ministry of Agriculture recommended that leaf heaps should be left to mature for a year and turned frequently. The Ministry strongly advocated creating compost heaps instead of the all too frequent bonfire; it took rather a dim view of bonfires and insisted that they should be kept small and restricted to woody material, old pea sticks, diseased vegetation and the underground parts of docks. However, the resulting ash was recognised as a valuable source of potash and instructions were given as to its use. Bonfire ash was to be incorporated into the compost heap or bagged up and stored in a dry place. The Ministry stipulated that bonfires were only to be started well before the blackout hour.

Artificial fertilisers became extremely popular and the use of National Growmore was particularly widespread. Since this fertiliser released nutrients slowly the goodness was not washed away by rain. National Growmore contained 7% nitrogen, 7% phosphate and 7% potash. The Ministry stated that 42lb of National Growmore was quite sufficient for a 10-rod plot if 30lb was applied for general use and 12lb was reserved as extra for potatoes, winter greens and spring cabbage.

The Ministry of Agriculture decided from the outset that the army of new gardeners, especially the inexperienced amateurs, needed advice on planning, cropping and of the best varieties to raise, so it unleashed a barrage of informative leaflets together with patriotic propaganda, literature and jingles to stimulate folk to take up the spade.

The 'Dig for Victory' campaign even had a jingle on the radio:

'Dig! Dig! Dig! And your muscles will grow big.
Keep on pushing the spade!
Never mind the worms
Just ignore their squirms
And when your back aches, laugh with glee
And keep on diggin'
Till we give our foes a wiggin'
Dig! Dig! Dig! To victory'.

A series of 'Dig for Victory' leaflets (26 in all) gave instructions on every aspect of vegetable and fruit cultivation and they were issued throughout the course of the war. The newspaper-quality leaflets were roughly 5 by 7 inches in format and were embellished with simple, woodcut-style illustrations of garden produce. Leaflets 19 and 20 were much more elaborate, printed on good-quality paper and, when folded, were pocket size (3 by 4 inches). They were illustrated with monochrome photographs giving step-by-step instructions on how to sow seeds and how to dig soil. By November 1940 the Ministry of Agriculture was distributing large 'Dig for Victory' posters, which for the most part were in red and white. Smaller posters were no less attractive and one depicted the archetypal father figure carrying a garden fork and basket brimming with vegetable produce. Circular adhesive 'Dig for Victory' stamps were also issued as part of the overall campaign. By 1942 around half a million 'Dig for Victory' leaflets had been distributed among the 1,400,000 plot-holders.

In 1940 Winston Churchill took over from Neville Chamberlain as Prime Minister, and he replaced Dorman Smith with Robert S. Hudson, together with Tom Williams and the Duke of Norfolk as junior ministers. Throughout the course of the war this team were on good relations. Williams was an ex-miner and he understood the persecution complex among the working classes and consequently revelled in his backslapping popularity with them. From 1940 onwards Mr Hudson's signature appeared on all of the 'Dig for Victory' leaflets.

Response to the 'Dig for Victory' campaign varied enormously in different regions. On 9 October 1939 the good citizens of Tunbridge Wells in Kent turned out in force to mark out and dig up plots at Bishops Down Park, an 8-acre site that had previously been used for pasture. Mr L. F. Kelly, a local resident, was largely responsible for developing the idea and he sought consent of the neighbours before embarking on the scheme. Since the land had always been pasture, clearance was a relatively simple operation and the light sandy soil proved to be ideal for growing vegetables. Plots of 5, 10 and 15 rods were cleared and let at 1 shilling a rod. Un-cleared plots smothered with gorse and saplings were let at half the price during 1939. By 1941 Mr Kelly had formed a 'Grow More Food' group and became Chairman of the Tunbridge Wells War Horticultural Committee, which largely consisted of members of the Culverden Golf Club. When part of the golf course underwent conversion to allotments, the Mayor of Tunbridge Wells drove the tractor that made the first furrows, not far from the clubhouse. From the beginning of the war the number of plots in Tunbridge Wells increased to

The citizens of Tunbridge Wells clearing pastureland at Bishops Down Park for wartime allotments.

Your own vegetables all the year round... if you

DIG FOR VICTORY NOW

The first 'Grow More Food' leaflet, published by the Ministry of Agriculture in 1939. (After HMSO)

1,900, which were governed by five allotment associations, one in each of the four wards, and one in a working-class district outside the town.

The Borough of Croydon had impressive allotment acreage, which was considered a major achievement since the region had undergone extensive development during the 1930s. At the start of the war the Borough had 2,500 acres of allotment gardens, but by 1943 the number had risen to 8,000. The Borough managed two farms and had more than 110 acres of parkland devoted to growing food. Local Victory Diggers raised more than 353,000 seedlings. The gardeners received exceptional help from Croydon Corporation, which supplied more than 14 miles of chestnut fencing, 300 gates, 12,000 wooden pegs, 300 notice boards, 8,000 yards of clinker for pathways, 17 tool sheds and 10 trading sheds. During the first year of war the Corporation supplied 4 tons of seed potatoes and 6 tons of lime. By 1943 the supplies increased to 69 tons of potato seed, 100 tons of potash and 15 tons of basic slag. In 1944 Croydon's Victory Diggers raised 25,000 tomato plants, which were expected to produce half a million tomatoes in the growing season. Alderman Maurice Stacey, Chairman of the Parks, Cemeteries & Smallholdings Committee, was largely responsible for finding plots and organising their cultivation.

In October 1941 the Mayor of Croydon, Alderman A. H. Harding, promised that after the war the whole matter of allotments within the Borough would be addressed. At the distributing of awards in the Allotments Amenity Competition, organised by the Croydon Housing Estates Garden Competition, Alderman Harding said that in the early part of the year none of them thought they would live to be prize-giving. He was full of commendation for Croydon's gardeners, and was surprised at the high volume of flowers cultivated, in spite of the Government's exhortations to grow food. He added that the tenants of the council estate houses had done remarkably well. In many districts the gardens were well kept and it was difficult to realise that there was a war on. He stated:

'When the war is over we shall have to tackle the whole idea of allotments. After the last war, it will be remembered, not so very many of the allotments then existing were allowed to continue. Now, I think we must make up our minds that after this war something in the nature of permanent allotments must be made part of our civic life and that land must be set apart for that purpose. So far as Croydon is concerned we shall have no reason to feel in any way dissatisfied with the effort we are making now. Our efforts will be a help in the future, as they are a help now.' (*Croydon Advertiser*, 1941)

In Lancashire the Allotment Movement was really booming, especially in and around the industrialised areas. By October 1939 more than 1,000 allotments were in cultivation in the Preston region, although 100 lay vacant. The Preston Allotments & Smallholdings Committee spent much time visiting sites to discuss new ways to increase vegetable production. Councillor Burgess, Chairman of the Smallholdings Committee, approached Alderman F. W. F. Matthew, Chairman of the Parks Committee, with a view to establishing a number of small allotments within the park grounds if there was sufficient demand. Morecambe & Heysham Town Council had already submitted an analysis on the amount of land available for food cultivation in wartime. Demonstration plots were established within the parks under supervision of the superintendent and advice was freely dispensed to allotment tenants and people with domestic gardens. At the time the amount of land available in the district amounted to 500 allotments.

The Borough of Stretford managed to develop 284 emergency wartime allotments and at the end of the year only 17 were left unattended. In addition 230 permanent allotments were also created, where flower cultivation was forsaken in favour of growing vegetables. Since the majority of new tenants were inexperienced at raising vegetables, the resulting 'bumper' crops far exceeded expectations. Both the wartime and permanent plots were under the supervision of Mr Chas F. Pragnell, Superintendent of Stretford Parks. Leaflets that were issued locally covered every aspect of gardening, from preparing the soil to the harvesting and storage of produce. Lectures were held imparting advice on good cultivation, and the latest innovation was a special newsletter, which was dispatched to all the plot-holders. The Borough's Parks Department also supplied the plot-holders with seed of brassicas, onions, leeks and celery, together with quantities of manure and lime at reduced prices. In September 1940 a vegetable show was held for the holders, which was a tremendous success. The show scheduled 41 classes and there were entries for 40 of them. More than 300 separate exhibits were submitted by the 63 participating gardeners.

The Horticultural Committee in Blackburn also decided to provide specimen allotments within the parks, so that people interested in growing food could use them as a template. The Parks Superintendent and his staff offered expert advice. In locations where more than 15 applications for allotments were made in any one district, the Blackburn Committee endeavoured to find sites for them.

Early in 1940 great interest was evoked at Parkside, on the edge of Wimbledon Common, when Mr Frederick Poke decided to plough up his lawn for the cultivation of vegetables. Mr Poke opted to use a machine that would enable the chore to be completed in a little under 2 hours, whereas digging with a spade would have taken a fortnight. A great many citizens turned up to watch the proceedings, including Mr H. A. Crowe, the Mayor of Wimbledon, and several Council colleagues. Mr Valentine Smith, a keen amateur gardener, who owned one of these machines and who had arranged for this lawn to be transformed into a vegetable plot, maintained that if the Councillors saw the machine in action, they might be induced to purchase one and hire it out to the Borough's plot-holders. The machine, a Swiss invention, was referred to as a 'rototiller', and some 6,000 were in use across the UK; Watford Council was one of the first local authorities to obtain one for hiring out to plot-holders and gardeners. It was powered by a petrol motor and said to work for up to 8 hours on 2 or 3 gallons. Since there were only two main controls, the 'rototiller' was easy to use and the Councillors watched girls using one. At the time there were three main models available, costing from £102 10s to £175.

By the early 1940s lawns were fast becoming a scarce sight as more and more land went under the spade. However, the disappearance of open grassy spaces had its critics. Stanley Christopherson, President of the MCC, drew attention to the demise of playing-fields through demand for wartime allotments. He argued that it was far beyond the scope for small isolated plots

By early 1940 lawns were fast becoming a scarce sight. Even the front gardens in affluent suburbia were turned over to vegetable production.

to contribute much to the overall food required by the country and urged both public authorities and local councils to carefully consider the undoubted need for allotments versus the destruction of sports grounds. Lord Davison, Chairman of the Executive Committee of the Metropolitan Public Gardens Association, backed Christopherson's views and strongly opposed the tearing up of recreation grounds for allotment usage until all other waste ground and dormant land had been taken. Mr Hampden of the Central Council of Recreational Physical Training was also aghast at the disappearance of sports grounds. The Central Council represented 115 national organisations associated with physical training and the social welfare of young people, and maintained that sports grounds were vital to foster abilities such as stamina, determination and mental alertness in young people, which it regarded as particularly important in wartime. The Central Council went to great lengths to point out that the process of reversing allotments to playing-fields would be looked upon as a waste of resources and money. The controversy influenced both the London County Council and Manchester Corporation to forbid the further destruction of sports-fields for allotments, and it was hoped that many other Town Councils would follow suit.

In the early 1940s the Government and the Ministry of Agriculture became increasingly concerned at the apparent lack of enthusiasm for growing food. During the 1940s the cinema was still pulling in greater crowds than the local allotment – starlets of the silver screen were obviously more appealing than rows of potatoes and carrots. The authorities were quick to point out that it was a free country and no civilian was forced to grow vegetables. Rather craftily, though, the Ministry underlined the fact that growing food was a patriotic and valuable service to both country and family:

> 'Dig for you and your family every week of the year. Never a week without food from your garden or allotment. Not only fresh peas and lettuce in June, new potatoes in July, but all the health-giving vegetables in winter, when supplies are scarce, savoys, sprouts, kale, sprouting broccoli, onions, leeks, carrots, parsnips and beet. Vegetables all year round, if you Dig Well and Crop Wisely.' (*Dig for Victory* Leaflet No 1, Ministry of Agriculture)

On 10 September 1940, after the disaster at Dunkirk, the Ministry of Agriculture intensified the 'Dig for Victory' campaign. In 1939 there had been approximately 815,000 allotments, but by 1942 there were 1,400,000 across England and Wales. In the early 1940s a survey found that half the working population cultivated some kind of garden or allotment. New regulations permitted the keeping of pigs, hens and rabbits on allotments. In *Growmore Leaflet No 5* (issued in November 1939) entitled 'Turning waste into eggs', the Ministry imparted advice on keeping poultry:

> 'House and allotment holders are urged to endeavour to keep a few laying hens to provide themselves with fresh eggs. It should be borne in mind,

however, that some local authorities have by-laws for preventing the keeping of poultry in such a manner as to be prejudicial to public health. Further, although some relaxation may be possible, many local authorities and private landlords have regulations or agreements in force relating to the keeping of poultry and preliminary enquiries should be made to the local authority or private landlord concerned. No attempt should be made to keep more birds than are necessary to consume waste materials available, supplemented with a little grain and meal, and as a rule no male birds should be kept.' (Ministry of Agriculture, *Bulletin No 5*, 1939)

By 1943-44 domestic hen keepers accounted for 25% of the country's supply of eggs. The keeping of pigs also became something of a craze. There were more than 6,900 pig clubs across the country and thousands of members fed their animals on kitchen waste. Wartime necessity had melted away the obstacles between the producers of bacon and eggs, potatoes and greens. In urban areas pig clubs were not always a great success as citizens living under air-raid conditions and having to attend to other work often found it difficult to look after the animals properly; many clubs had to be discontinued after a year or two. Some families managed extraordinary feats to produce food, as Roy Woolley recalls of wartime Romford:

'We had a modest back garden but also an allotment behind it and also two more allotments adjacent to Rush Green Road. They were at the end of Grosvenor Road. Dad had a full-time job at the brewery and was fire-watching in the evenings and overnight. On top of that he and Mum kept these four plots going to provide vegetables for a hungry family of four and, I suppose, two grandparents as well as neighbours. He had a trailer for his bike and would cycle from Crow Lane to Rush Green with me on the trailer. I would come back on top of a trailer full of potatoes on occasions but did have to walk if there was a slight uphill gradient.

How Mum and Dad did all this I will never know. We also kept chickens for the eggs and the pot as well as rabbits. We were never allowed to see Dad wringing their necks. The neighbours would trade for eggs and I suppose the money they paid kept us in chicken meal which was bought in those wonderfully smelling shops of Matthews Corn & Seed Merchants in Chadwell Heath High Road (near Dr Frew's and opposite the police station) or Beacontree Heath. There were the open sacks of all sorts of seed, feed and everything horticultural. It all smelled so terribly earthy. All the seeds were in little wooden drawers which lined the back wall. The day-old chicks were delivered by post! We had a wood and wire enclosure on the living room table and kept them warm with light bulbs. We kids loved it when a new supply of chicks arrived to play with.

Where did Mum and Dad get all this knowledge and skill? Was it Dad's Essex roots or did they learn from scratch? Sadly I never asked him. They never missed Mr Middleton's gardening programme on the wireless (battery delivered weekly from Silcock's in North Street even though we had mains electricity). When Mr Middleton died one of our gardening books was inscribed by Mum, "Dedicated to our friend on the wireless, Mr Middleton", so the programme obviously meant a lot. We also bought the Smallholder magazine.' (Roy Woolley, recollections of wartime Romford)

Meanwhile a remarkably similar picture emerged in Birmingham as 'Dig for Victory' posters appeared all round the city to encourage people to grow as much food as possible. Charlotte Tate recalls:

'All over Quinton allotments sprang up wherever there was spare land. My father had one of these pieces of land, adjacent to the high street, where vegetables and salad crops were cultivated. Like many Quintonians, we had a big garden as well as an allotment. My father grew potatoes, cabbage, sprouts, leeks, peas, beans and celery. When the potatoes were harvested he would dig out a big, straw-lined bury in which to store the potatoes for the winter. One could never be certain, in those times, that food of any sort would be plentiful in the shops. My mother would preserve the beans in salt inside screw-top jars. Apples were carefully wrapped in tissue paper and laid on a bed of straw in a cool place to keep for as long as possible.

The next point was poultry. My father built a large hen house at the end of the garden, and purchased five hens and a cockerel. We enjoyed watching the fowl take dust baths and listening to them cluck quietly to one another as they walked about. Sometimes a hen would go broody and sit her eggs. After 19 or 20 days we could hear the little chickens cheeping. Then a little later they would be brave enough to peep out from beneath the hen's warm, feathery wings. The females were kept for their eggs and the males were separated out and reared for the table – very precious additions to our wartime rations. My mother pickled the eggs in isinglass. The cockerels were sold at Christmas time. But the children were not allowed to see that side of the business.

We purchased a special meal for the fowl, mixed with a type of grit, from a shop opposite the Danilo. The grit was to ensure that the eggshells were strong, otherwise the hens might break the eggs. These two items were mixed with boiled vegetable peelings and table scraps then fed to the fowl. They also scratched around in the garden for worms, slugs, grubs and insects. Some people bred rabbits for the table, and would cure the pelts to make rugs, waistcoats and slippers.' (Charlotte Tate, courtesy of the *Quinton Oracle*)

In 1941 a comparison between households with and without allotments and gardens indicated that citizens with gardens tended to obtain and consume larger quantities of vegetables than people that relied on purchases alone. In urban areas the possession of a garden was the hallmark of a higher economic status, though it was noted that families in this class tended to consume more vegetables (excluding potatoes), whether they had a garden or not. Potato crops cultivated in gardens made a considerable contribution to the diet of the family, especially between July and October. The supply of fruit and vegetables varied in accordance with the season, ranging from 12% in winter (January-March) and up to 49% in summer (July-September). In rural areas the proportion was very much higher, up to 98%.

Gardening author Roy Hay said that every Victory Digger held the land in trust during wartime and those gardeners should attempt to use the land to their best advantage. In his book *The Spring Wartime Gardening Guide*, Mr P. Dyer urged gardeners to join local horticultural societies in order to save both time and money. He suggested that the more inexperienced gardeners and Victory Diggers should seek advice from horticultural experts, who were employed by the County War Agricultural Executive Committee, or subscribe to one of the many gardening periodicals. He impressed on the novice gardener the need to write to the Ministry of Agriculture or Royal Horticultural Society to solve important problems with cultivation. Most importantly, the novice was not to guess, for wasted effort, seed and money would only please the Germans more than anyone else.

One Worcestershire Victory Digger recalled wartime gardening at 24 Wavertree Nook Road:

'The front garden was dug up and planted with potatoes, cabbages, carrots, peas and beans... As the war progressed, shortages increased, and spurred on by Government exhortations to "Dig for Victory", we also rented an allotment beyond Thingwall Road, next to the Holt School field. A neighbour on an adjacent allotment grew corn on the cob, which was the first time I had ever seen it.' (Sandy Ellis, memories of Wavertree in wartime)

On 4 January 1941 'Mr P.', the correspondent to *Gardeners' Chronicle*, brought to readers' attention the merits of cultivating vegetables on refuse dumps. By 1941 there were more than 400 such allotments in his (unspecified) home town that produced excellent crops. Throughout 1940 many similar sites were laid out on marshy ground that had been reclaimed by the dumping of the town's refuse. Originally the sites were intended for use as sports grounds. However, impatient folk complained of the undulations that developed on the pitches superimposed over the strata consisting of paper, tins, ashes and other rubbish. 'Mr P.' suggested that it would be far more advantageous and economical to let the land as allotments over a period of years, since cultivation would enable humus to accumulate and thus level out the ground in a shorter space of time.

Even so, it was quite useless to attempt to set up an allotment on a recently filled-in site, since the heat generated from the decomposing material, especially on sites where the refuse was several feet deep, rendered the land useless for cultivation for at least five years. However, by covering the tip with a layer of heavy clay soil some 3-6 inches deep, the idle period was shortened. Such measures were not necessary on dumps that had been filled in several years earlier. On established sites the dumped material had decomposed to form highly fertile humus and a wide range of crops could be raised without the application of fertiliser.

Unfortunately the soil on municipal dumps tended to dry out very quickly during hot weather and it was recommended that sowing and planting was done as early in the season as possible. On some sites the planting of autumn potatoes was conducted, and not without some degree of success. Town dumps also enabled cultivation to be carried out at times when it would have been disastrous to attempt work on normal ground. Although the provision of water was not necessary, it was a great boon, especially during periods of drought. The perfect drainage on such sites enabled nearly all crops to over-winter in a satisfactory manner. 'Mr P.' added that allotments on refuse dumps were capable of yielding an extraordinary volume of crops that could scarcely be excelled on other types of land. At the time, there was, quite naturally, a desire to grow vegetables for large numbers of people, especially where there were numerous children in residence.

In 1941 Mr R. S. Hudson stated in Parliament that he had not encouraged the small cultivator or plot-holder to grow the maximum amount of food indiscriminately. He said that such a policy would have led to over-production of vast quantities of perishable produce. He advocated that the amateur grower should adopt a system of orderly cropping to ensure a year-round succession of vegetables and that any surplus was of a non-perishable type (carrots and roots) that could be stored for winter use. In rural regions where gardens and allotments were usually slightly larger than those in urban areas, gardeners often cultivated far more crops than they actually needed. The matter of distribution was given to the County Garden Produce Associations and Village Produce Clubs. Mr Hudson was adamant that the disposal of extra produce should remain a matter for local organisations – he insisted that the word 'surplus' should never be used in wartime, as there was no such thing. Mr Hudson also said that the underlying aim of the 'Dig for Victory' campaign was not to dig for profit, which he considered as very misleading.

In 1942 the *Growmore Bulletin* was re-published and Mr Hudson stated:

> 'As soon as war broke out it was realised that the contribution of food from well-cultivated gardens and allotments would be of vital importance. A drive for more allotments has already begun. But it is not enough merely to grow vegetables, unless they are grown in the right variety; the garden cannot produce food for the household all the year round and will not supply the range of vegetables that is so desirable from the health standpoint.' (R. S. Hudson, *Growmore Bulletin*, 1942)

Demonstration allotments within parks had gained in popularity by 1942 and often provided invaluable inspiration for the beginner. In Hyde Park the Ministry's own exhibition plot attracted much attention from the general public, the press and even the police. Birmingham closely followed suit and provided an exhibition allotment that became the 'Mecca' for all would-be gardeners seeking encouragement. This development led to the idea of establishing model allotments within domestic gardens where the private owners with plenty of gardening experience could dispense valuable information on the cultivation of vegetables. Mr T. Ellis Hughes, Mayor of Conway, wrote to the local press urging citizens to cultivate an allotment or garden to the best of their ability. The Mayor hoped that the townsfolk of Conway would make a strong case for the provision of allotments that could be offered at low rents and so provide themselves with food to the value of £10 per annum for the cost of a few shillings.

In Warwickshire the 'Dig for Victory' campaign was the cause of much pride among the county's plot-holders. There were 30,000 allotments covering 2,500 acres, but the Ministry of Agriculture pressed for further expansion, and to ensure that every allotment was cultivated to full capacity. Special demonstration allotments had become part of the County Council's educational activity during the previous 23 years. By 1943, 76 demonstration allotments had been set up and successfully managed in the county's parks and existing allotment grounds. Four plots were laid out in the grounds of schools and were tended by the pupils. Assistance also came from a special panel of advisors and lecturers from the Royal Horticultural Society, who dispensed information at meetings arranged by various allotments associations and garden societies.

The cultivation of spare or requisitioned land under military occupation became a compulsory activity for troops; however, cultivation of vegetables was not allowed to interfere with military duties. The Treasury met the cost of seeds, tools and fertiliser, and the produce raised was generally sold to the NAAFI at wholesale prices; any profits were divided between the Treasury and the units concerned. The Ministry of Agriculture supplied special 'Dig for Victory' posters for the camps, while patriotic householders were supplied with signs to affix to the garden gate, which read 'This is a Victory Garden'.

Even the disused land on airfields was turned over to the cultivation of vegetable crops, and larger areas that required ploughing were often made accessible to farmers. In 1941 a total of 1,700 acres was under cultivation on RAF bases, and by 1942 the amount of land had almost doubled. Samples of produce from the airfields were frequently sent to the Horticultural Halls at Vincent Square in London. The Horticultural Department of the RAF was awarded medals by the Royal Horticultural Society, and much friendly rivalry existed between the 300 different units. One bomber command in Eastern England devoted 37 acres for vegetable cultivation, and by 1942 a vast number of aerodromes had become self-supporting in vegetables. At one station expansion included the cultivation of virgin land, which a transport officer ploughed up during the evenings with much assistance from volunteers. Activity of this sort often culminated in horticultural shows. In 1943 the Duchess of Gloucester opened the Royal Air Force Horticultural Exhibition held at the Horticultural Halls in Westminster. She presented the trophy (in the guise of a man with a spade) to Captain K. C. Horner for the best RAF station with the highest food production record. In 1942 around 4,200 acres were in cultivation, but the following year there were 7,200 acres of vegetables, which were valued at £250,000.

Back on Civvy Street, the Metropolitan Public Gardens Association gave full support to the idea of turning the grounds of bombed churches into 'Gardens of Peace'. The Association pointed out that local organisations such as the ARP, the police and the fire services could help out with the cultivation of such open spaces. By 1942 it was noticed that garden produce often accidentally turned up in the most unusual places. Tomatoes, cucumbers, beans and even marrows were found ripening on the side of a crater formed by a bomb dropped a year previously. In November 1942 local councils were given the power to take over bombed sites, without consent from the Ministry of Agriculture, providing there was no sign of cultivation and that the owners or occupiers could not be traced or were unable to cultivate the land themselves.

Marrows growing on the side of a bomb crater in 1942.

Inspired by such events, the Bethnal Green Bombed Sites Association decided to set up an experimental plot in a bombed area where previously houses and shops had stood. The site only measured 150 by 80 feet, where 17 tenants had plots measuring 9 feet by 18 feet. In order to clear the land it was necessary to dig to a depth of 4 feet, occasionally through solid foundations and in some parts to a depth of 6 feet. Around 50 tons of rubble was cleared and carted away on War Department lorries (14 loads in all). The tenants only worked their plots during the evenings and at weekends. Work commenced on 7 June 1942 but the gardens soon became very productive, growing early and main crop potatoes, onions, shallots, turnip, beetroot, radishes, lettuce, peas, beans, rhubarb, cole and cabbage. The total cost of creating this allotment amounted to just £4, including the price of creosoting the fence and the supply of manure, seeds and plants. The Metropolitan Water Board laid on the water supply and charged 37s 6d per annum. Sir Wyndham Deeds, Chairman of Bethnal Green (Bombed Sites) Producers' Association, stressed that the success of the experiment emphasised the hunger for allotments.

Early in 1942 Mr Hudson was deeply concerned at the lack of proper planning among amateur gardeners in order to secure supplies for the advancing winter of 1942-43. He maintained that there was far too much emphasis by Victory Diggers on the growing of summer crops, especially main-crop potatoes, while little effort was made to cultivate leafy greens. Mr

Tenants gardening on a site at Bethnal Green previously occupied
by shops and houses. Wyndham Deeds, Chairman of the
Bombed Sites Producers' Association, said that the experiment was a great success.

J. D. Davison, Director of Agriculture, also stated that there were too many potato crops being raised by the small gardener, both on allotments and in private gardens. From 1941 onwards the civilian population had been inundated with information on the merits of cultivating and consuming potatoes in order avoid bread, as the greatest volume of wheat had to be shipped in.

During the spring of 1941 shipping losses were especially severe, but the following year the U-boat war reached a new peak and every ship that could be spared was needed for military action. Every SOS from a British ship on the high seas with the message of being torpedoed, bombed or mined was a challenge to the Victory Digger to ensure that no food that could be grown in the UK was imported. Before the war around two-thirds of food was imported, including thousands of tons of onions, carrots, lettuce, broccoli and cauliflower. There was even speculation that a dramatic cessation of the conflict would prevent further enthusiasm for growing food.

'Owing to the shipping position we shall need every bit of food we can possibly grow at home. Last summer many gardens had a surplus of perishable vegetables such as lettuce and cabbage. This winter those same

170

gardens are getting short, not only of keeping vegetables such as onions, carrots and other root crops, but also of fresh winter vegetables such as late cabbage, savoys and kale. We must try to prevent that happening this year. Next winter is going to be a critical period.' (R. S. Hudson, *Grow for Winter as Well as Summer*, Ministry of Agriculture, 1942)

In September 1942 Twickenham Allotments & Holders' Association held its second annual show at the Technical College. The exhibits within the 41 different classes amounted to roughly 300. In order to encourage wartime gardeners, the schedule was divided into two classes, one open only to holders of wartime allotments, the other open to any plot-holders and gardeners within the Borough of Twickenham. A special certificate of merit, bearing the crest of the Duke of Gloucester, was presented to Mr A. Howard for his magnificent set of six onions, which was placed first of ten entries; five others were also of outstanding quality. Beet also did exceptionally well on the Borough's wartime allotments. Twickenham's Mayor, Alderman C. W. Beckett (and that year's President of the Association), declared the show open at 2.30pm and the cups and shields were awarded at 6pm by the Mayoress. Afterwards the produce was auctioned off and the proceeds, together with the entry fees, were donated to the Red Cross. Mr Howard's first prize of six onions raised 6s 6d.

During the same year much wartime vegetable cultivation was undertaken at Kew, notably in front of Kew Palace. At the weekends in particular more and more people were taking an interest in the 'Grow More Food' campaign, and were asking questions. Most of the attention was focused on the official demonstration plot, where crops of beet, parsnips, onions, leeks and potatoes were compared with those that visitors were growing at home. A display of vegetable marrows trained over arches and poles illustrated a saving of space. However, the largest area, which drew special attention, was the plot devoted to the cultivation of carrots for seed. The variety was Early Market, a second early, stump-ended, half-long carrot, which had been one of the best types raised at Kew the previous year. Since this variety was successful and the need for vegetable seed rather pressing, it was decided to select the best roots to be grown exclusively for seed production. Half the roots were clamped in old coal ash and half in coarse river sand. When unearthed the following spring there was no apparent difference in the keeping qualities of the two materials, though the roots stored in the sand were of better colour.

By 1943 the mania for potatoes had reached epidemic proportions, which was partly due to the Ministry of Food placing much importance on it. The Ministry of Food created two cartoon characters, 'Potato Pete' and 'Dr Carrot', in order to get people interested in eating vegetables. Numerous 'Potato Pete' recipe books, posters, press advertisements and radio jingles enhanced the popularity of the potato. Betty Driver (more recently better known as Betty Turpin in *Coronation Street*) sang the 'Potato Pete' song, which was made into a record:

'Potato Pete, Potato Pete,
See him coming down the street,
Shouting his good things to eat,
"Get your hot potatoes from Potato Pete".'

The cartoon character 'Potato Pete' was created by the Ministry of Food. (After HMSO)

Since 1941 onions had become increasingly scarce and were almost unobtainable in the shops. Raymond A. Cook maintained that a farthing's worth of onion seed grown in the back garden of every house could result in half a million spring onions, which, after thinning, would yield 100,000 onions of cooking size. All that was needed was one small plot a yard long and a foot wide. Mr Cook suggested that the less ground the gardener had, the better he would cultivate it.

In 1941 the humble onion was front-page news.

In 1943 the Red Cross hoped to tackle the onion problem and established its Onion Clubs Committee, which operated from 29 Belgrave Square in London SW1. The plan was to get more than 1,000 separate onion clubs, consisting of children between 14 and 18 years of age growing onion crops on waste ground. The Onion Club Committee hoped that the various clubs might gain access to the odd half-acre or so and start planting onions. The formation of the Onion Clubs was loudly applauded, and the scheme had the full approval from both the Royal Horticultural Society and the National Allotments Society. The produce would be collected and dried at special centres prior to purchase by the NAAFI at fixed prices, and the money raised donated to the Red Cross Agriculture Fund. The Onion Clubs Committee was all too aware that in some regions there was a lack of land, which made the formation of an Onion Club almost impossible. However, it maintained that there were plenty of allotments still untended and that Young People's Onion Clubs could be established there. The Wisbech Onion Club, which was affiliated to the Wisbech Allotment Holders' Association, set out to raise 5 tons of onions. They issued a challenge to neighbouring boroughs of a similar size to match their target. All profits and finances raised from the venture were to be ploughed into the Red Cross Agriculture Fund.

Since the beginning of the war the National Allotment Society had enrolled more than 1,200 new allotment associations. The main purpose of the associations was to undertake the co-operative renting of land and the purchase of tools, fertilisers and seed at wholesale prices for their members. In Greater London alone 100,000 new allotments were prepared, which was considered to be a major achievement by citizens. The average value of produce, at retail prices for autumn 1941, worked out at £12 per plot. There was considerable variation, depending on the size of the allotments and amenities such as glasshouses, which greatly increased yields.

In 1943 the National Allotment Society strongly recommended to the Ministry of Agriculture that the price of potatoes needed to be regulated in order to prevent future despondency among the plot-holders and Victory Diggers. Many unscrupulous dealers often sold off sub-standard seed to plot-holders, and attempts were made to stamp out this contemptible trade.

Theft from allotments in wartime was dealt with in a stern fashion. When plot-holder William Lansdown of Bath stole vegetables worth 1 shilling from a neighbouring tenant he was condemned to one month's hard labour. Peter Hulme, a miner from Tyldesley, was sentenced to seven days detention at Leigh, Lancashire, for stealing two cabbages and eight onions from an allotment site. Sir Harry Speakman stated that the bench regarded such activity in wartime to be little better than common looting.

It was not only the menfolk who undertook to pilfering from allotments. In 1942, when Mrs Cicely Graham was apprehended on an allotment site, she was found to be carrying a basket full of onions, tomatoes, carrots, parsley and other vegetables, which included a bag of apples and pears. A little girl of infant years, clutching a bag of tomatoes, accompanied her. At Marylebone Police Court, Mrs Graham was fined £10. Her plea to the bench was that she thought the site was common land.

By 1943 an increasing number of people were noted trespassing on allotments with the intention of pilfering produce, and it was a trend that continued to rise in many regions. The Government passed a new Trespass Order, which came into force on 20 May, and after that date any person found trespassing on an allotment was liable to a fine of £50. The Government was determined to protect the nation's Victory Diggers from theft and damage to their crops and fully recognised the anguish of tenants who had devoted much time and effort in cultivating plots under difficult conditions on uncompromising ground. In one instance, an East London man was fined £20 by a Stratford magistrate for stealing one onion worth 2d, and a further 10 shillings for trespassing on the allotment.

In August 1944 members of the Billacombe & District Allotment Association complained bitterly about recurring thefts from their allotment gardens and raised the question of insuring against such events. R. J. Walsh, Assistant Horticultural Officer for the Devon War Agricultural Executive Committee, noted that a plot could produce foodstuff to the value of £20-£30 annually, which was the sum that the plot-holder would have to insure for, and since the majority of plots were open to the public the premium would have to be around 10 shillings in the pound.

One group of allotment-holders in Hull went a stage further to protect their sites and formed a vigilante society, which became known as the Newland (Hull) Allotments Protection Association. It was calculated that plants and tools to the value of £300 had been stolen; the Association Secretary had his shed and greenhouse broken into and substantial damage was caused. The aim was to wage war on the pilferer, and the society built a special hut on its 24-acre site and received a grant from the Corporation's Allotments Committee to use the building as a nightly rendezvous and social club. Following the formation of the vigilante group, together with much publicity, losses and damage were vastly reduced.

The new Trespass Order on allotments did not go down well with the Ramblers' Association. Mr L. Morris, spokesman for the Association, openly denied requesting an annulment of the Order; the ramblers claimed to be sympathetic toward the plot-holders and said they wished to avoid damage on allotments. Mr Thomas Levy MP pointed out that the damage needed to be proven before legal proceedings could begin. There was considerable opposition from gardeners when Mr Levy attempted to have the Trespass Order amended.

As in the First World War the railway companies were very accommodating with the provision of allotments both for their own employees and for workers from other professions. In 1943 alone food crops to the value of £200,000 were raised on lineside plots belonging to the London, Midland & Scottish railway company; this figure was the highest on record, and women employees rendered an invaluable service in this effort. One statistician stated that if all the railway plots across the country had been placed end to end they would have reached from London to Dumfries. In order to increase production the LMS decided to let plots on railway land to members of the public; particulars were available from the nearest station master.

Other patriotic gardeners helped to make life more tolerable for those with little time to spend on allotments. Victory Diggers at Yarmouth supplied more than 12½ tons of fresh vegetables to minesweeper crews through the Women's Voluntary Service, who organised the distribution. The WVS encouraged gardeners with vegetable plots living near ports to participate in the scheme; Grimsby and Plymouth were the main ports concerned, and the latter had no fewer than 110 collection points. Empty hampers were dispatched to the gardeners and, when filled with vegetables, were collected and taken to the WVS hut, which was usually located on the quayside. The crews of the minesweepers and other craft then obtained two or three days' supply of fresh vegetables. Occasionally a placard bearing the name and address of the donor was placed inside, which added that personal touch.

In February 1943 it was estimated that 4 million families were growing their own vegetables. The output from British soil amounted to more than 70%, which was well over the pre-war level. Potato cultivation increased to 80.4% and vegetables by 55.1%. The overall number of allotments across the UK (excluding domestic gardens) amounted to 1,750,000. It was calculated than an additional 3,500,000 food plots were located in domestic gardens, though the figure may well have fallen short of the actual amount. The entire volume of spadework conducted on cultivated sites was three times the surface area of the Isle of Wight. During the course of the war the total volume of produce raised by newcomers to plots was estimated to amount to more than 3 million tons.

'Food growing is not a job for the lazy man', declared the Duke of Norfolk at the presentation of the Bledisloe Cup to Yiewsley & West Drayton Council, Middlesex, for their outstanding effort in the 'Dig for Victory' campaign. He added that in this fifth year of war, the national demands made on the cultivators of gardens and allotments had become so heavy that it had become increasingly difficult to find the time to carry on with food production. The Duke (Joint Parliamentary Under-Secretary to the Ministry of Agriculture) told the Middlesex diggers:

'This is your part in the grand strategic plan. Even when the war on land, sea and in the air is won, the food situation will not be any easier for some time to come. Starving Europe will have to be fed and heavy demands will have to be made on all available transport.' (*Gardeners' Chronicle*, 1944)

The Duke added that although it was difficult for diggers to find the time, there should be no relaxing of the effort. He said it was important to maintain the physical standard and staying power at the highest pitch and that a continual supply of fresh greens was necessary to enable everyone to carry out their daily tasks under trying circumstances. The Duke rounded off by emphasising the need for planning to ensure a supply of green vegetables throughout the following winter, at a time when they were most needed.

In July 1944 a number of Kentish allotment holders were warned by the Ministry that if they grew too many flowers on their plots they could be dispossessed of their allotments. Eighteen months previously the Ministry of Agriculture had clearly stipulated that the primary purpose of an allotment garden was to grow food. The Ministry raised little objection to a token display of colourful blooms for the home, but local councils were given explicit instructions to take a firm line with tenants who cultivated flowers in quantity for sale in shops or markets. The penalty for engaging in such ventures resulted in forfeiture of their allotment. Mr Hudson was adamant that on no account were plot-holders to slacken their effort in food production. Mr Hudson stressed that flowers need not be completely banished from the garden or plots, for the Government recognised that in the austere wartime days flowers provided a ray of splendour in an otherwise drab existence. However, commercial flower-growers were only allowed to devote a small part of their plots to flowers.

Harrogate Town Council had long deliberated on the question of growing food or flowers. One Alderman said that the town had become a very dismal place during the war and suggested that a few flowers could be grown in the centre of town. By stark contrast another Town Councillor said that

Harrogate's shabbiness was a great credit to the townsfolk and something that local Victory Diggers should be proud of. He said Harrogate was 100% behind the 'Dig for Victory' campaign. Vegetables were even cultivated upon Harrogate's famous open space, The Stray, and one Town Councillor said it would be a terrible mistake to divert attention from growing food to flowers. In the previous year Victory Diggers in Harrogate had produced more than 420 tons of vegetable produce from 107 acres of land. This included 150 tons of potatoes, nearly 120 tons of sugar beet and more than 10 tons of tomatoes, which in total was valued at £1,800.

By March 1944 the Ministry of Agriculture came to realise that there was little chance of establishing new allotments or converting further domestic gardens to vegetable cultivation. Instead it turned its attention to ensuring that the existing army of Victory Diggers carried on to become more efficient. In 1944 an inspector from the Ministry of Agriculture noted that a considerable number of allotments were beginning to show a distinct deficiency of fertiliser; lack of manure was still a major headache. The composting of waste vegetation was not a widespread activity among plot-holders, even though the Ministry had given much publicity to the need to make compost. Having surveyed numerous Boroughs, one Ministry official stated that a good compost heap was as rare as a snowflake in summer.

The Ministry suggested that plot-holders should write to their local councils enquiring as to when the roadside verges were to be cut and so obtain supplies of grass cuttings, which could be added to the compost heap. It was even proposed that plot-holders in desperate need of composting material should cut the verges themselves and save the council much time and effort. At Weston-super-Mare, Mr G. Coles, who organised the town's demonstration plot, maintained that seaweed from the beach was ideal for compost if left to rot when spread over the ground. Gardeners along the coast in Devon also used seaweed for their potato grounds.

By 1945 thousands of allotments were located within London's parks and open spaces, and a commission from the National Allotment Society was awaiting the outcome of a decision on the future of allotments within the parks. Lord Latham, Leader of the LCC and Chairman of the Parks Committee, expressed great admiration and understanding of the problems faced by allotment tenants and in no uncertain way expressed every desire to help. The National Allotment Society received the promised letter regarding the future outlook for allotments. Plot-holders were told that should war terminate before 31 December 1945 they would not be disturbed before that date, but were warned that there would be no renewals afterwards. The National Allotments Society was happy with the result, as most of the park allotments were half-size (5 rods).

In January 1945 the Ministry of Agriculture released a new series of 'Allotment and Garden Guides' as part of the 'Dig for Victory' campaign. These eight-page pamphlets were more informative than the earlier leaflets, with elaborate diagrams and explanations of gardening techniques.

'In this new series of monthly "Guides" we are out to help you get better results from your vegetable plot and your fruit garden. Every month we shall try to do three things: first we shall remind you of things that ought to have been done, but may not have been possible because of the weather or for some other reason; secondly, we shall deal with gardening operations for the month; thirdly, we shall look ahead a month or two and remind you of what you need to do in readiness.' (*Allotment & Garden Guide*, Ministry of Agriculture, 1945)

At the beginning of 1945 the Minister of Agriculture expressed his deep appreciation for local authorities' efforts to stimulate food cultivation during wartime. The Minister also made it explicitly clear that there could be no relaxation in growing food, for the situation in 1945 was expected to remain difficult, whatever the course of the war. The demand for food was predicted to be as great as ever, and events in the previous year ensured that the need for allotments would remain. In 1944 agriculture suffered a major shortage of labour due to the war effort and thousands of tons of commercially grown vegetables, including main crop potatoes, could not be lifted. While farmers gave priority to harvesting cereals and sugar beet, the potatoes and other vegetables were left to rot in the fields.

Towards the end of the war the National Allotment Society anticipated a huge demand for allotments during the immediate post-war years, since many men who had served in the army and the RAF had developed a taste for gardening. Womenfolk had also come to appreciate the benefits of allotment gardening. The Federation of Women's Institutes set up more than 300 stalls in various villages and small towns to enable women gardeners to sell their surplus garden produce favourably. The Federation maintained that such sales made women gardeners realise the importance of rotational cropping to iron out over-supply and deficiencies.

During the last few weeks of the war many critics stated that the motto 'Dig for Victory' was becoming worn out and that a new slogan was required. There were many suggestions, such as 'Plant for Peace', 'Sow for Security' and 'Dig for Peace now Victory's nigh'. One northern gardener suggested 'Grow for Brighter Days'. Not one of the new slogans had quite the same ring, so the Ministry of Agriculture decided to stick with 'Dig for Victory'.

On 7 May 1945 Germany surrendered to the Allied forces. While Europe basked in triumph over the banishment of Nazism, the Victory Diggers continued with their battle to cultivate the land, unsure of the future for their allotments. In the June 'Guide' readers were informed:

'The Minister of Food has told us that this will be the tightest of the war years so far as food supplies are concerned, so readers of this guide, who are undoubtedly the "wise virgins" of the parable, will be patting themselves on the back that they did not rest on their spades, but continued to "Dig for Victory", not only victory in the fighting war but victory in the economic struggle for existence that will be the aftermath of war.' (*Allotment & Garden Guide*, Ministry of Agriculture, 1945)

By July 1945 there were reported outbreaks of potato blight due to the excessively wet weather, and the Ministry stated that the only safeguard was in spraying. In most parts of the country only the main crop varieties were at risk as the early varieties had been harvested before the disease became prevalent. The Ministry's 'Dig for Victory' leaflet No 17 explained how to utilise sprays against blight. So the nation's Victory Diggers continued to garden for King and Country, not to mention the family.

In December 1945 the Ministry issued the very last edition of the 'Allotment & Garden Guides' and urged gardeners to keep their copies as they would not be re-issued in 1946. In this publication the Ministry summed up the bad season endured by the Victory Diggers:

'The weather is always with us to grouse about, and 1945 was on the whole a pretty poor year. In the first place we got off to a bad start. The Januarys of 1940 and 1945 were the coldest of the last half century, and those of us who were putting off doing things before Christmas were less inclined to do anything for a long time afterwards. The beginning of the year's offensive was far too long delayed on many allotments with the result that the "diggers" were forever trying to catch up on jobs to be done and seldom succeeded, and the soil lacked the weathering influence that benefits the land during winter.

Too much rain, not enough sun – that was 1945. Tomatoes loomed large in the minds of most of our gardeners. They were late in most places owing to the lack of ripening sun, and numerous were the enquiries for hints on speeding up ripening. Some people had trouble with their runners: the flowers would not set. In built-up areas there were no bees to do the job of pollination and some allotment-holders were unable to give the flowers the fine misty spraying that could have helped. Or it may have been that watering, where possible, was irregular and the land dried out too quickly, which was a trouble on the Ministry's own demonstration allotments in Hyde Park. On some plots marrows suddenly died off and there was little that could be done about that.' (Allotment & Garden Guide, Ministry of Agriculture, 1945)

As the clouds of war cleared a new sinister shadow crept over the allotments. A growing number of councils, both local and metropolitan, began to seize emergency allotment land for building purposes, for sport fields and development schemes. In many cases the plot-holders were not provided with alternative sites. While the future of many wartime allotments remained uncertain, the nation entered into a new peacetime era of chronic shortages, bleak austerity and economic gloom.

9
Austerity to leisure gardens

A s peace settled over the land once again, the sense of urgency attached to allotment gardening quickly evaporated, and as a result the 'Dig for Victory' campaign disintegrated. Thousands of wartime gardeners rapidly lost interest in cultivation and relegated their spades to the garden shed. By 1947 half a million wartime allotments had simply vanished, almost overnight, as many sites were reclaimed for their previous use. No strategy was implemented to reverse the trend. Whereas the 'Great War' had fuelled a healthy desire for allotments, the conclusion of the 'Dig for Victory' campaign curtailed it. The greatest majority of citizens had been patriotic during the war and their reward was a wearisome continuation of crippling shortages, and drab austerity.

The food shortages were prolonged by excessively cold weather in the winter of 1946-47. After weeks of heavy snow and hard frost, a sudden thaw in March 1947 brought severe flooding to many parts of the country. Thousands of tons of potatoes in clamp, together with vegetables such as spring cabbages, Brussels sprouts and kales, were destroyed. While destitution prevailed, the Ministry of Agriculture warned that the shortages would last well into June. The situation was so bad that potatoes were placed on the ration books. The following year housewives were still queuing up at the greengrocers for their weekly allowance of 3lb per person.

The Ministry of Agriculture still continued to advise plot-holders to plan their cropping to ensure a continuous supply of vegetables, and usually insisted that three rows of early potatoes and six rows of main-crop varieties were sufficient, together with space for early vegetables. In 1948, due to the potato shortage, the Ministry advocated the cultivation of extra potatoes on land usually reserved for parsnips and carrots, which could be transferred to space allocated for summer crops. The Ministry also pointed out that in regions infected with eelworm, potato crops should not be extended.

Fortunately, wartime gardening created a core of serious enthusiasts who stoutly refused to give up their allotments:

'In the immediate post-war years there was still tremendous interest in growing vegetables, among serious gardeners, that is, due to the continued rationing and shortages. Most of the gardeners were senior age groups,

179

usually people between 45 and 60, who found health-giving activity and great pleasure while cultivating vegetables during the war and they wanted, often pleaded, to be able to continue gardening. It was still tremendously rewarding to obtain bumper crops of peas, carrots and potatoes.' (Recollections of a post-war plot-holder, author's interview)

During the late 1940s it became the Government's priority to keep down imports for the sake of the national economy, and emphasised the importance of allotment cultivation. The Minister of Agriculture stated that the need to grow vegetables was still as great as it was during the worst days of the war. He said that there should be no slackening of effort in growing vegetables, especially in the light of the recent devastation caused by the flooding.

In 1947 the National Allotment Society became the National Allotment & Garden Society (NAGS) in order to foster a more up-market image, and it became the main organisation representing the Allotment Movement in England and Wales during the post-war years. In 1949 there were around 296,098 members, but 20 years later membership had dwindled to around 170,000, which coincided with a rapid drop in the number of allotments. By this time Tom Williams had taken over as Minister of Agriculture and he was anxious to redress the imbalance in allotment cultivation. He said that it was in the national interest to delay the restoration of emergency allotments to their former use as recreation grounds or otherwise.

Many of the wartime allotment sites were given extensions, while others were not. Even though the Government insisted that vegetable cultivation was vital to the nation's economy, they provided little in the way of material support for the plot-holders. Tenants often had to fight very hard to keep their allotment gardens. In one example, the approval of the Ministry of Agriculture was sought by Fulham's allotment-holders in order to retain their plots on Hurlingham Polo Club's No 1 ground for another two years, due to the food shortages. Permission was granted but subject to re-assessment when the extension period expired. Plot-holders at Eastbrook Allotments lodged a complaint to Portslade Urban District Council during the same period. The Council had consented to allow the Central Electricity Board to acquire the land for the construction of a power station. Accusations were made at the meeting of the Allotments Committee that no vote had been taken and that the Portslade UDC had issued notices for the plot-holders to vacate their site before permission from the Ministry had been obtained. If the Council was not prepared to negotiate, the site would be compulsorily acquired. Around 80 allotment holders would have been displaced and would have had to find alternative land.

In the immediate post-war years, the Borough of Croydon had its ups and downs with allotment issues. In February 1947 Norwood Grove Allotment Association toyed with the idea of acquiring a mechanical cultivator for use by the plot-holders. Mr W. H. R. Green, who conceived the idea, stated that a 10-rod plot could be turned over in the space of one Saturday afternoon and save the gardener from losing interest in his plot. He hoped that the Croydon Federation of Allotment Holders might assist with the purchase of such a machine, but, failing that, the Norwood Grove Allotment Association would buy one themselves. Another suggestion that found favour among the plot-holders was the cultivation of flowers, especially sweet-peas, which could help to cover up the rusty tin cans and old baths. In spite of such plans, Croydon's Mayor, Alderman Harry Regan, insisted that the question of cultivating food was just as important as it was during the war. At the annual meeting of the Croydon & District Federation of Allotment Societies, the national organiser, Mr S. J. Merreil, said that if they could influence young men returning from the forces to take an interest in allotment cultivation, they would be doing a great thing.

On 31 May 1947 Tom Williams arrived in Croydon to open a new model allotment on the outskirts of town (not far from the sewage farm). He was greeted by Alderman Stacey, Councillor Todd and the Mayor, Alderman Harry Regan. The 10-acre site was neatly divided into plots that could accommodate 160 tenants. This site had 9-foot-wide concrete paths, and was surrounded by 2,800 feet of 5-foot-high chain-link fencing to provide adequate protection. A central concrete pavilion comprised a spacious trading room complete with fertiliser bins, a committee and rest room, a kitchen in which to prepare light refreshments, and toilet facilities. Eight groups of concrete cubicles in which tools could be stored were placed within easy reach of the plots, each with a water tank attached. Some 3,000 feet of water piping lay below the ground. There was also a section for rubbish as well as two modern incinerators.

Alderman Stacey hoped to extend the scheme and supply the Borough's 2,500 holders with permanent plots, and that allotments would eventually be placed in the same category as parks, municipal swimming baths and libraries. However, allotments were only permanent until someone else wanted the land for development.

Mr Williams described the model allotment site as the epitome of all that plots should be:

'Permanent plots in adequate numbers are the best thing the Movement can have and the initiative shown by Croydon in laying stress on tidiness is most commendable. There is no need for allotments to be unpleasing to the eye.'
(*Croydon Advertiser*, 1947)

Mr Williams said that the opening day should be one of profound satisfaction for Alderman Stacey. Sadly, the ground proved to be unfit for cultivation and, sandwiched between affluent housing and light industry, the allotments never really caught on. By the middle of the following decade the allotments had all but disappeared.

While plans were made to expand the Movement in the Borough, more than 50 holders had been displaced from their allotments at New Addington to make way for a housing project, and were to be allocated a new site.

Alderman Stacey said that he had attempted to visit the new site but was unable to continue due to the heavy snowfall.

At the seventh annual show of the New Addington Horticultural Society, it was noted that the produce was not up to the usual standard of previous years. Gardeners blamed not only the unusually dry season but also Croydon Council. Alderman Stacey, Chairman of the Parks & Smallholdings Committee, expressed regret that the ground had proved unsatisfactory for the plot-holders and promised that his Committee would do everything in their power to put matters right. He had hoped that the ground would be excellent and that the new allotments would become a permanent feature. However, Mr George Crackel, the Society's President, said that although the soil in the region was not very good, the Council had given the plot-holders the worst area.

In October 1947 Alderman Stacey and his colleagues came under heavy criticism from the angry Addington plot-holders, who found the new area at Castle Hill to be quite unsuitable for cultivation. At a meeting between the Allotment Federation and Croydon Council (held at Addington) the plot-holders said that the ground had not been properly tested, that there was not more than 8 inches of topsoil overlying the chalk bedrock, and that Croydon Council had simply ignored their interests. The tenants stressed that they had invested much time, money and energy, but the plots had yield no food whatsoever. Some of the plot-holders had even dubbed the 10-acre field 'Starvation Meadows'. When Mr G. Whitting implied that there was evidence that the plot-holders were not cultivating their land properly and that no work of any kind had been done for many weeks, disorder broke out and the Addingtonians were forced to leave. Mr S. M. Harlow, Chairman of the Croydon Allotments Society Federation, claimed that the plot-holders had abused the officials of the Federation.

Meanwhile, Spa Hill Allotment Society in nearby Thornton Heath faced the prospect of losing 2 acres of its allotment land for the development of an infants school. At the Society's annual meeting, Mr H. W. Rose said that every effort was being made to oppose the Education Committee's plans. Mr A. Mitchell, of the Education Committee, maintained that the new school could be built on the Lawns Estate, thus saving the allotments. However, Mr J. M. Allen argued that the children would then have to walk to the top of Spa Hill. He considered it essential that the new school should be as near as possible to the Ingram Road School and pointed out that Spa Hill Allotment Society would be compensated by a slightly larger area on the Lawns Estate. Mr Allen added that every scrap of vacant land in the Borough should be cultivated in view of the devastation brought on by the flooding. Spa Hill's Allotment Secretary, Mr R. W. Slatter, said that membership had increased by 43 and that the trading results were well above the previous year.

In 1948 Tom Williams made a dramatic plea to delegates at the annual conference of the National Allotment & Garden Society and stated that they were digging for food, their lives, dollars and self-respect. His speech may well have fallen on deaf ears.

'The greatest majority of people were tired of "Digging for Victory", or anything else for that matter. Allotments had come to symbolise wartime and depression when the cultivation of "spuds" and "greens" was vital to keep body and soul together. Plot-holders were also discouraged by the constant gnawing away of allotment land for development schemes.' (Personal communication with the author)

Lack of a centralised and cohesive allotments policy led to total confusion, and the demise of interest resulted in the collapse of the new 'Dig for Plenty' campaign. Some individuals took note of the muddle surrounding the provision and maintenance of allotments. In January 1948 Mr C. W. Whately of Wroughton, Swindon, stated that it was quite illogical that acres of rural allotments should lie idle during a serious potato shortage. The underlying cause was largely due to the Parish Council's lack of funds to tackle the problem. George W. Giles, Secretary of NAGS, drew attention to the scarcity of allotment sites in regions where land was readily available. He pointed out that local authorities could still exercise their far-reaching powers under existing legislation to obtain more land for use as allotments. He suggested that funds for the purchase of allotments could be obtained from the Public Works Loan Commissioners, but the Ministry of Agriculture preferred to adopt the more permanent but slower method.

Many local authorities dragged their heels over the matter of allotments and preferred to allow temporary wartime sites to revert to their previous use. While the Minister of Agriculture insisted that it was still imperative to produce food on the highest possible level, numerous local councils, including the LCC, ignored this request and thought it was more important to have open space for recreation and walking. Of the 14,000 wartime allotments situated in London County Council Parks, only 3,000 remained in 1951. Their utilisation was due to expire by December and all land held for use as allotments in the Royal Parks had been reclaimed the previous year. The Commons, Open Spaces & Footpaths Preservation Society was overjoyed that recreational land taken for allotments was being restored to its former use. NAGS attached less importance to growing food, and placed more concern on the supply of allotment land, especially to the elderly, who found health and happiness while cultivating their urban plots. By the spring of 1951 safeguard of tenancy lay at the very heart of the allotment issue. Although wartime plots were regarded as a great success in their own right, many people felt that more should be done to provide permanent plots in peacetime. Numerous allotment associations insisted that secure tenancy would give the gardener incentive to develop their plots on a long-term basis, which would result in the erection of glasshouses, and the planting of fruit trees or bushes.

At a riverside site in Airedale, West Yorkshire, the benefits of enduring tenancy were very apparent, as tenants had mature fruit trees and glasshouses containing vines that must have been 50 years old. On this noted site, continuing generations of gardeners had built up an affiliation with the soil. The well-established allotments also had ornate summerhouses, where tea and cake were taken, little lawns graced with flower borders at the forecourt of presentable sheds, and a reliable hand pump from a deep-sunk pipe to irrigate the land in times of drought. This indeed was a fertile locality, for the tenants, like their crops, had roots that ran deep.

It was hoped that the Town & Country Planning Act of 1947 might stimulate not only playing-fields for the younger age groups, but also address the needs of energetic older generations, who wanted to 'grow it' themselves. In many urban areas there were long waiting lists for permanent plots, while scores of temporary sites lay abandoned. Mr A. C. Richmond, Chairman of the Land Settlement Association, endorsed the need to obtain secure tenancy but pointed out that the unpopularity of allotment sites was partially due to their unsightliness. He noted that in Holland ugly allotment sites had been replaced with carefully planned gardens, fully provisioned with amenities such as playgrounds for children, canteens and recreation rooms, and saw no reason why such schemes should not be implemented in Britain. Mr Richmond insisted that with due consideration and the planting of fruit trees and shrubs, allotments for the raising of pigs and poultry should not be displeasing to nearby communities. He stated that such work had already been carried out on many of the LSA's own holdings, which were solely devoted to the rearing of livestock.

A year on and warnings of food shortages still made the headlines. George W. Giles, General Secretary of NAGS, stressed that more should be done to grow food. During 1942-43 allotment gardeners had raised a staggering 995,000 tons of food, yet by 1948 this figure had dropped to 619,000 tons, and the downward trend continued. Mr Giles estimated that an all-out drive could result in the production of 500,000 tons of food. But he also stated that it was not simply a question of obtaining more allotment land, but fully utilising existing sites. He thought that the excuse of insecure tenancy was no longer viable, and that a normal 10-rod plot (300-odd square yards) could provide enough vegetable produce for a small family for most of the year.

In February 1952 Mr Giles wrote to *The Times* and stated:

'I cannot understand why so many able bodied men do not exercise their statutory right and obtain an allotment. A well-worked 10-rod allotment could produce £20 worth of food annually, based on the current retail prices. The value of an allotment is increased where pigs, poultry or rabbits are kept because they convert waste vegetation into good wholesome food. The National Allotment & Garden Society have a scheme where old-age pensioners, the disabled, the blind, widows and the unemployed can, thanks to charitable support from the public, obtain gardening necessities at reduced rates and so gain the full benefit from their allotments. There is simply no reason why people should not start growing their own food and so help to alleviate some of the pressure from the nation's overwrought economy.'

On 14 May 1948 the Allotments Advisory Committee (AAC) was asked to formulate a report to consider and make recommendations with regard to the provision of allotments. The Committee included representatives from NAGS, the Country Landowners Association, and the Local Authorities Association. George Brown MP, joint Parliamentary Secretary to the Ministry, chaired the Committee. Its report was published in January 1950, and formed the basis for the 1950 Allotment Act.

'The AAC suggest that the provision of 4 acres of land per 1,000 citizens as a general target for allotment land. The ACC realise, of course, that in many regions that figure will be unrealistic, but, a number of "allotment minded" local authorities have provided land exceeding the recommended figure above and the sites are fully tenanted.' (Report of the Allotment Advisory Committee, Ministry of Agriculture, 1950, p5)

The Allotment Advisory Committee thought that local authorities should fully uphold the supply of allotment land where there was a demand. The AAC also wanted allotments to be re-classified in order to eliminate the possibility of continual disturbance in the form of reclamation.

The AAC recognised that there were three kinds of allotment that needed assessing differently. Permanent land acquired by a local authority under statutes was considered to be adequately protected under existing legislation. On temporary land requisitioned under the defence regulations, the AAC maintained that it was best for plot-holders to be relocated to alternative sites as soon as possible. The AAC maintained that wartime plots should be relinquished even if alternative sites were not found, as the compensation rate was often out of context with the rental value. The AAC still hoped that the Ministry of Agriculture would ensure tenants were found alternative sites.

Allotments on private land let to the local authority, allotment association or individuals were often the cause of much contention. The AAC noted that on a number of occasions the tenants got their land in good condition, only to discover that the owner has served notice to quit and subsequently re-let the land to a farmer or market gardener. Thus, the tenant lost not only his plot but also compensation for residual manures.

'The Committee suggests that it should be made illegal for plot-holders to be dispossessed in this way on non-statutory allotment sites. However, the AAC also realises that a complete ban on such activity will not work. The AAC understands the need for building and for new sports grounds. In theory, no allotment land is supposed to be taken without consent from the Ministry of Agriculture. Since this is not the case, the Committee cannot support the conversion of allotment land under private management for use as a market garden or for agricultural purposes.' (Report of the Allotment Advisory Committee, Ministry of Agriculture, 1950, p7)

The AAC noted that most councils largely ignored the matter of rating on allotment association huts used for storing, raising and distributing of crops, and thought that this was the right attitude to take. In a number of cases, though, local authorities insisted on rating huts, whether they were used just for storage or otherwise. Problems also arose where the communal hut was not actually on allotment land but adjacent to it. The Committee stated that communal huts should only be used for storage and for allotment matters, and if utilised for other social events they would be liable for rating, even if they were currently exempt. The AAC maintained that communal huts should be classed in the same category as a church hall. Rating also varied on greenhouses, poultry holdings and pig holdings, which the AAC thought should be excused from any rates.

'It was suggested that the AAC consider preparatory plans for a series of "standardised" types of buildings and greenhouses for construction on allotments, with a notion of getting them approved by the Ministry of Town and Planning, so that plot-holders would avoid unnecessary expense in putting forward individual proposals. The Committee fully backed this suggestion, which would enhance the tidiness of many sites.' (Report of the Allotment Advisory Committee, Ministry of Agriculture, 1950 p13)

The Land Settlement Association said that there was a great desire among townsfolk to keep small livestock. The AAC recognised the grave possibility of the spread of disease through such schemes, if there was no authorised or proper control, and that closer liaison between the National Farmers Union and Town & Country organisations was needed. The kind of holding the LSA wanted to see extended was on plots not bigger than a quarter of an acre in groups on not less than 2-3 acres with half a dozen devoted to gardens and half a dozen for livestock. The AAC implied that a miner might be able to manage a holding of this size but it would be quite unsuitable for the industrial or factory worker operating on a shift system. Easy access to the site was vital, and if the occupier in full-time employment and his holding were more than a quarter of a mile away from home there would be a great danger that the stock would become neglected and the general appearance of the holding become an eyesore.

The Committee also recommended that group holdings should be fostered by local authorities, providing the individual plots were not more than a quarter of an acre, and in effect make them allotment gardens. The AAC insisted that equilibrium between group holdings and 10-rod allotments was required so as not to prejudice vegetable cultivation in favour of large holdings for the keeping of livestock.

The Allotment Act of 1950 was the last major legislation pertaining to allotments, and was aimed at improving the security of tenure for plot-holders. Under Section 1 of the Act, the period of notice to vacate was extended to 12 months, which had to expire during the winter months. Sections 2-6 dealt with the amount of compensation a plot-holder should receive, according to the season in which his tenancy expired. Plot-holders that allowed their plots to deteriorate were liable to pay compensation for dilapidation on quitting. Local authorities were only obliged to provide 'Allotment Gardens', thus making 'Farm Allotments' non-statutory. Section 10 of the Act amended the rent collection system and local authorities were given jurisdiction to charge such rent 'as a tenant may reasonably be expected to pay for the land'. Local authorities could also charge lower rents if they were satisfied that a holder's circumstances warranted such a reduction. Section 12 of the Act permitted the keeping of small livestock (poultry and rabbits) on allotments, though this was often restricted by local by-laws.

By the mid-1950s the majority of citizens were earning more money than ever before, food was cheaper and more plentiful, and new leisure activities made allotment cultivation less appealing. Between 1950 and 1964 the number of allotments slumped from 1,100,000 to 729,013. Many local councils and town planners began to see allotments as an unrelenting hindrance to town development schemes, while others made a half-hearted attempt to encourage allotment gardening by maintaining the fencing, pathways and laying on basic facilities such as a water supply and installing huts. Under the 1950 Allotment Act, local councils were obliged to provide 4 acres of land per thousand citizens (as recommended by the AAC), but the scheme was never fully implemented. By 1960 the actual figure amounted to 67,804 acres, roughly equivalent to 1 acre per thousand citizens. By the mid-1960s almost 20% of allotment sites were derelict and had run to grass.

In order to drum up support for allotments, NAGS stated that cultivation of a plot was more justifiable and of greater benefit to a larger number of people than any other form of recreation. In 1951 W. J. Gibson stated in his book *The Right to Dig* that an allotment could accommodate more gardeners, as opposed to a sports facility that would be used by a handful of people at any one time. He compared the amount of land required for certain recreations against allotment gardening: for instance, a golf course of 50

A 1950s plot-holder.

In the 1950s, long before environmental awareness,
allotment tenants lit bonfires at any time of day.

acres could be used by 60 people at any one time, averaging 1.20 persons per acre. Cricket took up 3 acres (without the cow), with 13 people using the ground, averaging 4.33 persons per acre. Football required 1⅛ acres and enabled 22 people to play, averaging 19.55 persons per acre. Allotment gardening on a 2-acre site enabled 81 people to occupy a site at one time, averaging 40.50 persons per acre. NAGS realised of course that the way to raise awareness of allotment cultivation was to gain wider publicity. In 1966 the society took a stand at the Chelsea Flower Show to illustrate an allotment garden, though it was mainly composed of flowerbeds and a lawn with a small vegetable plot tucked away in a corner.

During the 1950s the Allotments Advisory Committee still made continual references to 'The Ordinary Vegetable Allotment', which induced plot-holders to avoid cultivating flowers. Legislation was unclear on the subject, and many tenants believed that they would be breaking the law by growing flowers on their allotments. However, in the 1960s the domestic garden was often regarded as complimentary to the allotment. For every five plot-holders, only one lacked a domestic garden of any kind.

'There was a feeling among plot-holders that the growing of flowers on an allotment was a bit stupid, since flowers could be grown in one's own back garden. The point of having a plot was to grow vegetables and some fruit, strawberries, currants and gooseberries, that is. Mind you, the odd patch for sweet-peas wasn't out of the norm 'cos they needed training up poles and wires but they were usually grown for the horticultural shows.' (Personal communication with the author)

By the early 1960s roughly 3% of plot-holders were women and nearly 2% were housewives. Women preferred domestic gardens, since they were fonder of cultivating flowers. Women were also more fastidious, and they found the derelict condition of many allotment sites rather off-putting. On tidier allotments, where a sense of communal vitality flourished, women tended to be more in evidence.

Around 80% of plot-holders lived in urban areas, yet most had some kind of rural childhood, which greatly influenced the decision to take up an allotment garden. More than 50% had parents that had been allotment gardeners. Almost 72% who had been born in rural areas also had parents that were allotment gardeners. Some 22.3% of pensioners said that the allotment was a hobby.

In fact, the allotment often enabled the elderly to overcome the boredom of retirement, especially for active individuals, and where pensioners met on a daily basis a sense of comradeship developed. Other gardeners insisted

A 1960s plot-holder.

that the allotment provided an escape from the pressures and mental strain of modern living. One tenant stated:

> 'A trip to the allotment simply washed away all the tensions of the day; even if there was nothing that needed to be done, one could always just potter about, do a little weeding, which never goes away, or possibly have a bonfire or something. Gardening provides a tremendous boost to my morale and even after only 20 minutes or so I feel calm and relaxed again.' (Personal communication with the author)

During the mid-1960s the allotment still made a considerable saving in the weekly budget of working-class families, for supermarkets were few and those that did exist certainly did not cater for fresh vegetables and fruit. The value of allotment produce roughly amounted to £25 per annum, or 10 shillings a week, depending on how well the land was cultivated. In urban districts 57% of plot-holders in England and Wales were earning more than £16 per week, while the others secured a pay packet of £12-£16 per week. Yet the value of produce raised was not the main incentive for working allotments. The majority of plot-holders stated that they regarded the upkeep of an allotment as a cheap, keep-fit hobby.

A 1960s allotment garden.

'There's nothing like a sunny Saturday afternoon on the plot, fresh air and a bit of exercise. Beats going to the football match any day, though I do enjoy watching our local cricket team play. Then of course one has an end product, wonderful fresh veg that is better than the stuff from the greengrocers. I can pick my own parsnips Sunday morning and they can be on my dinner plate at lunchtime – can't get any fresher than that!' (Personal communication with the author)

Some tenants often utilised their plots for seemingly bizarre purposes, and growing vegetables was not always the primary reason for taking tenancy of an allotment. A number of tenants said their plot was a place for drying the washing (during summer at least!), as a place for sitting out, or as a safe place where their children could play.

On average a plot-holder would spend up to 10 hours a week on his plot during spring, making around four visits lasting up to 2½ hours. In summer, as the growing season progressed, the number of hours per week rose to 12½, with five trips of 2-2½ hours. During the autumn the figure dropped, especially after harvesting, to about 8 hours per week with four trips of 2 hours. Few plot-holders had a desire to tend their plots in foul, wet weather. During winter they usually only made one trip a week, lasting for 2-3 hours.

Although the greatest majority of plot-holders received little help from their families, a few treated the allotment as a substitute day out. Sunday was extremely popular for this activity and some families made a day of it, where the mum would bring along sandwiches and a flask of tea. This was generally only a summertime event, especially during the fruit-picking season. Throughout the early 1960s soft fruit was still highly valued as many housewives still had time to make jam.

In the 1960s the average annual rent for a 10-rod plot was between 10 and 25 shillings. In urban areas 60% of plot-holders paid less than 15 shillings and 39% paid 15 shillings. Tenants gardening on model sites generally paid £2 per annum. About 83% of tenants considered the rent to be reasonable, but those paying between 15 and 20 shillings a year were happiest. In rural areas about 58% paid less than 10 shillings a year for a 10-rod plot. In some cases the urge to take an allotment was purely financial. One plot-holder said that if his local authority provided him with enough land to grow all the vegetables he needed for 15 shillings a year, he would be foolish not to take it.

During the 1960s the social problems surrounding allotment gardening still prevailed. Many sites suffered from want of proper fencing, roads and other facilities. Almost 85% of sites lacked any suitable road from the entrance, and many were too narrow and soft-shouldered to allow access for vehicles. Other pathways had degenerated to the extent that they were barely usable during winter, with ruts and potholes. Some paths were surfaced with compacted cinders or rubble that provided a foothold for weeds. Pathways between the plots were often too narrow for tenants with wheelbarrows. Rather like their counterparts of the 1930s, tenants adopted all sorts of items for use on their allotments. Muck pens were often made from rusted sheets of corrugated iron or in some cases asbestos. In the 1950s and '60s cold frames made from old window frames were another commonplace feature. During the immediate post-war decades the white enamelled bath tub came into general use on allotments as a holding tank, and was usually located beside a standpipe or tap. It wasn't unusual for one allotment site to have three or four bath tubs. So the allotment retained its ramshackle image, at a time when many authorities implied that much could be done to improve the image of sites.

A 1950s improvised cold frame and rhubarb patch.

Two dramatic events subtly altered the allotment landscape during the mid-1960s. The arrival of mass-produced plastic was regarded as a major advance within the horticultural industry. Suddenly gardening had become less of a strain and plot-holders eagerly embraced this new lightweight material. Almost overnight, plastic items in the form of flowerpots, seed trays, watering cans and hand tools littered allotment sites. Even standard spades and forks had handles that were made of plastic.

The white enamel bath tub was a prominent feature on allotments in the 1960s.

'The old heavy cumbersome frames and cloches made from wood, metal and sheets of glass gave way to the polythene tunnel cloche. They were very easy to construct, being held in place with a series of wire hoops. The only snag, though, was that the polythene needed replacing after a couple of growing seasons, but some tenants simply took to patching them up. Polythene was also less appealing to vandals. By the end of the decade the use of polythene cloches had become almost universal and very few allotments were without them.' (Personal communication with the author)

When West Indian tenants took up allotment gardening, they introduced sweetcorn (maize) as a main crop. At first rows of these tall leafy plants looked very alien to the British allotment, but gradually they became more common during the following decades. Tenants of ethnic origin also grew peppers, chillis and gourds as well as pumpkins, and favoured plants with hot spicy seeds. They also largely took a casual attitude to allotment gardening, and placed little emphasis on tidiness. For West Indian tenants, the owning or renting of a patch of land meant a rise in social status, even if cultivating the land was regarded as being a low-born activity among the islanders.

During the 1950s and '60s the use of chemical pesticides and artificial fertilisers was widespread. Environmental awareness had yet to be born, and words like ecology and recycling were only used by the scientists of the day. Alarmingly, DDT was the most widely used of all pesticides and was regarded as a cure-all for every kind of pest and crop disease. If plants displayed symptoms of ailment or disease, out came the can of DDT. Eventually, concerns were voiced and DDT was withdrawn from general sale in 1968, though not completely banned from agriculture.

'Ah! "Derris" dust was another of the wonder potions to deal with all kinds of pests. Plot-holders would think little of giving their raspberries, potatoes and anything else a liberal squirt of this noxious substance. National Growmore was the most widely used fertiliser, largely because it was so easy to use. Unlike bulky manure this fertiliser did not need digging into the soil. A few tenants did use leaf mould for their potato ground. For gardeners, the emphasis of allotment cultivation was placed on bulk quantity of produce rather than quality.' (Personal communication with the author)

During the economic crises of 1967, the National Allotment & Garden Society claimed that allotment gardening was vital to the country's economy. When the 'Dig for Britain' campaign was launched, to get more people interested in allotments, a quarter of a million leaflets were distributed. Although there was no official census of the feedback, it was noted that response was better in urban areas, and for a brief period it became stylish to cultivate a vegetable patch. However, this gardening activity was short-lived. Many young allotment enthusiasts had visions of a higher social status and said that the Government should help to provide them with weekend chalets for their plots. One plot-holder stated that he wanted to get away from the dreary railway sidings image. However, with the grim reality of many allotment sites in the 1960s, complete with panoramic view of the gasworks, not to mention the trains thundering past and the smut-covered strawberries, the picture fell short of idyllic. Many plot-holders, though, insisted that their activities could make a tiny dent in the nation's balance of payments, and that if they were treated properly they would continue to raise foodstuffs. As for the chalets, they would have to wait, though for some that delay was not to be long. While the younger newcomers had high trendy aspirations for their allotments, seasoned tenants in the North and the Midlands had more practical ideas.

Since the 1930s numerous pigeon-fanciers had built their crees on allotments as a matter of convenience. Legally, the lofts were not supposed to take up more than a quarter of the allotment and the remainder of the land had to be cultivated. In most cases the pigeon-fanciers were not at all interested in gardening and only made a token gesture to comply with

A depressing view of a decrepit allotment site dominated by poultry huts and pigeon crees. (After HMSO)

regulations. Many of the crees were very ramshackle, while others were well constructed but imposing. Allotments adorned with crees were usually very unkempt, though sites with poultry runs were kept in a better state of cultivation. Vegetable gardeners often complained of the ravaging of crops supposedly inflicted by the pigeons, but the fanciers insisted that their birds were not to blame, as racing pigeons needed a balanced diet and rarely settled on the plots. However, they attracted local wood pigeons that did, and the resulting damage was often widespread. On smaller sites the combination of crees and gardeners resulted in much agitation and unrest between the two groups. Gardeners were generally of the older generation, while the pigeon-fanciers were much younger, often in their 20s, so the combination of the two groups was far from harmonious. In fact, many gardeners gave up their plots and the land fell vacant.

Much contention also existed between vegetable gardeners and livestock breeders, who had different objectives. Tenants that were only interested in cultivating vegetables insisted that that livestock keeping drew in vermin, which in turn led to disease and damage to their crops. Vegetable growers also claimed that pig-swill attracted flies and maggots, while unkempt buildings to house the livestock debased the locality. Tenants keeping livestock were undaunted as they found their ventures far more profitable than growing vegetables, and gradually livestock breeders extended their

194

areas when the gardening tenants gave up. In some cases livestock keepers were renting blocks of five or six plots at a time, which they invariably fenced in. One such tenant even had the audacity to advertise his venture on the door of his hut. Pig and poultry rearing on plots of up to half an acre was nothing unusual in the Midlands and the North and the notion often began as a wartime expedient. At Accrington in Lancashire one tenant made £220 a year by raising hens in batteries. Another enterprising tenant had a unit of three poultry huts measuring 20 by 60 feet that housed more than 600 hens; his annual profit was well over £500. Some of the animal breeders kept high-quality stock for exhibition at shows. The greatest majority of keepers were only concerned with the profit from the sale of meat and eggs. In many cases the blocks of allotments came to resemble farm holdings and local councils readily accepted this situation where gardening was on the decline. Some councillors maintained that an economic rent was better than taking action against livestock holders and ending up receiving no rent at all. However, animal rearing was in the minority and accounted for roughly only 3% of allotment tenants across the UK.

In 1950 around 75,000 allotments existed on roughly 4,000 acres of land owned by British Railways. Throughout the 1960s the number of railway plots declined rapidly at the rate of 3,000 a year, although BR still owned more allotment land than any other corporate organisation in the UK. During the 1960s a number of railway sites were let to local authorities or allotment associations for use as temporary plots. Only railway employees (in theory) were supposed to cultivate plots alongside the tracks, but this rule was frequently relinquished to enable residents of houses along the railway line access to their plots, providing there was no need to walk alongside the rails.

Except for the North Eastern Region, all railway allotments were administered at the British Railways Board's Regional Headquarters in London. By the middle of the 1960s the Board regarded the mountain of paperwork attached to administering the railway allotments as an uneconomical headache, since there was very little in the way of financial return. By 1967 it no longer became British Rail policy to renew tenancies on railway plots. BR did not provide a very high standard for its plots, and very few sites had piped water, which was usually supplied and paid for by the tenants. Tenancies were secured by written agreement, which adhered to the Allotment Acts. Many of these contracts carried a clause that stated that in an emergency land could be re-possessed within 24 hours, though the term 'emergency' was ill-defined. BR also operated different rent schemes and charged its employees 10 shillings per annum while non-BR plot-holders paid 20 shillings for a 10-rod plot. The final death knell came when Dr Beeching's axe fell on many of the branch lines and the railway plots simply vanished with the line closures.

A similar story applied to allotments let by the National Coal Board. Originally allotments were a conspicuous feature of mining districts, though they had developed during the time of the independent coal companies. After the Second World War there were roughly 7,000 allotments over 560 acres of NCB land. These sites were usually administered from nearby offices and for this reason NCB allotments were usually more accessible than those on BR land. However, by the mid-1960s the Coal Board had little inclination to extend the provision of allotments.

During this period of decline, the Ministry of Land & Resources decided, once and for all, to sort out the controversy surrounding allotments. On 2 August 1965 the Ministry appointed Professor Harry Thorpe of Birmingham University to chair a special Committee of Inquiry to address the allotment problem. Mr B. V. White was nominated as the Committee Secretary, and the Committee of six was to review the general policy on allotments in the light of present-day conditions across England and Wales. A controversial questionnaire was dispatched to 900 Urban Councils and 8,500 Parish Councils.

One sub-section of the questionnaire asked for details regarding the growing of flowers on allotments, the purpose being to determine whether flower cultivation took place over a quarter, half, the entire plot or none at all. Mr F. Horsley, clerk to Denby Parish Council, Derbyshire, stated that if the Minister thought that they were going to count the flowers on every allotment in the country, they had another think coming. Another parish clerk described the questionnaire as a useless waste of the taxpayer's money during a time of economic crisis. Many parish clerks responded with disparaging remarks like, 'There are no poor people in the parish', 'Pensioners need rest, not work,' and 'The allotments have no amenities'. When asked whether the allotment had any model plots that were on view to the public, another clerk replied by saying that it was rather unfortunate that all the allotments were on view to the public.

Professor Thorpe responded to the feedback by stating that parish clerks were intelligent people, but they were often overworked, underpaid and that eventually they would realise the need for such an inquiry. He added that many clerks had managed to fill out the form without difficulty and had written to say that such an inquiry was long overdue. A separate questionnaire was sent to plot-holders, which met with a much better response. Their replies indicated that the majority of plot-holders were unhappy over the issues surrounding the security of tenure and the lack of amenities on their sites.

Few plot-holders devoted their entire plots to growing flowers, and those that did grew them in rows with little thought of creating a beautiful garden; most of the blooms raised were simply destined for the horticultural show table. Professor Thorpe found that flowery sites were less prone to vandalism than plots assigned purely to vegetables. Plots for flowers prevailed at Wolverhampton, Norwich, Malvern, Sunderland, Stoke-on-Trent and Normanton in West Yorkshire. Younger tenants usually experimented with flowers, especially in Newcastle-under-Lyme. In contrast, there was very little evidence of flower cultivation on sites at Grantham, Lewisham and Northampton, and plots that did have flowers were restricted to very small areas.

Professor Thorpe found that vandalism was more prevalent in urban regions. In Bristol a site with a high fence and a locked gate was regularly assaulted, while another allotment area with a flimsy hedge was rarely touched – the thief or vandal obviously enjoyed a challenge. Allotments adjacent to playgrounds were also prone to frequent vandalism. Where a public right of way crossed an allotment site, much produce was often lost through pilfering. A regular trespasser said:

'A bunch of flowers, a bag of tomatoes and the odd swede now and then is never refused at home and the missus never asks where they come from. Besides, the gardeners had got so much of the stuff anyway, they probably never miss it.' (Correspondence with the author)

Well-managed tidy allotments were less troubled by this problem.

The Departmental Committee's report was finally published on 4 November 1969. It recommended that the Continental system of allotment gardening, prevalent in Germany, Holland and Denmark (all very neat and tidy), should be adopted and the name of allotment changed to 'leisure garden'. The report stated that local authorities within urban areas should provide half an acre of leisure garden per thousand citizens. The Committee suggested that such gardens should be fully landscaped and have facilities such as hard-surfaced roads, car parks, communal areas or centres and toilets, and noted that such improvements would have to be paid for by the tenants. The Committee maintained that a rent of £5 per annum for a 10-rod plot on an improved site or 30 shillings to £2 a year for a plot on an unimproved site was a fair rate.

Professor Thorpe and his team re-designed an allotment for the second part of the 20th century. They chose a working-class region at Bordesley Green in Birmingham, which was set amid heavy industry and housing. Initially the plot-holders were very unhappy with the plan, which involved the felling of mature trees, and felt that this would rob the site of its wildlife, which was deemed to be part of the attraction. After a meeting between the tenants and the University team, the plans were re-structured, and the tenants had a 40% say in the proceedings. Eventually the new site was established, and became known as the Bordesley Green Ideal Allotment Holders' Association. The venture was held as a great success and many tenants were prepared to travel miles in order to work on this former market garden.

At about the same time, Bristol District Council decided to embrace the leisure angle and create a special pilot site. Plot-holders were provided with spacious cedarwood chalets, complete with porches, curtained windows and seating. The concept was to create a beautiful garden for recreation and rest as well as a place for cultivating vegetables. The gardens had colourful flowerbeds, lawns and sitting areas in addition to vegetable plots. Car parking facilities and toilets were also provided. Eventually many similar schemes were established across the country.

Overall the picture was less encouraging, for most allotments were strewn with an array of 'shanty town' sheds. Any attempts to tidy up the allotment sites were held back by the singularity of each tenant. In December 1969 Birmingham Allotments Committee designated up to £100,000 over a period of years to improve plots across the region. However, Birmingham's 6,000 plot-holders refused to abandon their individual tool sheds. Councillor Alan Hope, the Committee Chairman, declared that although most tenants were willing to accept improvements, such as surfaced roads and adequate fencing, they would not relinquish their home-made sheds. Mr William France, Secretary of the National Allotment & Garden Society, stated that the tenant who built his own shed regarded it as the finest 'do-it-yourself' feature and little would persuade him to part with it. Mr France added that it would require a very good public relations job on the part of the Councils to persuade tenants to change their minds over this issue.

The following year (1970) Birmingham's plot-holders responded angrily to the accusation that they were delaying the modernisation of sites by refusing to demolish their individual tool sheds. Alan Hope stated that plot-holders would not be persuaded to agree on the improvements. John Lewis, Chairman of the Birmingham & District Allotments Council, said that the existence of 'shabby sheds' was not the real reason for the discontent, and maintained that the dispute arose over the poor state of fences, gates and roads on sites. He said that if facilities were improved, the tenants would be only too happy to remove their hideous huts and sheds from their plots and co-operate in the cleaning up and modernisation of their allotments.

In spite of the controversy surrounding the refurbishment and development of allotments, overall precious little was actually done to improve most of the sites across the UK. The Government was largely dismissive of Professor Thorpe's recommendations, and the greatest majority of allotment sites retained their air of discordant tattiness, complete with their vistas of eyesore shacks and sheds. Pensioners and seasoned gardeners, too, were less enthusiastic about the leisure garden idea:

'Calling allotments Leisure Gardens, with exercise as the only incentive, is utter nonsense. We want crops as an aid to domestic economy. The Continental idea of land outside towns with chalets, playgrounds, landscaping, car parks and all weekend amenities is of no value to old age pensioners, who may have no transport and cannot carry home vegetables in bulk. What a racket!' (E. S. Jefferies, *A Brief History of West Wickham Allotments Association*, 1974)

Years after the publication of Professor Thorpe's radical facelift for allotments, the majority of sites remained unchanged and unimproved. Allotment gardens, like their tenants, appeared impervious to change. The patchwork of unkempt plots with their accompaniment of ramshackle sheds and assorted paraphernalia remained an inherent part of the British landscape.

Postscript

In 1946, shortly after the 'Dig for Victory' campaign, a gardener from Tunbridge Wells asked whether the future of allotments was in the balance as numerous plot-holders across the nation were becoming increasingly concerned about the fate of their plots. This gardener suggested that, instead of trying to preserve existing wartime plots, the entire allotment situation should be reviewed, with the possibility of establishing new, well-equipped sites of a permanent nature. The plan was to establish a series of modern allotments that could be walled in and subdivided into sections. The walls would provide protection and if anyone objected to them they could be screened. Within such a walled garden there could be well-laid-out paths and greenhouses for each portion, together with tool stores, sheds and a system of controlled heating. Such an undertaking would require the presence of a resident supervisor or attendant, but there was little reason why such a scheme could not be implemented in some of the larger towns. These modern allotments or leisure gardens could have been located near or around horticultural institutions. The Tunbridge Wells gardener said that such facilities would provide seasoned gardeners with a valuable amenity and introduce younger people to the marvels of horticulture. Unfortunately, such concepts were never put into practice, partly due to the country's economic difficulties in the aftermath of war. The other factor was the lack of interest in allotment cultivation among the general population.

In 1968 a parks superintendent in Hertford drew attention to the argument for providing Continental-style chalet allotments, but asked whether such a scheme would work in Britain. He noted the fall in allotment tenancy and was convinced that this was largely due to the dispersal of the population to the new suburbs. He implied that many allotments were located too near the inner city and that older gardeners often found the journey from suburban areas to their town plots both tiring and expensive. Whether or not pensioners would prefer weekend gardens or allotments, he implied that landscaping could provide the answer to the declining interest in allotments. At the time Hertford Borough Council Allotments Committee had agreed to the planting of small trees on one of their sites, in order to create an attractive and natural appearance. The superintendent insisted that simple chalet gardens without landscaping were too similar to the modern housing estates and therefore unappealing to prospective tenants. However, if the garden was landscaped then plot-holders could look upon their weekend garden as a 'little breath of the country.'

Mr R. C. Macmillan MBE, Director of Parks in Manchester, was horrified to discover that few planners knew anything of allotments and that they had made no provision for them in new town development schemes. With 35 years experience of public park administration, he realised that the value of open space for recreation was unquestionable. Although the majority of gardeners had no interest in allotments during their youth, this outlook often changed following home ownership, and by middle age the gardener was often an expert. Mr Macmillan recognised that although allotments provided solitude and peace of mind, he insisted that it was the local authorities' responsibility to make sites as pleasing as possible.

Throughout the decades numerous plans to improve allotments, with a few exceptions, have largely failed. Even after the publication of Professor Thorpe's proposals, local authorities were still providing temporary sites with little or no amenities. Part of the reason lay with the lower number of prospective tenants seeking allotments. After 1945 allotment cultivation entered a long period of decline from which there has never been a recovery, though the slump evened out a little during the 1970s.

By the 1990s, according to one allotment association, there were roughly 400,000 allotments left, which was less than the figure for the 1890s, and the downward trend continued throughout the remainder of the decade. Miraculously, allotments survived into the 21st century, though many sites were more decrepit than ever before.

When contemporary plot-holders are asked if they see a future for allotments, their replies fall into two categories. Some gardeners insist that there will always be a place for some type of communal gardening scheme, even if the traditional 10-rod plot fades to obscurity. One tenant stated that the nation's love for gardening would prevent allotments from disappearing completely. Less optimistic tenants imply somewhat despondently that the Allotment Movement has had its day and that it is only a matter of a decade or so before allotment gardens become consigned to memory or the pages of history books.

Over the past 20 years or so westernised society has experienced consumerism on an affluent scale that would have been unknown to previous generations. A few years ago a lady plot-holder complained in a most disparaging letter to *The Times* that the only cheap vegetables were the ones in the shops. Today a tin of economy garden peas can be purchased for just 9p at any supermarket. By comparison, a packet of pea seed costs around £1.25p (1998 price). Added to that, there is the effort of sowing, nurturing and harvesting this crop, which is prone to attack from pigeons, rodents and the dreaded pea maggot. Little wonder then that gardening journals, periodicals and occasionally newspapers carry woeful tales of allotments ending up under car parks or tenants being evicted to make way for other development schemes. When such events occur there is often a furore over the loss of allotment land and a cry that something must be done to ensure the safety of the remaining sites, as in the case of Harborne Lane Allotments in Birmingham.

Harborne Lane Allotments had always been popular with gardeners in the past, in spite of more than 30 years of planning blight in one form or another, which did much to discourage prospective tenants. Eventually Birmingham City Council sold the largest portion of the grounds to a well-known supermarket chain, leaving only a tiny fragment of land enough for 40 plots, hardly sufficient to warrant the funding required to maintain such a site. Even so, plans to lay out the gardens for cultivation have, so far, remained unattended to and the displaced tenants have moved to other sites or given up gardening altogether. While some allotments have apparently prospered, others have fallen into serious neglect when plot-holders have moved to different locations. The vacated land temporarily became a grassy haven for wildlife before ending up under concrete as a supermarket, car park or similar facility.

Personal views and opinions on the merits of the allotment system are still as diverse as the range of tenants that garden on them. Some sites are regarded as great success stories, such as Uplands Allotments at Oxhill Road, Birmingham, while other plots are ignored or looked upon as little more than a blemish on the landscape. Variations in tenancy also contribute vastly toward the usage and thus the appearance of allotments. While the majority of older gardeners often mourn the loss of land and the lack of funds to keep many associations going, others adopt allotments as a money-making venture, just as the livestock breeders did during the 1950s and '60s. Allegedly, on one Midlands site it is not unknown for conglomerates of Asian businessmen to rent blocks of vacant allotments and employ their countrymen to cultivate commercial mono-crops of coriander or Egyptian onions. Since three crops can be lifted during the course of one growing season, a businessman can make an annual profit of more than £500 from one 10-rod plot. In such locations the number of genuine tenants is often so minimal as to make the formation of an association almost impossible.

Some allotment spokesmen maintain that if it were not for the activity of Asian and West Indian tenants, who have a closer affinity with horticulture and farming, even more land would be lost. In other words, the commercial cultivation of allotments enables local retailers and restaurants to avoid entering the unsustainable food supply chains that encourage the supermarket economy. What some see as an immoral money-making enterprise, others regard as a sustainable resource that benefits the local community. The Handsworth Allotments Information Group (HAIG) has pointed out that large-scale cultivation helps to keep the land productive and therefore less tempting to the developers.

The ethnicity of tenancy has also introduced a more diverse range of crops on allotments. At one location in particular, tenants now cultivate asparagus (this always sells well), dhania, Egyptian onions, grapes, methi, mooli, coriander and dill. Ethnic tenants have perhaps a greater appreciation of the land and they are very industrious on their plots, which may be the most productive on many sites. Ethnic tenants not engaged in commercial enterprises also have a more relaxed attitude to gardening and possibly a more optimistic outlook.

The financial restrictions facing many associations will probably influence the development of allotments in future years, and generation of revenue will be at the forefront of any association's aspirations. Even during the 1990s some associations had developed the leisure angle in a small way, such as opening a small cafeteria on Sunday mornings, holding local fetes or bring and buy sales. Others promoted their activities by exhibiting at county or craft fairs.

Some allotment associations have developed their gardens with the leisure idea very much in mind, and their sites often resemble miniature theme parks. It is possible that this idea may be taken further with permanent facilities to entertain visitors, with cafeterias, amusements, horticultural souvenir shops and open spaces for games and relaxation as well as plots where gardeners can indulge in their hobby. Who knows, just maybe trading association huts could become the venue for a social club. If an enterprising allotment association was successful in gaining a license to sell alcohol, it could open a clubhouse that would enable plot-holders to socialise in much the same way that J. B. Lawes allowed his tenants to do during the Victorian era.

Cost and ecological factors will invariably influence future developments. Water payments, if switched to the metering system, could well be the death knell for the smaller associations. Some ecologically minded associations have already found ways to combat the ever-increasing water charges by introducing devices to catch and hold rainwater on their grounds. Other plans, such as the placement of solar panels and wind turbines to generate electricity for the lighting and heating of the association trading or communal hut, are not beyond the realms of possibility. Thus the allotment would well and truly become a self-sustaining enterprise. All this is

With organic gardening methods, compost pens and bins
have become an integral part of the allotment scene.

speculation – or is it? Numerous allotment organisations have already accepted these ideas in order to develop their sites further. Some allotment societies and associations have found that there is an insatiable demand for organic produce, especially at shows and fairs. Why then should an association not be able to market its produce and thus create wealth that could be ploughed back into the funds, enabling the allotments to become an even greater benefit to the local community? This concept could be a way forward for many of the ailing associations. Such schemes would require a great deal of work, but some associations appear ready to accept this option. Certainly, if an allotment association became a viable business enterprise, then problems like security of tenure (that age-old problem) would be overcome and the threat from developers vastly diminished if not eradicated altogether.

Robins find organic gardens particularly appealing.

Sadly, at the start of the 21st century many allotments have retained their tatty characterisation of the 'cloth cap' tenancy of the 1930s, complete with vistas of rotting, dilapidated shacks. Such images do little to promote the benefit that allotments could provide to the community. To the non-gardening British public, allotments are something of an enigma and they find it difficult to understand how cultivation of fruit and vegetables could possibly be appealing, let alone a rewarding hobby. This notion has been ingrained within society for so long that the current green gardeners are having an uphill struggle to bring the benefits of their activities to the fore. Only when an allotment becomes threatened or destroyed through the actions of local government does the Movement gain any sympathy. Events of this nature often inspire people to suggest that the remaining allotment gardens should be given the same status and degree of protection as that applied to parks, pleasure grounds and historic gardens.

Green gardening has encouraged wildlife to move in on allotments. The sight of a fox cub is one of the most endearing.

A contemporary allotment garden, where composting and design have subtly altered the appearance of most sites.

Throughout history the humble allotment garden has played its part in the wellbeing and survival of the British people. Countless multitudes of allotment tenants have found economic benefit, comfort, relaxation and salvation while tending their little plots of earth. Allotment gardens may not fall into the same category as historic gardens, but perhaps they should, as their social history forms a rich part of the nation's cultural heritage. Allotments provide an insight into the ideas and innovations applied to the most basic form of horticulture by previous generations. There is no other feature of the British landscape quite like the allotment garden.

Appendix 1
Development of allotments in Great Britain, 1873-1999

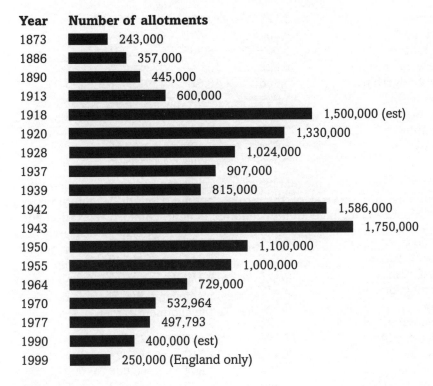

Year	Number of allotments
1873	243,000
1886	357,000
1890	445,000
1913	600,000
1918	1,500,000 (est)
1920	1,330,000
1928	1,024,000
1937	907,000
1939	815,000
1942	1,586,000
1943	1,750,000
1950	1,100,000
1955	1,000,000
1964	729,000
1970	532,964
1977	497,793
1990	400,000 (est)
1999	250,000 (England only)

Sources:
1873-1918 Board of Agriculture
1920-1943 Gangulee
Others: Ministry of Agriculture

Appendix 2
Number of allotments in Great Britain by county, 1873-1890

County	1873	1886	1890
Bedford	8,364	12,602	15,194
Berkshire	5,007	8,305	10,231
Buckinghamshire	6,632	12,346	17,225
Cambridgeshire	5,396	10,579	13,428
Chester	929	2,603	3,239
Cornwall	1,762	3,127	2,539
Cumbria	410	676	1,125
Derbyshire	5,628	7,128	10,702
Devon	7,063	10,264	10,407
Dorset	7,322	9,135	10,875
Durham	1,000	4,294	9,077
Essex	8,269	12,228	12,770
Gloucestershire	7,552	11,144	14,653
Hampshire	6,712	8,590	12,614
Herefordshire	5,197	8,316	1,440
Hertfordshire	5,197	8,316	1,014
Huntingdonshire	3,376	5,402	6,980
Kent	4,150	6,613	11,660
Lancashire	992	3,706	4,447
Leicestershire	17,168	18,496	23,396
Lincolnshire	7,430	11,710	15,921
Middlesex	689	1,844	3,098
Monmouthshire	569	767	1,502
Norfolk	6,400	9,130	11,855
Northamptonshire	16,447	19,535	26,229
Northumberland	968	4,124	3,247
Nottinghamshire	11,317	14,795	21,253
Oxfordshire	9,088	14,062	17,947
Rutland	1,252	1,878	2,197
Shropshire	1,002	1,714	2,584
Somerset	9,503	14,908	16,477
Staffordshire	5,444	6,312	10,517
Suffolk	11,664	15,258	17,658
Surrey	1,263	3,163	5,266

County	1873	1886	1890
Sussex	2,782	4,852	6,822
Warwickshire	12,794	17,174	17,731
Westmorland	52	295	950
Wiltshire	15,445	20,760	23,723
Worcestershire	4,919	7,322	9,983
Yorkshire, East	1,781	4,333	3,200
Yorkshire, North	4,731	6,812	8,480
Yorkshire, West	6,876	10,704	12,985
Total, England	242,542	348,872	441,024
Total, Wales	1,726	4,949	7,562
Total, Scotland	2,130	3,974	6,419
Total Great Britain	246,398	357,795	455,005

Source: Board of Agriculture 1890

Appendix 3
Glossary

Acre A unit of land of 4,840 square yards, usually enclosed as a field.

Board of Agriculture (old) A Government-sponsored organisation established by Sir John Sinclair in 1793 to assist the Improvers to make country reports and agricultural censuses. The Board was deemed to be a failure and was abolished in 1822.

Board of Agriculture (new) Established in 1889, largely through the work of Henry Chaplin, who became the Board's first president. In 1903 the Board became the Board of Agriculture and Fisheries, until 1919.

Bushel A unit of dry measure (volume) equivalent to 8 gallons.

Conacre The sub-letting of ground already prepared for cultivation.

Coombe A unit of dry measure (volume) equivalent to 4 bushels or 32 gallons.

Cowgate Pasture for one or more cows. Set-aside pasture for communal use in the 19th century. Also referred to as cow runs or cow allotments.

Crome A garden tool with tines bent to an angle of 90 degrees and used like a rake.

Crown A coin with the value of 5 shillings.

Cultivation of Lands Order Legislation passed in December 1916 to permit the cultivation of waste ground by civilians in order to grow food during the First World War.

Demense Owner's land worked by tenants, which might or might not include the tenants' holdings.

'Dig for Britain' A half-hearted attempt to interest people in growing vegetables during the economic crises of 1967. The plan faded to obscurity after a few months.

'Dig for Plenty' A post-war campaign launched in 1948 that attempted to revive flagging interest in allotment gardening and food cultivation, in order to keep imports down. This enterprise was a monumental flop.

'Dig for Victory' The Government's massive Second World War campaign encouraging citizens to cultivate home-grown food in order to boost supplies and reduce dependence on food imports while shipping was vulnerable to attack.

DORA Defence of the Realm Act, passed on 8 August 1914. This legislation gave the Government the right to suppress criticism, imprison persons without trial and commandeer economic resources for the war effort. DORA was also used to control civilian behaviour, which included alcohol consumption and the regulating of food supplies.

•••

Enclosures The process of enclosing open fields and commons between 1750 and 1870.

Enclosure Commissioners Officials appointed to regulate and supervise the enclosure of the fields and commons and award allotments where required.

Farthing A small coin with the monetary value of one-quarter of a pre-decimal penny. Withdrawn from circulation in 1961.

Foot A unit of linear measure consisting of 12 inches.

Gallon A unit of dry measure (volume) equivalent to an eighth part of a bushel.

Glebe From the Latin term 'glaeba' meaning a clod of earth or soil. Glebe land was either given in entirety to the Church or was land purchased by the Church.

Guinea A gold coin with a value of 21 shillings, originally cast with gold from Guinea. In circulation as currency until 1813.

Half-Crown A coin with the value of 2 shillings and 6 pence (pre-decimal).

Inch A unit of linear measurement roughly equivalent to 2.5cm.

Justices of the Peace Knights appointed to receive oaths from all men over 15 years of age for the maintenance of peace, which originated from a proclamation of 1195.

Manor A territorial unit originally held by feudal tenure, which in later times was used to describe a landed estate.

Ministry of Agriculture Established in 1919 to replace the Board of Agriculture. During the Second World War the Ministry was largely responsible for increasing food production and optimising the use of the land. In 1955 the Ministry absorbed the Ministry of Food and became the Ministry of Agriculture, Food & Fisheries (MAFF). In 1965 the functions of the Ministry regarding allotments, commons and forestry were passed to the Ministry of Land & Resources, until 1967. After that date allotment matters were dealt with by the Ministry of Housing and Local Government, while duties relating to the Forestry Commission were handed back to MAFF. In 2001 MAFF was abolished and replaced by the Department for Environment, Food & Rural Affairs (DEFRA), which the farming press quickly dubbed 'The Department for the Eradication of Farming and Real Agriculture'.

Overseers of the Poor Supervisors of the Poor Laws, who reported to the Vestry, which consisted of ratepayers (occupiers of land, not owners).

Parish An ecclesiastical unit that served for administrative functions from the 16th century.

Penny A bronze coin being the twelfth part of a shilling. Remained in circulation until the change to decimal currency in 1971.

Potato patch A remnant of ground usually allocated within a farmer's field for the cultivation of potatoes. Tenants were responsible for raising the crop, but only entitled to a fraction of the produce harvested.

Poor Laws Various measures taken to relieve the needs of poor folk.

Rod A unit of linear measure equal to 5½ yards. Also referred to as a lug, perch or pole.

Rood A term used in the 19th century to describe a quarter of an acre or 40 rods (1,200 square yards).

Security of tenure Security for the tenure of plot-holders, which could only be achieved if the holders purchased their land outright. Relative security could be gained through obtaining a long lease or when a local authority purchased land for allotment purposes.

Shilling A silver coin with the value of 12 old pennies.

Speenhamland system A relief system developed by Berkshire magistrates in the 18th century, which was quickly adopted in most southern counties. Allowances of bread were allocated on a sliding scale regulated by the price of bread and corn, enabling farmers to pay their workers less than a living wage.

Tenant A person holding a portion of land or tenement from a landlord.

Tenantry Part of an estate under common or field husbandry.

Tithe A tenth part of the agricultural produce raised each year that was appropriated by the Church as payment. This measure was made compulsory in the 10th century. Tithe did not extend to the mining of ores, or the manufacture of items derived from minerals, since that was part of the earth and not the produce from it.

Ward An electoral or administrative division within a town, city or borough. Thought to originate from Wapentake, first mentioned in 1278.

Vacant Land Cultivation Society (VLCS) An organisation formed by Joseph Fels in 1907 to utilise waste ground for the cultivation of food by unemployed folk. The organisation came to prominence in the UK during the First World War.

Yard A unit of linear measure comprising of 3 feet.

Appendix 4
Imperial/metric equivalents

Land measurement (approximate equivalent)
1 rod, perch or pole = 5½ yards = 5.027 metres
10-rod plot = one-sixteenth of an acre = 0.025 hectares
20-rod plot = one-eighth of an acre = 0.050 hectares
40-rod plot = one-quarter of an acre = 0.101 hectares

Irregular plot sizes (approximate equivalent)
5-rod plot = 0.031 acres = 0.012 hectares
8-rod plot = 0.050 acres = 0.012 hectares
9-rod plot = 0.056 acres = 0.012 hectares
15-rod plot = 0.093 acres = 0.037 hectares
16-rod plot = 0.100 acres = 0.037 hectares
25-rod plot = 0.156 acres = 0.050 hectares
30-rod plot = 0.186 acres = 0.075 hectares
60-rod plot = 0.375 acres = 0.151 hectares
100-rod plot = 0.625 acres = 0.253 hectares

Area (approximate equivalent)

Acres	Hectares	Acres	Hectares
½	0.202	9	3.642
1	0.405	10	4.047
2	0.809	50	20.234
3	1.214	100	40.469
4	1.619	200	80.937
5	2.023	300	121.406
6	2.428	400	161.874
7	2.833	500	202.343
8	3.237	1,000	404.686

Linear measurement (approximate equivalent)

Inches	Centimetres	Inches	Centimetres
1	2.5	8	20.30
2	5	9	22.86
3	7.5	10	25.50
4	10.16	11	27.94
5	12.70	12 (1 foot)	30
6	15.25	24 (2 feet)	61
7	17.78	36 (3 feet = 1 yard)	91

Feet inches	Metres	Feet inches	Metres
3 6	1.067	7 6	2.286
4 0	1.219	8 0	2.438
4 6	1.372	8 6	2.590
5 0	1.524	9 0	2.740
5 6	1.676	9 6	2.900
6 0	1.829	10 0	3.048
6 6	1.981	5,280 0 (1,760 yards,	1609.344
7 0	2.134	1 mile)	(1.61km)

Square feet	Square metres	Square feet	Square metres
1	0.0929	5	0.4645
2	0.1858	6	0.5574
3	0.2787	9 (1 sq yd)	0.8361
4	0.3716		

Currency (approximate equivalent)

1 farthing = ¼ penny
 = 0.10 pence
2 farthings = 1 halfpenny
 = 0.20 pence

1d (old penny) = 0.41 pence
3d (threepence) = 1.25 pence
6d (sixpence) = 2.5 pence
12d = 1 shilling = 5 pence

Shillings pence	Decimal	Shillings pence	Decimal
2 0	10p	12 0	60p
2 6 (half-a-crown)	12.5p	13 0	65p
3 0	15p	14 0	70p
4 0	20p	15 0	75p
5 0 (crown)	25p	16 0	80p
6 0	30p	17 0	85p
7 0	35p	18 0	90p
8 0	40p	19 0	95p
9 0	45p	20 0	£1
10 0	50p	21 0 (guinea)	£1.05
11 0	55p		

Weight (approximate equivalents)

Pounds (lb)	Grams	Pounds (lb)	Grams
1	454	6	2722
2	907	7	3175
3	1361	8	3629
4	1814	9	4082
5	2268	10	4540

Pounds (lb)	Grams	
14 (1 stone)	6456	
112 (1cwt)	50848	
2,240 (1 ton)	1016960	(1.017 metric tonnes)

Tons	Metric tonnes
2	2.03392
3	3.05088
4	4.06784
5	5.08480

Dry measure volume (approximate equivalent)
1 bushel = 35.239 litres = 0.035239 cubic metres
8 bushels = 281.912 litres = 0.281912 cubic metres
12 bushels = 422.868 litres = 0.422868 cubic metres
14 bushels = 493.346 litres = 0.563824 cubic metres
16 bushels = 4 coombes = 563.824 litres = 0.563824 cubic metres
18 bushels = 4½ coombes = 635.274 litres = 0.634302 cubic metres
90 bushels = 3171.516 litres = 3.171510 cubic metres
105 bushels = 3700.102 litres = 3.700095 cubic metres

Liquid measure volume (approximate equivalent)

Gallons	Litres
1	4.55
2	9.1
3	13.6

Appendix 5
Allotment Acts

1782

A Parliamentary Act enabled the Guardians of the Poor to enclose up to 10 acres of waste ground around the poor house for cultivation by parish paupers.

1790

A Private Members Bill proposed the supply of small plots of land to the poor.

1796

The General Enclosure Bill, which would have compelled future Acts to set aside land for the benefit of the poor, but it failed to pass into law.

1819

The Select Vestry Act gave Churchwardens and Overseers of the Poor the authority to purchase or hire any plot of land up to 20 acres in extent and let it to the poor and unemployed of the parish.

1831

An Act of Parliament empowered Churchwardens and Poor Law Overseers to supply land not exceeding 20 acres for the employment of poor folk. Where demand exceeded supply, the Act allowed provision for an extension to 50 acres.

1832

In further provisions to the previous Act, it became lawful for the Poor Law Overseers to apportion land not exceeding 1 acre to an individual.

1845

The General Enclosure Act, whereby land was granted for the use of the poor within a parish in the form of a field garden.

1882

The Allotment Extension Act required trustees holding charity land for the use of the poor to set apart a portion for use as allotments.

1885

Under this Act land held in the parishes could be let in the form of allotments at the same rate as the surrounding agricultural land.

1887

The Allotment Extension Act enabled the local Sanitary Authority to provide allotments and if necessary acquire the land by compulsory purchase. Any six registered electors, who were qualified to vote for Members of Parliament, could appeal to the local Sanitary Authority that there was a need for the Act to be put into force. Allotment tenants were also given the right to install buildings on their allotments and to remove any constructions on vacating.

1888

Established County Councils, and as a result local Sanitary Authorities were, in theory, compelled to provide land for use as allotments. This was not always the case.

1890

County Councils had to have a Standing Committee on allotments and it became the duty of the Committee to hold an inquiry if the local Sanitary Authority failed to obtain land for allotments by voluntary agreement.

1894

Under the Local Government Act, any Parish or Urban District Council had the power to provide land for allotments by voluntary agreement. Hired land could be let in allotments not exceeding 1 acre to one person (voluntary) or 1 acre arable and 3 acres pasture (compulsory).

1907

The Smallholding & Allotment Act made amendments to the previous Acts of 1887 and 1890.

1908

The Smallholding & Allotment Act repealed and consolidated the Acts of 1907, 1887 and 1890. It remained the duty of the Parish or District Council to provide allotments to inhabitants of the parish who required them. The Board of Agriculture became the central authority for all allotment matters (except for finance).

1919

The Land Settlement Facilities Act made Metropolitan Borough Councils allotment authorities. Local authorities were also permitted to supply and improve land for use as allotments.

1922

This Allotment Act compelled allotment authorities to set up allotment committees. It also covered the release of requisitioned land and gave some security to tenants and improved the terms for compensation.

1925

This Act established statutory allotments, which local authorities could not sell or convert without consent from the Ministry of Agriculture.

1926

The Smallholding & Allotment Act improved the law, mainly with regard to smallholdings.

1929

Under the Local Government Act, agricultural land ceased to be liable to assessment for local rates and allotments shared in this benefit.

1931

The Agricultural Utilisation Act reinforced the Allotment Act of 1925.

1950

This Act consolidated previous legislation of 1925 and was confined to allotment gardens. Notice to quit was extended to 12 months, though plot-holders were liable to pay for dilapidation of their allotment on vacating.

1971

The Town & Planning Act covered planning with provision of allotments.

1974

The Local Government Bill ended the need for statutory Allotment Committees.

Bibliography

Allen, Lady Marjory FILA *How Allotments could be made an Amenity Asset to the Community* (London, 1936)

Arch, Joseph *The Story of His Life – As Told by Himself* (London, Hutchinson & Co, 1898)

Ashby, Arthur W. *Allotments & Smallholdings in Oxfordshire* (1917)

Aylesbury News 'Land Allotments' (article, 1844)

Bateman, John *Great Land-owners of Great Britain & Ireland* (Victoria Library Ed, 1883; Leicester University Press, 1971)

Bath Southern Counties Society, Pamphlet 8, *Gardens & Allotments in Wartime* (1943)

Bathurst, Sir Charles, 'Allotments and Gardens' (article, 1918)

Berwick Sayers, W. C. *Croydon and the Second World War* (Corporation of Croydon, 1949)

Brazier, R. H. & Sanford, E. *Birmingham and the Great War* (Birmingham, Cornish Brothers Ltd, 1921)

Broderick, George C. *English Land and English Landlords* (1881; David & Charles, 1968)

Burstow, Henry *Reminiscences of Horsham* (Free Christian Book Society, 1911)

Butcher, G. W. *Allotments for All: The Story of a Great Movement* (London, 1918)

Bury Post 'Town Farm Allotments' (article, 1844, courtesy of Walsham Village History Group)

Calder, Angus *The People's War 1939-1945* (London, Jonathan Cape, 1969)

Chambers, J. D. & Mingey, G. E. *The Agricultural Revolution 1750-1880* (London, B. T. Batsford, 1966)

Cobbett, W. *Rural Rides* (1830; Penguin Books, 1979)
A Treatise on Cobbett's Corn (1828)

Cook, Raymond A. FRGS ARHS *Plots Against Hitler* (Gateshead, Northumberland Press, 1941)

Davies, David *The Case of the Labourers in Husbandry* (London, 1795)

Dent, Robert K. *The Making of Birmingham* (London, Simpkin, Marshal & Co, 1894)

Dyer, P. *Spring Wartime Gardening Guide* (London, 1943)

Ellis, E. T. FRHS *Jottings of an Allotment Gardener* (A. C. Black, 1919)

Ellis, Sandy, memories of Wavertree in wartime, from his autobiography (Worcester, 2003)

Food Production Department 'Economy in the Use of Vegetable Seed' (leaflet, HMSO, 1917)

Forbes, J. *All about Allotments* (1922)

Gangulee, Prof N. *The Battle of the Land* (London, Lindsey Drummond, 1943)

Genders, Roy *The Allotment Garden* (London, John Gifford Ltd, 1976)

Gibson, William John *The Right to Dig* (London, Gibsonian Publications, 1951)

Gray, D. *Nottingham through 500 years* (1960)

Green, F. E. *A History of the English Agricultural Labourer* (London, P. S. King & Co, 1920)

The Allotment Movement (*Contemporary Review*, Vol 114, 1918)

Green, J. L. *The Life of the Right Hon Jesse Collings* (London, 1920)

Grey, Edwin *Cottage Life in a Hertfordshire Village* (St Albans, Fisher, Knight & Co)

Reminiscences of Edwin Grey (St Albans, 1911)

Gunston, James *Successful Gardening Without Digging* (London, 1960)

Herbert, Paul *History of Modern England* (London)

Hobsbawn, E. J. & Rude, G. *Captain Swing* (London, Lawrence & Wishart, 1969)

Hodson, H. V. (ed) *The Annual Register of World Events 1976* (Longman, 1977)

Hugget, Frank E. *The Land Question & European Society* (Thames & Hudson, 1975)

Hutton, W. *The History of Birmingham* (1835)

Huxley, Anthony *An Illustrated History of Gardening* (London, 1978)

Impey, Frederic, *Three Acres and a Cow* (Birmingham, Allotments & Smallholders Association, 1890)

Jeffries, E. S. *A Brief History of West Wickham Allotment Association* (1975)

Journal of the Board of Agriculture (HMSO, 1894, 1908, 1912, 1913, 1916)

Journal of the Ministry of Agriculture, 'Allotments' (HMSO, 1933)

Keatley Moore, H. BA BMus JP *Croydon and the Great War* (Corporation of Croydon, 1920)

Kemp, T. *Manual of Field Gardening (in Sussex and Yorkshire)* (Huddersfield, 1846)

Langford, J. A. *A Century of Birmingham Life* (Vol 2, 1870)

Lawes, J. B. 'The Rothamsted Allotment Club' (article, *Royal Agricultural Society Journal*, 1877)

London Evening News 'A Fable for Today' (article, 1917)

Loudon, J. C. *Encyclopaedia of Gardening* (1836)

The Second Tour (1831)

Lyte, Charles *The Kitchen Garden* (The Oxford Illustrated Press, 1984)

Majendie, Ashurst, Poor Law Report (HMSO, 1833)

Maidstone Journal 'Bearsted Allotments' (1844)

Middleton, Cecile Henry *Wartime Allotments* (London, 1940)

Ministry of Agriculture, The Allotment Act 1922 (HMSO)

'Dig for Victory' leaflets 1-26 (HMSO 1939-45)

'Allotment and Garden Guides' 1-12 (HMSO 1945)

Food From the Garden (booklet, HMSO 1939; re-issued 1942)

Growmore Bulletin No 1 (HMSO, 1939; re-issued 1942)

Potato Wart Disease Order (HMSO 1923)

Ministry of Agriculture & Fisheries, *Urban Working Class Household Diet* (HMSO, 1951)

'National Service' Industrial Army *Our Stocks are Low* (leaflet, HMSO, 1917)

Nottingham & Midland Counties Daily Express 'Allotments in Nottingham' (1971)

Onslow, William Hillier, *Landlords & Allotments* (London, Longman & Co, 1886)

Orwin, C. S. & Whetham, E. H. *History of British Agriculture* (London, Longman, Green & Co, 1964)

Pollock, Prof Frederick, *The Land Laws* (London, 3rd ed, 1896)

Queries Concerning Cottagers, with Answers (Board of Agriculture, 1796)

Rackham, Oliver *The History of the Countryside* (London, J. M. Dent & Sons Ltd, 1986)

Report of the Allotments Advisory Committee (published for the Ministry of Agriculture & Fisheries, HMSO, 1950)

Report of the Departmental Committee appointed by the Ministry of Agriculture into the provision of Allotments by Local Authorities (HMSO, 1922)

Report of the Land Division, Board of Agriculture, Pt II, Cd 6832 (HMSO, 1912)

Report of the Land Enquiry Committee (London, 1913)

Return of Allotments and Smallholdings in Great Britain, Board of Agriculture, Cd 6144 (HMSO, 1890)

Royal Commission on Labour 'The Agricultural Labourer' (*Board of Agriculture Journal*, HMSO, 1894)

Salman Redcliffe, N. *The History and Social Influence of the Potato* (Cambridge University Press, 1949)

Sanders, T. W. FLS FRHS *Allotments* (London, One & All Garden Books, 1907)

Allotment and Kitchen Gardens (London, W. H.& L. Collingridge, 1919)

The Book of the Potato (London, 1905)

Senior, Nassau W. & Chadwick E. Poor Law Commissioners' Report (HMSO, 1834; Penguin, 1973)

Showell's Dictionary of Birmingham (1885)

Stephen, Sir Leslie *Life of Henry Fawcett* (Smith, Elder & Co, 1886)

Stoney, J. FRHS *Allotments*, Bulletin 90 of the Ministry of Agriculture & Fisheries (HMSO, 1936)

Stratton, J. M. & Houghton Brown, J. *Agricultural Records* (3rd edition, ed Baker, J., London, 1978)

Talbot, F. A. *Those Amazing Allotments* (World's Work, 1919)

Tate, Charlotte 'Dig for Victory' (article, *The Quinton Oracle*, Birmingham, 2003)

The Penny Magazine, Penny Encyclopaedia Vol 14 (1845)

Thirsk, J. (ed) *The Agrarian History of England & Wales*, Vol V, 1640-1750 (Cambridge University Press, 1985)

Thirsk, J. (gen ed) & Mingey, G. E. (ed) *The Agrarian History of England & Wales*, Vol VI, 1750-1850 (Cambridge University Press, 1989)

Thorpe, Prof H. Departmental Inquiry into the Provision of Allotments, Cd 4166 (HMSO, 1969)

Timmins, Samual, Local Committee of The British Association (1866)

Townsend, J. *A Dissertation on the Poor Laws* (1786)

Trevelyan, G. M. OM *English Social History* (London, Longman, Green & Co, 1947)

Tuckwell, Rev W. *Reminiscences of a Radical Parson* (London, 1895)

Walsham Village History Group Quarterly Review 'Town Farm Allotments and the Poor' (article, 2002)

Warner, T. *Landmarks in English Industrial History* (Blackie & Son, 1949)

Williams, John *The Home Fronts 1914-1918* (London, Constable & Co, 1972)

Young, A. *Annals of Agriculture*, Vol XXXVI (1800)

Ziegler, P. *The Black Death* (London, Collins, 1969)

Other reference sources consulted

The Agricultural Gazette (1846, 1850)

The Croydon Advertiser (1941, 1947)

Gardeners' Chronicle (1880-99, 1917-18, 1920-38, 1943-48, courtesy of Horticulture Week)

The Times (1885-99, 1915-18, 1939-43, 1948-52, 1965-66, 1969-70, courtesy of Times Newspapers NI Syndication, London)

Tunbridge Wells Courier 'Tunbridge Wells Digs for Victory' (article, 1939, courtesy of Courier Newspapers, Kent)

Acknowledgements

Special thanks to: Simon Baddeley, Handsworth Allotments Information Group (HAIG), Birmingham; Sandra Brind of NI Syndication (*The Times*) London; Giles Broadbent, Editor of Kent & Sussex Courier Newspapers, Tunbridge Wells; Ian Carter, Editor of the *Croydon Advertiser*, Croydon; Ted Clarkson of Shakespeare Street Gardens Ltd, Coventry; Sandy Ellis of The Wavertree Society, Liverpool; Margaret Ferre of Her Majesty's Stationary Office, Norwich; Irene Gellet of Spa Hill Allotment Society and Alf Walters of SHOGG; Sarah Gore, Exhibitions Officer of The People's History Museum, Manchester; Sheila Hughes of Westbourne Road Leisure Gardens Association, Birmingham; Stuart Kelly, Associate Publisher of *Horticulture Week*, London; Alex Kerr, Managing Editor of The Contemporary Review Company Limited; John & Jean Mantle of Sturminster Road Allotments Association (Spadeworks), Bristol; Julian Mills, Information Team Librarian of Tunbridge Wells Reference Library, Kent; Suzanne Nicholls, Archive Library Assistant, Hertfordshire County Council; Linda Nicol of Cambridge University Press; Mr J. Parfitt of West Wickham Allotment Association, Kent; Charlotte Tate and the Editor of the *Quinton Oracle*, Birmingham; James Turner and Audrey McLaughlin of the Walsham Village History Group, Suffolk; Roy Woolley, Romford Then and Now (website); the Chief Librarian and Staff of the Local Studies & History Dept, Central Library, Birmingham; the Chief Librarian and Staff of the Local Studies Dept, Central Reference Library, Bromley; the Chief Librarian and Staff of the Central Reference Library, Croydon; the Chief Librarian and Staff of the Royal Horticultural Society, Lindley Library, London; Amanda J. Robertson, Chief Librarian, and Staff of the Reading Room, Dept of Printed Books, Imperial War Museum, London; the Chief Librarian and Staff of the Museum of Rural Life (Reference Library), Reading.

Extra-special thanks to: Kerrie Clarke and Grace Corne for diligently proofreading my manuscript, and to David Gibbs, Publicity Officer and Editor of the *National Allotment & Leisure Gardener* magazine for providing inspiration and encouragement with this project.

Thanks also to the 50 or so plot-holders who have supplied me with snippets of information.

Index